SHARK

SHARK

THE BIOGRAPHY
OF GREG NORMAN

LAUREN ST JOHN

RUTLEDGE HILL PRESS®
NASHVILLE, TENNESSEE

Published in Nashville, Tennessee, by Rutledge Hill Press®, 211 Seventh Avenue North, Nashville, Tennessee 37219.

Typography by E. T. Lowe Publishing Company, Nashville, Tennessee.

Library of Congress Cataloging-in-Publication Data

St John, Lauren, 1966–
    Shark : the biography of Greg Norman / Lauren St John.
      p. cm.
    Includes index.
    ISBN 1–55853–583–7 (hardbound)
    1. Norman, Greg, 1955–   . 2. Golfers—Australia—Biography.
  I. Title.
  GV964.N67S8   1998
  796.352'092—dc21   98-11089
  [B]   CIP

Printed in the United States of America

1 2 3 4 5 6 7 8 9—02 01 00 99 98

"I hate failure. The idea of failure is, I think, my driving force."

Greg Norman, November 1989

For J,

Who makes everything possible

CONTENTS

ACKNOWLEDGMENTS xi

PROLOGUE xiii

1. THE MILKY BAR KID 1

2. BLUE SKIES AND 65s 14

3. NORMAN CONQUEST 29

4. LOVE AND WAR 44

5. THE YEAR OF LIVING DANGEROUSLY 64

6. STORM WARNING 81

7. THE SATURDAY SLAM 99

8. OPEN SEASON 115

9. GREEN JACKET BLUES 131

10. LONE SHARK 149

11. FLIRTING WITH DISASTER 166

12. KING OF THE HILL 183

13. POWER STRUGGLE 202

14. DEATH IN THE AFTERNOON 222

15. GHOSTS OF AUGUSTA 239

16. THE POLITICS OF ENVY 259

INDEX 281

ACKNOWLEDGMENTS

The success and authenticity of almost any biography of a living person depends largely on the cooperation of the people who have shaped and influenced him. For that reason, I am indebted to Greg and Laura Norman, who not only gave generously of their time but were much kinder and nicer than they actually needed to be while doing so. Also to Frank Williams, who is that rarity in professional sport—a manager who returns phone calls—and who went above and beyond the call of duty in attempting to ensure that this book depicted Greg fairly and as a whole human being—with all the charms and flaws that that implies.

I am enormously grateful to Merv and Toini Norman, to James and Lois Marshall (thanks for the kindness, the lift to the station, and the chocolate biscuits), to Hughes Norton, Tom Ramsey, Bill Longmuir, Nick Price, Bruce Edwards, Butch Harmon, David Leadbetter, Charlie Earp, Robinson Holloway, Tom Callahan, and Bart Collins.

Thanks to everyone at Transworld, especially my editor Adam Sisman, Shona Martin, Hazel Orme, Sheila Corr, Shawna Newman, and Katrina Whone. Also to Debbie Beckerman, for persuading me to do the book, to Rhod McEwan, the best bookseller in the world, and to my agents, Lyn Tranter in Australia and Sara Menguc and Georgia Glover at David Higham, for keeping faith in me.

Anyone who has been through the nightmare that is writing books knows that it is not only the author who feels the strain. Thanks to my Nashville family, Jack Daniels, Steve and Kim Byam, Jan, Steffi, Debra, Anabel, and Mike and Jan Blaustone, my London support group, Jane and

Chris, Liz and Joan, and my friends in the AGW, especially Peter Higgs and Derek Lawrenson. Lastly and most importantly, thanks to Ken Johnson, my mom, dad, sister Lisa, and my cats Felix and Mommy-Cat, who weather the storms, cope with the crises, and, hopefully, share in the good bits.

PROLOGUE

"Power is what it is all about and no one likes relinquishing that."

Mark McCormack, *Golf World,* 1988

Greg Norman had taken New York. Eyes narrowed, black hat pulled down low, he stared down the tramps, Trumps, and shoeshine boys of Gotham from a king-sized neon billboard on Times Square. "I had completely forgotten all about it," Norman told *Golf World* magazine. "Then the limo driver told me to look up, and there it was. It was a lot bigger than I expected. It looked like a football field up there."

Norman was everywhere in 1995. His ice-blue eyes and Lone Ranger stance were plastered on subway stations in Brooklyn and buses rolling down Broadway. He was a sepia-toned success story on the cover of *Men's Journal* and the PGA Player of the Year. He put his adventure hat on for Chevrolet in America and Holden in Australia. He urged people to write with Le Boeuf pens, use Cobra clubs, consider Maxfli balls, play eighteen holes at the Medalist, buy Norman turf, sail Norman yachts, fly Qantas, wear a Rolex, and Attack Life in Greg Norman clothes.

Two years earlier in a villa on the other side of America, the cornerstones of this success story—International Management Group and the man they once marketed—had collided. Then nobody was smiling. Norman, his chiseled face intent, was talking to his agent, Hughes Norton. Norman's elegantly beautiful wife, Laura, sat beside him. They were discussing the successful outcome of the biggest gamble of a career founded on risk. In 1990, Norman had invested two million dollars of his own money in Cobra Golf,

Inc., acquiring a 12 percent stake in the company. Even before the primary shares were offered in September 1993, it was clear that Norman's stake was worth almost twenty million dollars. By January 1, 1996, it would be worth nearly forty-four million dollars.

In the meantime Norman had left IMG and the small matter of a commission had arisen. Earlier, they had reached a stalemate, but now Norton believed he had a temporary solution in mind, a destination for the million dollars in question, a safe house, as it were, on the way to IMG.

"Greg," he said slowly, "you're wrong not to pay IMG. But if you can't bring yourself to pay it to them, why don't you pay it to me?"

I

THE MILKY BAR KID

"The guys who want to be great players learn, from the age of fifteen, that if you're not willing to totally fall on your face with the whole world watching, and deal with it, and stay up, then you don't become a champion."

Dr. Bob Rotella, sports psychologist, 1996

When Toini Norman played her last round of golf, the bougainvillea were in bloom, crowding the tees with their scarlet and purple blossoms as she walked wistfully from the eighteenth, her pregnant belly heavy and awkward. She had managed to keep playing for more than seven months, holing out weekly amid the ghost gums and sand greens of Mount Isa, but when the summer came with scorching metallic skies, she was forced to admit defeat. On February 9, 1955, she was admitted to the hospital with high blood pressure. Gregory John Norman was born the next day, arriving in the world with fine milky hair and a piercing scream. He weighed eight pounds, eleven ounces.

"He was a terrible baby," Toini laughs. "He cried all the time. He kept us awake for about twelve months. Finally, we moved into a new house and I said to the neighbors, 'I hope you aren't light sleepers because I'm going to just leave him to cry.' Greg cried for two whole nights, and then he never cried again."

Both Toini and her husband, Mervyn, were of Nordic ancestry. Toini's carpenter father, Seth, and her mother, Tyyne Hovi, were Finns who migrated to Australia in the thirties, while Merv's heritage was Norwegian, Danish, German, and English. They met and fell in love on the tennis court;

1

and when Greg was born, Merv was working as an electrician for Mount Isa Mines in Northwest Queensland, a noisy jumble of slagheaps and shuddering pipelines. The largest city in the world in terms of surface area, Mount Isa sprawled over rich deposits of zinc, silver, lead, and copper. "As the only place of consequence for seven hundred kilometers in any direction," reports the *Rough Guide to Australia*, "the smokestacks, concrete paving, and sterile hills at Mount Isa assume oasis-like qualities on arrival, despite being undeniably ugly."

Perhaps fortunately, the Normans moved away when Greg and his older sister, Janis, were still tiny, taking up residence in Townsville, an arid and muggy but altogether more convivial spot near the translucent waters of the Great Barrier Reef. Merv set up his own engineering practice, and Toini played golf again and tried to cope with Greg and Janis. "Both my children were little horrors," she says.

Her son was barely six when he discovered the joys of Magnetic Island, a vividly beautiful granite triangle just off the coast. The Normans had a small holiday house among the palms there, and Greg and Janis spent every spare hour of their childhood skin diving and spearfishing among the coral reefs, roasting their catches over an open fire. "That's all I did," Norman says, "if I wasn't playing football or cricket or rugby or Australian Rules. I definitely wasn't studying, that's for sure."

School was the bane of his life. He remembers a certain fondness for engineering, geography, and physics, but his mind was always elsewhere. He despised French. "He didn't like school," Toini says. "He'd rather have been outside. He didn't apply himself. His father tried to get him to, but he'd rather play sports, to the despair of his teachers. I ran into his headmaster years later and he said, 'I often wondered what was going to happen to Greg.' They always thought he could have tried harder."

"He was always occupied and physically active," Merv recalled. "The bloke was never sitting down reading books. The simple thing is that his co-ordination was so good that any sport he touched he could have played it well. Picked up a billiard cue and he could play billiards well. Always had that good hand-eye coordination."

As a young man Merv had been a talented rugby footballer who received several offers to go south to Brisbane and play, but his priorities lay elsewhere. Stern and uncompromising, with wide, powerful shoulders, he labored toward a degree in electrical engineering and then threw himself into

Family portrait: Greg poses with his parents, Merv and Toini, and his sister, Janis.
(Merv Norman)

work at Mount Isa Mines. Norman describes him as "dictatorial," the kind of man who would bang his fist on the table and say, "That's it, boys. No more talk. Let's do it now." A man to whom actions spoke far louder than words. "To win anything," Merv would inform his small son, "the first thing you need to do is control yourself, then the environment around you. Do that, and you're on your way to improvement."

At that age the only thing Greg was interested in improving was his sporting skill. He proved an adept rugby league footballer at Townsville Grammar and was chosen to represent Northern Queensland against Southeast Queensland in a match in which he scored the only try. A series of strains and minor injuries persuaded him that rugby wasn't for him, but by that time he had developed a passion for bareback riding, galloping along the beaches in a wild flurry of spray. He and his friend Peter Rawkins kept horses in a paddock behind Greg's house, a location that would have been convenient had it not involved a three-mile hike to the gate. To facilitate matters Greg cut a hole in the fence and, after being caught red-handed by the furious park ranger, was banished forever from keeping horses there.

Like a lot of young boys, Greg saw his father as dull and authoritarian. It came as a huge surprise to him to discover, years later, that Merv had been a bit of a prankster in his time, rigging up sticks of gelignite so they would explode when the lighting he had fitted in the new Mount Isa Golf Club was switched on in a solemn ceremony. Merv's engineering skills also enabled him to build a little Sabot yacht for his water-mad children, who were members of the Townsville sailing club. Greg was already steeped in the machismo of Australian society and he immediately appointed himself captain of the *Peter Pan*, shouting down his older sister. After they had sailed to victory in the B grade club championship, Janis punished him by joining the crew of a boat whose owner allowed her to be skipper.

"It was always the same," Janis laughed. "I'd beat him and he'd beat me up."

Asked on the television program *This Is Your Life* if there had been much competition between them, she said, "Absolutely. I used to have bruises up my arms. He was a ratbag!"

"I'VE LOST ALL MY FRIENDS IN AUSTRALIA THAT I GREW UP WITH, WHICH IS TOUGH. THAT'S THE OTHER SIDE OF THE COIN PEOPLE DON'T KNOW OR SEE OR UNDERSTAND."

"My sister and I were close, but like any brother and sister, you've always got a love-hate relationship," Norman says. "We did a lot of things brothers and sisters wouldn't usually do together, like sailing. But you know we drifted apart. Distance is a killer for me because I live in the States. I've lost all my friends in Australia that I grew up with, which is tough. That's the other side of the coin people don't know or see or understand. You'd like to go back and see your friends you grew up with and see what happened and what they're doing. But I don't do that."

Greg was influenced most by his mother, who remembers him as a thoughtful and considerate child. "At one stage I was sick with flu. He was about seven at the time and he said to me, 'Mum, you stay in bed and I'll make you some tea.' "

"Greg and Toini have always been close," says Charlie Earp, who would become Norman's mentor. "They're the same sort of characters. Greg's lucky in that he's got his father's determination and ability to keep gnawing away, and he's got Toini's sporting gift."

Merv was substantially stricter, not least because he was hoping that his son could still be persuaded to apply himself to his studies. Struggling to puzzle out a math problem at thirteen, Norman recalls asking his father for help. "Go in there and figure it out," Merv said, pointing to his bedroom. Minutes later young Greg was back. "Dad, I can't figure it out," he said. Merv just pointed. "Get back there and try again," he snapped.

"They had their altercations," Toini admits. "Merv had his ideas of what he expected, and he was a bit on the strict side."

It was always something of a relief when the school holidays came and Greg could return to the rainbow reefs of Magnetic Island or go out fishing and island-hopping for weeks on end with his schoolfriends Peter and David Hay, whose father, Dr. Bob Hay, owned an oceangoing cruiser. It was on one of these trips, skin diving and cautiously watching sharks feed, that Greg lost his front teeth for the first time. Rushing toward the killing pit—the hold where fish were dumped as they were heaved aboard—he slipped and fell against the edge. Amid the gore it was discovered that a tooth of his had been cracked diagonally from the bottom to the gumline, and the other tooth had broken in half. Dr. Hay charted a rapid course to Townsville, where the teeth were temporarily capped. Those caps were promptly knocked out in an Australian Rules game, and it was six years before Greg could afford to have them properly fixed again.

On another, more successful school holiday, Greg spent several weeks at an immense cattle station rounding up strays and indulging a brief flirtation with the idea of becoming a station hand, what the Australians call a "jackeroo." Years later Norman recalled, "It was hard bush work and I loved the chase, but any thoughts I had of a jackeroo's life ended when I found myself assigned to a team castrating bulls."

By 1969, Merv had resigned himself to the fact that it would be years, if ever, before his son was sufficiently educated to take over his thriving engineering practice, so he reluctantly gave it up to accept another job with Mount Isa Mines, Ltd., in Brisbane. "Greg was never that way inclined," Toini says, adding: "An engineer knows if a person's got the qualities needed. Greg didn't have the mathematics to be an engineer. I think Merv was a bit disappointed when he realized that Greg wasn't going to follow him into engineering. He would have kept the practice if he had done."

In the breeze from the open window, the little airplanes twirled, straining at the twine that tethered them to the ceiling and the walls. There were P-51 Mustangs, Spitfires, balsa-wood gliders and jets, all made with the same loving precision, some occupied by granite-faced pilots intent on circumnavigating the bedroom, others fitted with tiny motors that helped them bump along the paddock behind the house and reach for the sky on the sultry Australian evenings.

Greg Norman lay stretched out on his bed, picturing his future as a fighter pilot. He had tried collecting stamps and building balsa box cars, but it was flight, and particularly fighter jets, that fascinated him. He had already joined the air cadets at his new school, Aspley High in Brisbane. "That's my earliest recollection of what I wanted to be—a fighter pilot," he says. At fifteen Greg had long, finely muscled brown limbs, faraway blue eyes, a gaptoothed grin, and a shock of straw-blond hair. He didn't dream, he focused. He didn't fret about getting from A to B. To Greg, B was attainable simply by wanting it badly enough.

"I was a very single-minded individual," he says. "Once I put my mind to it, I'd get the job done. I've never been a quitter in my life, even when I was a kid. I've always told the truth because that's what my father instilled in me—tell the truth whether people like it or not. You know who your friends are when you tell the truth." But already he was discovering that not everybody enjoyed the truth quite as much as he did. "At school I'd get the cane across my fingers because I was too honest," Norman laughs. "Because I'd tell them what I thought. But in the long run, it's been very beneficial for me."

The Normans had moved into a two-story house in Aspley, Brisbane, just a few months earlier, and this afternoon Greg was lonely and bored. His

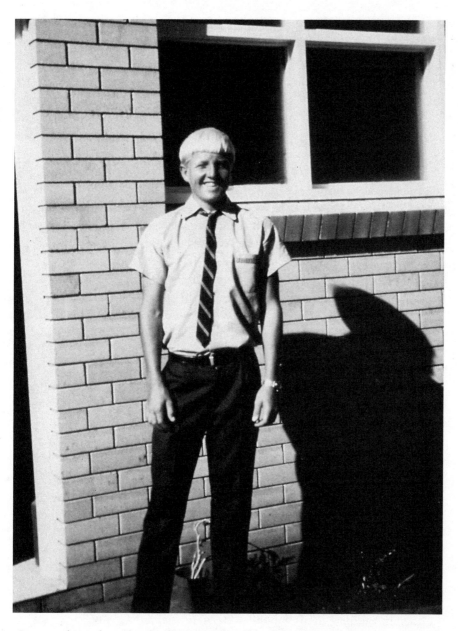

Greg, complete with pudding-bowl haircut and school uniform, dreams of stardom.
(Merv Norman)

friends had been left behind in Townsville, and his mother had joined Virginia Golf Club and was on her way out to play. Hearing her gathering her clubs, he jumped up. "Do you mind if I caddie for you?" he asked.

It was not his first introduction to golf. Janis still teases him about the time she beat him at crazy golf when they were kids. There had been a nine-hole course on Magnetic Island where, Toini says, "he would hack around and hit the ball a mile. But he wasn't really interested, unless the water was too rough to go spear fishing."

Norman's memory of golf prior to that day at Virginia is largely restricted to a shot he hit into a pandanus palm tree. In Brisbane when he carted Toini's clubs around the course, he enjoyed watching her play. Afterward, when his mother went into the clubhouse for a drink with her partners, Greg borrowed her clubs and attempted a few holes on his own. Years later he would say that he could reach par-fives in two on the first day he ever played, but he also had his share of duffs and slices out of bounds. By the time his mother emerged, he was hooked.

"I'm a type-A personality," Norman says, "and it was one of those things that I knew I could beat. I just loved the challenge of it."

"He only caddied for me once," says Toini. "He stole the clubs for himself after that. He had such dedication. He wanted to do everything well."

At Aspley High School, Greg had started playing Australian Rules, a game based on Gaelic football, eventually representing Queensland as a half-forward. But when he discovered golf, he realized that he preferred individual sports to team games. "Everything I did outside surfing was a team sport," Norman says. "I could put in many great games playing Australian Rules and rugby and cricket and lose the matches, and you feel down. Or vice versa—put in a lot of poor performances, and when we won and everybody's elated, you know you didn't perform. Whereas, in golf you have all the highs and lows every time, every shot, every putt. It's so spontaneous. It's here and now, and it's only you who experiences it, nobody else. That's what I loved when I was a kid."

At first Greg borrowed Toini's clubs, but it soon became clear that golf was a passion that wasn't going to go away, and after he had left his mother waiting on the darkened clubhouse steps a few times, his parents bought him his own set for $150. It was August 8, 1970. When he joined Virginia, his handicap was twenty-seven.

"Once he made that decision, he went all out for it," says Toini, who picked him up from school at 3:00 P.M. every day and drove him straight to the club, where he would hit balls until twilight obliterated them. "He was there from daylight to dawn. Weekends, you wouldn't see him. He loved to practice. I don't think anyone in the world has practiced more than Greg."

Greg's first action was to enroll himself for lessons with John Klatt, the pro at Virginia, who charged juniors twenty cents apiece for a group session. His second was to start devouring every piece of golf literature he could get his hands on, starting with Jack Nicklaus's classic *Golf My Way*. "The [Nicklaus books] taught me the art of hitting down the line and using my body naturally. You want to keep the clubface going down the line and then let the automatic rotation after impact just happen."

At school he sat reading golf magazines behind his desk. Gail Horne, a teacher at Aspley High, remembers confiscating them. His academic record plummeted.

"He would have failed my subject, Math II," Clive Evans told *Time* magazine, "but that was the hardest of the lot. It wasn't a matter of ability. He just wasn't interested. His main asset was always his confidence." He remembered Norman sitting sprawled out in his airy classroom, the louvered windows thrown open. "He'd sit right next to the doorway with those long legs of his stretched across the aisle. Not the greatest student. Had ability, but you could see him sitting there dreaming. A natural sportsman: Australian Rules, cricket, everything. Always very respectful, polite. One of his favorite sayings if you suggested he might do better if he did some work was: 'She'll be right, sir.' And you know, he was darn right."

The 1972 Aspley High yearbook shows Greg with a slightly bored smile on his face, his straw-blond hair framing a narrow face. He looks older than his years. The picture caption informs the reader that "Greg is such a good golfer that he made the state team at Easter. Lately he played with Billy Dunk. As well as golf, Greg has other interests. He is in Grade 12A and after matriculating would like to get a job with a golf firm or take up professional golfing. He is also Kenny's House Captain this year. Greg enjoys playing Australian Rules and has been center half-forward for the past two years on the A-grade team."

Klatt remembers his athletic blond student as having "a lot of raw talent, very strong. Hit the ball hard but not straight. He was very positive in his outlook. Believed in himself and that he could beat anyone."

On April 25, 1971, nine months after taking up the game, Greg won his first trophy, teaming up with Merv in a fourball stableford event at Virginia for fifty points. "That's the first [newspaper clipping] I have in the scrapbook," Toini said proudly. Greg's twenty-one handicap was immediately slashed to seventeen. By July 1 he was an eleven, and Virginia nominated him for a Queensland junior squad for which the handicap limit was six. By the time he left school in 1972, he was a scratch.

When he wasn't playing golf or Australian Rules, Greg spent his time surfing with his friend Greg Lyons. They were both prefects, and they abused their privileges by playing truant in the afternoons and riding the waves down at Noosa Heads. It was Lyons who found them holiday jobs at the Australian Match Manufacturing Company. They earned fifty dollars a week for slicing up thirty-foot logs with chain saws and depositing the chunks in vats of boiling water, working stripped to the waist in jeans and army boots. Greg kept himself going through the back-breaking days with dreams of the gleaming set of clubs he planned to purchase.

AS A SIX-YEAR-OLD, NORMAN HAD EXPERIENCED ALL THE FEARS THAT LURK IN THE MINDS OF SMALL CHILDREN. IN HIS NIGHTMARES SNAKES LAY COILED AND DEADLY BENEATH THE BED.

"There was always something about Greg," Merv said. "I thought the kid had something special. He always enjoyed himself with his mates but he liked to lead."

As a six-year-old, Greg had experienced all the fears that lurk in the minds of small children. In his nightmares snakes lay coiled and deadly beneath the bed, and when darkness fell, his bedroom became a place of nameless terrors. But unlike most children, he steeled himself to do something about it. One night he plucked up the courage to run from the door to the bed without turning on the light. Nothing grabbed him, no snakes reared their heads. The next night he walked a little slower and didn't cower beneath the covers. From then on the darkness held no fear for him.

As he grew older, he tested himself continually, and each time he walked away unscathed he grew braver. A lifesaving course at Magnetic Island had equipped him to deal with minor emergencies, and ultimately it was that training that helped him save the life of a friend. Sitting around a swimming pool with his Queensland Golf Union teammates one afternoon, Norman, variously nicknamed the Milky Bar Kid, the Strawberry Bull, and Buster, was watching Steve Perrin demonstrate his ability to swim six lengths underwater. After three lengths, Perrin slid slowly to a stop and sank to the bottom of the pool.

"He's in trouble!" cried Greg, and he dived fully clothed into the water. While Glen Cogill ran to call an ambulance, Greg gave Perrin mouth-to-mouth resuscitation. By the time the ambulance arrived, Perrin was breathing again.

"I remember the guy in the pool," Norman told golf writer Chris Hodenfield. "Everybody was either mesmerized or joking about the situation. Nobody wanted to take the responsibility of going in. So . . . from that day I never heard from him again. Completely disappeared from the game of golf, from surfing, from life."

It was the second time Greg had saved a life. Janis's favorite memory of her brother is the time she was skin diving and found herself tangled in deadly box jellyfish. Greg, "my knight in shining armor," leaped in, pulled her free, dragged her aboard their boat, and rowed as fast as he could to get help.

Greg's third brush with death had no happy ending. He and a young friend were at football training at Aspley High, running laps around a track in the Queensland heat, when the other boy fell over suddenly. He had had a heart attack. Greg gave him resuscitation before the ambulance arrived. But he died. "He was my buddy, we were running together, and thirty-five minutes later I'm seeing his mother arrive at the hospital and I'm saying, 'He didn't make it.' Those exact words. I didn't go out and change my whole lifestyle, but it had an impact. It strengthened my mind. You never forget the face, the smell. Those are the things that build your stamina, your character, and all that stuff."

Cogill remembers Greg, who had his first victory in the 1973 Queensland Junior Championship at Royal Queensland (shooting 73, 74 to win by five strokes), as a very confident, gregarious teenager. "And he was very aggressive with the girls," he said. "Aw, yeah. Very aggressive guy. He used to get into a few scraps with the blokes over the girls. And he would not back off from anybody. Tough as nails."

Toini's recollection is that Greg was outgoing to an extent but also quite conservative. "Greg was never one to party. I never had to worry about him coming home late at night, or drinking."

Mostly, Greg just loved to be outdoors, soaking up the sunshine with his black Labrador Pancho, and breathing in the freshly cut grass on the range at Virginia or the clean, salty smell of the ocean. He enjoyed being alone. Years later, long after he had achieved wealth and fame beyond his wildest dreams, almost nothing gave him greater pleasure than a hunting holiday with people he cared about in Queensland. "I love to be out walking," he said. "May not even shoot a thing. Just to be out there in the solitude and the peace and quiet, where you can hear the birds and see the flowers and smell the rain coming from forty-five miles away."

NORMAN . . . TOLD HIS FRIENDS OF HIS AMBITIONS. "BEFORE I'M THIRTY, I'LL BE A MILLIONAIRE. I'LL BE THE BEST GOLFER IN THE WORLD AND I'LL BE MARRIED TO AN AMERICAN."

In the months after he left Aspley High, Greg took to pitching a tent on the beach at Noosa with his friends, lying in front of the campfire, waiting to catch a good wave. Bored and soon broke, he nonetheless enjoyed the untrammeled freedom of his existence. One morning he left the camp and tripped down to the sea alone. A day earlier a cyclone had blasted through the area and the surf was high, rising up in a towering wall of indigo and foam and then crashing lustily onto the rocks. Greg left his surfboard behind and took his flippers and hydrofoil hand controls.

"There was some great surf coming in," Norman recalls, "because any time you had a cyclone you had a great groundswell. At Noosa, the only way you could get out to the break was to go out onto the headland and jump in. I was a big bodysurfer in those days and I wanted to go out where all the surfboarders were. When you're a kid, you never think of those things as being dangerous."

Poised on the headland, Greg waited for a smooth, high wave and leaped. His last conscious thought, before he was caught up in a churning tunnel of white water and smashed against the sea bed, was that he'd chosen the wrong wave. The flippers and hand controls were ripped from his body, and the sea whirled him around like a washing machine. He was terrified. Clawing his way to the surface, he found that he had been swept half a mile out to sea. When he finally managed to half-swim, half-drift to the beach, he collapsed exhausted on the sand, unable to move for a quarter of an hour. It was the last time he ever surfed.

Lying wet and drained on the beach at Noosa, with the sky curving silent and blue above him, Greg realized that his life was going nowhere. When all was said and done, there was one thing he wanted more than anything else and that was to play great golf. "Like I said, I'm a single-minded individual," Norman says with quiet determination. "That challenge came to me, and there was nothing that was going to stop me from getting to where I thought I could be."

It was on a six-hour bus journey to Grafton for one of his last amateur events that Greg, full of optimism for the future, told his friends of his ambitions. "Before I'm thirty, I'll be a millionaire. I'll be the best golfer in the world and I'll be married to an American," he announced suddenly to Kevin Flanagan and Kevin Murphy.

There was a second's silence as they digested this. Then the jeers began. "Who the hell do you think you are?" they demanded of Norman, who was a one-handicapper at the time and had never left the country. "What the hell are you talking about?" And with the careless savagery of young men, they tore his goals to shreds.

Norman, lanky and tousle-haired, glared at them defiantly. "When I've got my first million in the bank, I'll call you and let you know," he promised.

A decade later, he did exactly that.

BLUE SKIES AND 65s

"I think we may have a helluva player back home. He may not win five Opens because the competition is greater, but this kid is going to be world class."

Peter Thomson to the British press, 1976

The road to Royal Queensland leads through a lonely wasteland of warehouses, scrub, and run-down factories. A concrete arch dominates the horizon, rising out of the ground like a bridge to an uncertain future, and it is not until the visitor turns up the drive that the club's oasis effect is felt. Lush trees shade the low-lying gray clubhouse; palm fronds cast spiky shadows. Above the putting green, glasses clink on the balcony and golfers wilt in the relentless heat.

Nowadays the shelves of Charlie Earp's pro shop are stacked high with Shark merchandise. Above the Akubra hats and boiled sweets, there are framed photographs of the teacher with Jack Nicklaus, Corrine Dibnah, Wayne Grady, and Norman himself, and the changing-room door bears a crudely printed quote from Sam Snead: "If a lot of people gripped a knife and fork like they do a golf club, they'd starve to death."

In 1974, Earp's favorite adage was DIN and DIP: "Do it now and do it properly." A product of the red parched earth, as wiry and sun-scorched as Crocodile Dundee, he would stand behind the counter dispensing homespun wisdom in a flat, earthy twang. He has never forgotten the day that Norman walked into his shop, broad-shouldered and loose-limbed, with a gap-toothed grin and determined blue eyes.

"I'm going to be the best player in the world," he announced calmly.

Norman once said that as a teenager he "turned to the surf as an escape route for the problems I was trying to sort out in my mind." Exactly what those problems were he doesn't remember, but there is little doubt that his father's bitter opposition to his love affair with golf was the root cause of them.

Norman emerged from high school without any direction in life, feckless and fancy-free. Initially, he just "lay around for twelve months, mostly doing nothing." Nothing, that is, except surfing—hours and hours of skimming the waves in a bid to chase away the shadow that descended over the Norman household the day he turned down a career in the Royal Australian Air Force.

For the best part of twenty years, Norman has been describing how, in the grip of a "burning desire to be a fighter pilot," he was sitting in the RAAF's Brisbane recruiting office with Merv, pen poised to sign the enlistment papers, when he froze. To this day he has no idea what stopped him. "I never consulted anybody, I never spoke to anybody, I just decided to say no. You've got to trust your instincts. And I'd have regretted it. If I'd joined the air force, I would have known deep down inside that I was doing something I didn't really want to do."

But according to his mother, Norman, whose academic record hardly suggests a fast-track entry into the top-gun ranks, was never on the brink of committing himself to a career as a fighter pilot. "He and his father went to talk to the air force people, and they suggested he finish his final year at school, his grade twelve, before applying," she remembers. "But by then he was more interested in playing golf."

Merv drove Norman home, tight-lipped. He had hoped against hope that Norman would scrape through school with enough academic qualifications to be able to go to college and perhaps follow him into engineering. When that failed, he had clung to the idea that Norman would fulfill the ambition he himself had once had of being a fighter pilot. Now that hope too had been extinguished. Instead, he had to watch his carefree son, overlong hair in salty rats' tails, rise at his leisure every morning and saunter down to the beach with his surfboard tucked under his arm.

It was during this period that Norman became fixated on the idea of a career in professional golf. "I was never particularly good up to that point. There wasn't much to go on except I had confidence in myself." After nearly twelve months of sun and sand, he announced to his parents that he was thinking of becoming a professional golfer: "The greatest player in the world." Merv, and to a lesser extent Toini, took the news badly. "I hadn't given them a lot of reason to believe I could make it as a professional golfer," Norman said, remembering the scenes that followed this announcement. "I was this big lump who hadn't done anything for a year."

Laura, Norman's wife, who understands better than anyone else the long-term effect Merv's disapproval had on his son, can see both sides of the story. "His dad comes from the old school," she says of Merv's depression-era severity. "His dad really wanted Greg, his only son, to be successful, which is normal. Greg didn't play golf until he was fifteen years old, so when all of a sudden one day Greg wanted to play golf, his father was like, 'Wait a minute, you can't just all of a sudden be a professional golfer.' I guess he didn't realize the talent that Greg had. No parent would. He was afraid that he would fail. It would have been different if he had been playing since he was nine or ten years old, but he was going to start playing golf and he was going to be the greatest golfer in the world. Well, his father was just afraid for him."

Earp sighs. "Old Merv didn't know anything about golf. Toini used to play. He's a workaholic, Merv, and he was a bit keen to get Greg into the air force, so he'd have some profession behind him. He'd be a bit like my father. My father had never heard of golf, so the second day I worked as a golf professional was the second day I'd been on a golf course in my life. I was never an amateur. And Greg was sort of in that situation. His father couldn't see the value of going into golf. In fairness to Merv, it wasn't that he didn't want his son to do that, he just thought, 'What future is there?' "

"I'd be the same way if it were my son," Norman says now. "Believe me, now I have kids I can understand how my father felt. Of course, I didn't at the time."

In 1973, Norman took a job as a packer in the Brisbane warehouse of Precision Golf Forgings, an equipment manufacturing company run by an amateur golfer named Sommie Mackay, the brother of the test cricketer Ken "Slasher" Mackay. The atmosphere at home was strained, to say the least. With his pockets empty and his father's disappointment hovering like a palpable and accusatory presence in the house, Norman had been forced grudgingly out to work. Winning the Royal Queensland Club title had done nothing to allay his parents' worries. Merv, with his neatly pressed shirts and fanatical work ethic, saw Norman's golf dreams as a dilettante extension of his interest in surfing. Partly for that reason and partly because he was afraid of being left off of amateur teams if his ambitions were known, Norman felt he had no choice but to conduct his inquiries about turning professional in secret, and he used his breaks at PGF to make clandestine phone calls to golf's governing bodies. He planned to present his new career to his father as a fait accompli.

In the meantime, practice was Norman's priority. Soon after dawn broke he would make his way to the factory, and there in the cool gray light he would parcel equipment furiously, hurrying to subdue unwieldy golf carts, clubs, and bags so that when his shift ended, he could be gone. It was a contest of wills. In Norman's mind, a four-hour shift was a four-hour shift, but as the hands of the clock ticked toward 11:00, more and more tasks would suddenly be produced for him. Boiling with frustration, he would work even faster. At the last conceivable second, Mackay would acquiesce reluctantly and Norman would be out on the streets of Brisbane, racing for freedom, a breathless blur dodging disapproving suits and women trapped in high heels.

He had more than a mile to run, and often the 11:20 train was pulling out of Roma Street station as he leaped aboard, collapsing winded among the hot, curious commuters. If he missed that train, there were no others for an hour and Virginia station was twenty minutes away. He was determined to practice for five hours a day.

Norman remembers approaching golf aggressively even as a youngster. He had only one aim and that was to beat the living daylights out of the ball. "Hit it three hundred meters without any problem," he says. That year, he entered the Australian Open at Royal Queensland. To Norman, who had made rapid strides in an incredibly short period of time, it was an opportunity to gauge how much he had to improve as an amateur before he could consider the professional ranks. For the first three rounds it seemed he was already there. He scored 71, 76, 71 and was drawn with Terry Gale, one of Australia's leading amateurs at the time. Norman was determined to beat him.

At the tenth hole in the final round, Norman's approach found a greenside bunker. He splashed out, not noticing that his friend Roger Dwyer, who was caddying for him, had left his golf cart unattended and was talking to someone in the gallery. His ball ran over the green, down the hill, and struck the cart for a two-stroke penalty.

Norman was wild with anger. He racked up an eight, and as he walked to the next tee, turned angrily to Dwyer and demanded to know why he had been so stupid. Dwyer was mortified. "One day, you're going to be a great player," he said placatingly. "Rome wasn't built in a day, and you will have many more bad breaks. I'm sorry."

"ROME WASN'T BUILT IN A DAY, AND YOU WILL HAVE MANY MORE BAD BREAKS. I'M SORRY." NORMAN BURST INTO TEARS. HE PUT A TOWEL OVER HIS FACE TO HIDE HIS MISERY.

Norman burst into tears. He put a towel over his face to hide his misery and made a double bogey at eleven. Gale finished as leading amateur and Norman was runner-up after a 77. To the annoyance of the Australian Golf Union, he didn't appear at the presentation ceremony. "I just wanted to get away," Norman said.

Finally, his perseverance paid off and Billy McWilliam, the pro at Beverley Park in Sydney, took him on as an assistant. This was a coup for several reasons. Not only did McWilliam have a reputation for discovering and nurturing talent—Bruce Devlin and Bruce Crampton, the first Australian to win a million dollars on the U.S. Tour, had both benefited from his guidance—but the New South Wales PGA had gone a step further than the PGA's Queensland division and assured McWilliam that Norman would be given releases to play in tournaments. To Norman, to whom three years as a trainee sounded like a life sentence, there was no better justification for heading south.

In March, a few weeks after his twentieth birthday, Norman put his belongings in the back of the little Cortina he had bought for twenty-three hundred dollars, kissed his mother, shook hands with his father, and set off on the long drive to Sydney. Six hours later he was back again. Halfway to his destination, he remembered the two thousand dollars he had saved. He had not heard the message his mother put out on local radio, but Toini maintained it was telepathy: "Would Greg Norman, heading south to Sydney, please return home. He has forgotten his money."

In Sydney, Norman shared an apartment in Kogarah with Doug Murray, another trainee. Initially, he set the alarm for 4:00 A.M. every day without fail and was hitting balls into the sunrise within the hour. At 7:30 he would unlock the pro shop, and then he would repair clubs and sell balls to members until 5:00. McWilliam then decided his assistants should help run his floodlit driving range. Since it rarely closed before 11:00 P.M., at which time Norman and Murray, working alternate evenings, had to gather up about four thousand balls, it was usually midnight before they were in bed.

Most nights they drifted off to sleep complaining about the drudgery of their lot. Their lives had become a monotonous, not to say murderous, regime of dealing with customers, with hardly a moment to spare for practicing or playing. Norman felt he was going nowhere fast. He was. Three months after his arrival in Sydney, the New South Wales PGA reneged on its promise to grant him releases to play in tournaments while he was still a trainee. He would not be allowed to enter a professional event for three years.

It was a crushing blow. McWilliam, whose admiration for Norman's gift and hard work had been masked by his stern manner, was furious. "Greg Norman is one of the most talented assistants I have ever had, but he is going back home because he cannot play in pro tournaments in Sydney," he told reporters. "He has been waiting for invitations to play that have never arrived, so now he is going back to Queensland."

The first Earp knew of it was when Norman phoned him and asked if he could see him. "Is it important?" the older man asked. "Very," Norman said.

In Brisbane, Norman sat in Earp's lounge and begged him to let him finish his apprenticeship in Queensland. "He had a girlfriend then and he was a fairly homey sort of boy," Earp remembers. "I said, 'You're welcome to come back.' And he got in his car, saw his mother and father, drove to Sydney to pack up all his gear, and came back again. And that's when we really became close."

In Sydney, Norman loaded up the Cortina and, determined not to waste another second of his life, set off on the five-hundred-mile drive home at 10:00 P.M. Suburbs gave way to tropical beaches and barren red landscapes. Norman kept himself awake by wondering whether Earp would really be able to help him, and how his parents and the members of Royal Queensland would feel about his working in the pro shop.

The kangaroo came out of nowhere. Norman saw a blur, yanked the wheel hard left, hit a road sign, and went into a spin. When the car finally stopped, jammed up against the embankment on the opposite side of the road, Norman sat in his seat trembling, the night unfurling all around him.

The next afternoon, after a long, exhausted sleep, he went to inspect the car. It was totaled. Somehow he had managed to drive it home, but he wouldn't be driving it again. Uninsured, it cost twelve hundred dollars to repair, and afterward Norman sold it.

Life at Royal Queensland was fair but hard. Norman was paid thirty-eight dollars a week, for which he spent half a day in the shop and the rest hitting balls or working with Earp. "The way you can hit a golf ball, we're not going to worry about the long game," his teacher told him. "We're just going to worry about your short game."

Norman threw himself into his new practice regime with a discipline and ferocity that was astonishing even to the ambitious young assistants he worked alongside, Wayne Grady and Mike Ferguson. "He was quite impressive," recalls Grady, an enormously likable, salt-of-the-earth Australian. "He was a much bigger kid than the rest of us and could hit it a very long way at that time. It was always fun watching him hit the driver off the ground, because the old equipment and the old balls used to take off very low and then rise, peak, and fall down. Greg was always a couple of years ahead of myself and the other guys, and he was the best."

"His idea of practice was to practice," said Cogill. "He didn't just go muck around and have a drink. His hands would nearly bleed." He remembered Norman as being very organized. "He knew where he was going and he wanted it real bad. That's the kind of guy he was. You could nearly call him cocky. At the junior pennants he'd say, 'I'm going to beat this guy 5 & 4.' He was cocky for an Australian. We're a pretty negative people."

In the first six months at Royal Queensland, Norman sat for and passed all the trainee exams he would normally be expected to complete in three years. In September he won the Queensland trainee championship in a play-off at McCleod Country Club, a course built for women by women. "He had that flair," Earp says.

Encouraged, Norman beat balls behind the bamboo curtain of the practice range at his own club with religious intensity. Soon he provoked the ire of the greens committee. There is something about exceptional young-sters that arouses the pettiness inherent in all golf clubs, and at Royal Queensland it was led by the chairman of the greens. He wanted Norman banned from the range for taking so many divots it looked like it had been mauled by pigs. "We had a bit of a barney," recalls Earp, who refused to stand by and see his most disciplined assistant punished for his dedication.

It was incidents like these that cemented their relationship. While the other assistants were letting their hair down in the pubs or on the beach, Norman wrestled with his game. He liked to give himself projects. There was a gnarled old Moreton Bay fig tree near the practice ground, and he liked to see how close he could stand to it and still clear it with a five-iron. "He learnt to play the shot that made him under that tree," says Earp.

Watching his pupil one morning, Earp said, "Gregory, you need to learn to hit the ball lower."

"I'll be all right," Norman said, launching a ball into the blue. "I'm designing my game for America."

"Yes," retorted Earp, "but if you play that shot in Britain, it'll end up in Paris."

But Norman always required proof for everything. It was not enough for him to be told that a technique was wrong or a clubhead was right. He had to know *why*. On that particular occasion Earp called over a Scottish member who assured Norman that, when playing at Turnberry or Troon, "You'll be needing to keep it quail high," but there were numerous others. He needed confirmation from Kel Nagle that Earp was right when he said the shaft in his driver was too stiff to work the ball effectively, and he nearly had a stroke when Earp suggested he change his grip.

"Nobody plays with a grip like that," Norman growled.

"Well, Jack Nicklaus does, Norman von Nida does, Kel Nagle does, Gary Player does, Arnold Palmer does," Earp snapped back.

21

Secretly, he thought Norman had it all—power, talent, focus. "Determined, really determined," Earp told *Time*. "He'd look at you with those palomino eyes that he's got and you knew, you could see him pumping up."

Earp had a fuse as short as Norman's, which inexorably led to clashes. One lunchtime, when Norman had worked hard all morning and felt he was owed a few hours' practice, Earp ordered him into the back of the store to clean some sets of clubs. Norman exploded. Any assistant who didn't measure up was shown the door and occasionally helped there by the scruff of his neck, and Norman might have received the same treatment had he not grabbed Earp by the front of his shirt and lifted him off his feet. Reason prevailed before any damage was done. When his mother came into the shop ten minutes later, Norman stood sweetly behind the counter and sold her a golf ball.

PLAYING FOR MONEY THAT HE COULD NOT AFFORD TO LOSE . . . TAUGHT HIM HOW TO HANDLE PRESSURE AND WIN; AND THE BETS GREW LARGER BY THE DAY.

He grins at the memory. "Charlie always pushed me, which was great. There were times when I wanted to fight him, but you knew that the guy loved you and knew where you wanted to go, so he was just being your blinkers for you."

When Norman wasn't hitting balls or waiting on customers, he went fishing with Earp and a couple of friends in a little wooden dinghy with an outboard motor. Earp remembers those trips as being among the few social settings in which Norman was truly comfortable. "A lot of people who are shy are outgoing until they get to a certain barrier, then they go back the other way. He was never a person to be pushing in. He'd wait till he was invited, which is a sign of shyness."

Earp encouraged him to come out of his shell on the course, teaching him the value of sport as entertainment by coaching him to adopt "the aura of a clown. . . . The clown in the circus is making people happy. Gary Player is like that, and so are Seve and Greg."

One area where Norman showed no sign of reticence was in his on-course gambling, which he had started while still a boy at Virginia. Playing for money that he could not afford to lose, often with local businessman Cyril King, taught him how to handle pressure and win; and the bets grew larger by the day. The most he ever earned in one round was twelve hundred dollars, and in April 1976, when the Queensland PGA announced that he was now eligible to compete in state-controlled tournaments, he used the money to pay for his travel arrangements. He won his first pro-am title in Dalby in June. Even now Earp can remember the hostility that greeted Norman's success in those early events. "They didn't like him because he was good. In Australia, we have that: knock the tall poppy down," Earp says.

In August the PGA of Australia invited him to join the circuit. Norman celebrated by regaining his state trainee title at Keperra by fifteen shots. His first real event was held in Bateman's Bay and had a purse of fifteen thousand dollars. He finished third. The following week he returned to Keperra for the Queensland Open, shot 70, 73, 74, 70 and again shared third place.

"Throughout the tournament he missed only ten greens," reported the *Brisbane Courier Mail*. "He laid into his tee shot off the eighteenth for a gain of 360 meters and hit a nine-iron in. For a twenty-one-year-old not yet out of his time, it was downright arrogance."

It was a lightning beginning. Brimming with confidence, Norman finished in the top ten in the New South Wales Open for the third successive week. He was ready.

When the starter called his name, Norman strode onto the tee box and smashed his drive down the first hole at the Grange. Cogill was caddying for him. Norman was up against the cream of Australian golf in the $35,000 West Lakes Classic, his first major event, and he felt he needed all the help he could get just to make the cut.

It was not a day conducive to settling the nerves of rookies. Not only was Norman paired with Crampton, who attracted a large gallery, but there was a strong gusting wind and a forty-minute delay. Norman eyed the tree-lined fairways with alarm. A Perth player named John Clifford had set a course record of 67, an outstanding score in the conditions, particularly when the field featured players like David Graham, Graham Marsh, Jack Newton,

Bruce Devlin, and Bob Shearer. Norman calmed himself by focusing on Clifford's score. "I'll have to beat that," he thought.

Until he teed off that day, Norman's progress had gone largely unnoticed by the media and even by most players. The only reason Bill Longmuir, a young Scotsman in the group ahead, had heard of him was because his friend Doug McClelland had been paired with Norman the week before. "Doug said, 'Have you heard of this Greg Norman?' " Longmuir recalls. "He said, 'God, he's just unbelievable. This is the best player I've ever seen.' "

Longmuir, struggling in the high winds that swept through Adelaide's Grange club that first day, shot 77. "I got in and this kid had shot 64. I thought, 'That's just not possible on this course, not on a day like that.' My memories are that it was a score that just wasn't possible. A 69 would have been brilliant, but a 64 was phenomenal."

In the second round Longmuir struggled to concentrate and kept glancing back at the group behind, awed by the length of Norman's drives. Norman, who was determined not to defend his lead, played aggressively and twice incurred Crampton's wrath. First, he was shouted at for memorizing rather than marking his ball's original position when he dropped away from a path at the short eighth. Fortunately, Norman was supported by an official who also noted the exact spot. But Crampton found fault with him again when they reached the green.

"You're not allowed to do that," Crampton snapped as Norman carefully brushed a few grains of sand off the green.

"Yes, I am," Norman said. And a small row developed.

Once again the official stood by Norman, assuring Crampton that the rules of the Australasian Tour differed from those in the United States and that Norman was quite correct.

"I watched him come up the last," Longmuir says, "and he hit it in the water off the tee. I thought: 'He's gone today. He's probably shot 76 or 77.' He put his scorecard in and he'd had a 67, with a ball in the hazard at the last. It was mind-blowing stuff, really. That was my introduction to him. Everyone was going, 'This is definitely the next Jack Nicklaus.' He was always going to be great, was how it was viewed. I mean, it was a bit like Tiger Woods now. Everywhere he goes, people are talking about him and watching him. Well, it was the same with Greg."

After two rounds Norman was leading by five strokes. After three he led by ten at sixteen under par, an unbelievable achievement in a field of that

strength. He had made twenty-two birdies in fifty-four holes, and his nearest challengers were Crampton and Chris Tickner. Marsh and Devlin were a
distant twelve shots behind. It was national news. Even the conservative
Peter Thomson, winner of five British Open
Championships and the greatest golfer Australia
has produced, was moved to say that Norman
was the best-looking young player he had seen.

"He was an instant star," Thomson remembers. "I thought he was phenomenal. We're
now in awe of Tiger Woods coming out of the
forest, but Norman was the same at the time.
He was a long hitter and he seemed to have
everything in his favor—good looks, good
physique, nice personality. I thought that he
would be the dominant figure after Nicklaus. In
fact, I was the one who said he would beat
Ballesteros, but everybody in Europe scoffed at
that because right away it was Ballesteros who
started doing things. 'Course Greg didn't."

"HE WAS AN INSTANT STAR," THOMSON REMEMBERS. ". . . WE'RE NOW IN AWE OF TIGER WOODS COMING OUT OF THE FOR-EST, BUT NORMAN WAS THE SAME AT THE TIME."

Rodger Davis, another successful Aus-
tralian, was struck by the dramatic improvement in Norman's game. "Within
a matter of eighteen months, he had gone from being one of the wildest
long hitters to one of the straightest long hitters."

On the final day Norman woke up with Player's words running
through his mind—"The toughest, loneliest place in the world is out in
front of a golf tournament." Cogill did his best to reassure him, and together
they decided that Norman should stick to the aggressive strategy that had
rewarded him so far.

And so it was that when the gun went off, Norman played with complete
abandon, sending every tee shot past the three-hundred-yard marker with scant
regard for the consequences, aiming every iron shot at the pin. It was an expensive play. He notched up six bogeys and a double bogey and, had he not also
managed five birdies, would have handed the tournament to Graham.

"It might have destroyed him forever if he had blown a ten-shot lead,"
Graham said melodramatically.

"I felt the pressure today," admitted Norman, who had a new car and
eight thousand dollars in the bank after just four events. "My stomach was

25

tied in knots." He described victory as "an unreal feeling." He also said, "It's been a great experience and now I know what to do—I think."

Thomson was lavish in his praise. "His rounds of 64, 67, 66, 74 speak for themselves, but the manner of his getting them revealed that here we have a young golfer in the Nicklaus mold—dare I say better? What incredible heights must now be before him . . . what an income this man will earn by the time he reaches thirty."

Back in Brisbane his mother was beside herself with joy. No victory before or since in his career has brought her greater pleasure, and it was compounded when she sank a putt to win the mixed-foursomes championship at Virginia just as Norman won the West Lakes Classic. Her partner was Sommie Mackay, Norman's old boss.

"When I put on the radio and heard that Greg had won, it was so incredible," Toini says. "I couldn't believe it. I was stunned."

So was Norman. "It was a great catalyst for my career, winning as quickly as I did," he says now. "I was Tiger Woods. I went through the same thing that Tiger's going through; I got off to a fast start. . . . At West Lakes, when I blew away the field—ten shots in front in a field with the strength of the Bruce Cramptons, the David Grahams, and Bruce Devlins, those guys who were the icons of Australian golf—I went straight up to the roof and then I was off. I just knew. When I won that seven-thousand-dollar check I thought I was the richest man in the world."

Norman was twenty-one, weighed 185 pounds, and had the unstoppable momentum of greatness. He not only played like a young Nicklaus, he looked like him. A photograph of Norman meeting his hero at the Australian Open a couple of days after West Lakes shows an uncanny resemblance—the same broad faces and tanned, uneven features, the same eagle eyes and chapped lips, the same rough-cut, wind-streaked blond hair, and the same stubborn stances. But none of it helped when Norman was drawn with the Golden Bear in the first round of the tournament. So nervous that he thought he "might die," he shot an 80 to Nicklaus's 72 and died only of embarrassment.

Angry and disappointed and scarcely able to speak, he retreated to his hotel room at the first opportunity. Lying in bed, he relived the anguish of the round over and over again, beginning with his first tee shot, which he had cold-topped, dribbling it thirty yards into a tree. What must Nicklaus have thought of him?

Nicklaus actually thought a great deal of him. "He shot an 80 today, but you'd never know it by his manner," he said of Norman, who was already being nicknamed "the Golden Cub." "The score was not a reflection of his game. He's potentially a very good golfer." He described Norman as having "the physique of a durable athlete."

When Norman recorded a 72 the following day, Nicklaus spent twenty minutes talking to him in the locker room, telling the young Australian that he felt he was good enough to play the PGA Tour in America. "Why don't you think about doing that?" he suggested. Norman was overwhelmed. He would have loved to have told Nicklaus that the first golf book he ever read was his, but instead he just nodded shyly. The trauma of the previous day had been entirely worth it.

Norman finished second behind Bob Shearer on the Australian Order of Merit that year, presenting a unique problem for the PGA. For the first time ever they had to select a trainee professional to represent Australia in the World Cup, held at Mission Hills, California, in mid-December. When Norman and Shearer finished a respectable seventh, the former was given permission to play the professional circuit full-time. If he ever decided he wanted to teach or work in a pro shop, he would have to complete the last eighteen months of his three-year apprenticeship.

Even at that stage it was unlikely Norman would ever find himself so down on his luck that he would have to go back to selling tee pegs, but he was already discovering that life on the road had its own set of problems. Six months after the West Lakes Classic, the company whose equipment he used had still not honored its agreement to pay him a victory bonus of $750. In perhaps the most shortsighted decision any business ever made, the company heads resorted to blackmail, telling Norman that unless he entered into a contract with them he would forfeit the bonus. The contract? A return fare to Europe and $1,500. Norman told them he would "rather die" than sign for that amount.

It was Thomson who came to his rescue. He was already guiding Norman through the formalities of full PGA membership, and when he heard about his predicament, he phoned Norman at a motel in Melbourne where he was staying and asked him to meet him on the tenth tee at Victoria Golf Club.

At the appointed time Norman waited on the tenth. When Thomson appeared, he was walking briskly through the shady avenue of trees from the ninth, talking to the British player Guy Wolstenholme and another sturdy man. Up close, the young Australian took the stranger's measure, noting his sharp eyes and aura of no-nonsense strength. He was smoking a pipe. They shook hands.

"Meet James Marshall," Thomson said.

3

NORMAN CONQUEST

"He will become the world's greatest golfer. He has weaknesses in his game but these will not prevent him from reaching the top."

Norman Von Nida on Greg Norman's potential, 1980

It was barely dawn when Norman rose, pulled a thick shirt over his wide shoulders, whistled to the dogs, and set off across the fields with his shotgun, dew spurting like smoke from his heels. Behind him, Beaurepaire House was etched against the skyline. Its castlelike structure, moat, and manservant lent it an austere but faintly exotic air. Peacocks paraded around the garden, dark trees huddled on the grounds. It resembled a building from fiction: Wuthering Heights or Northanger Abbey.

"It was like one of those English jumble sales," recalls the Australian golf writer Tom Ramsey, who once stayed in Norman's bedroom there, "full of antique furniture and antlers. Parts of the house looked like it belonged to the Addams Family. You just expected the hand to come out of a box and grab you as you walked past."

In a matter of months Norman's life had changed out of all recognition. It had been doing so ever since he first laid eyes on James Marshall at Victoria Golf Club. A former stevedore in Canada and lieutenant in the British Army in Malaysia, Marshall was now a director of two Rolls Royce engineering companies and an Australian company, and it was through his friendship with Thomson and Guy Wolstenholme that he became interested in golf management. Thomson had remarked that his business experience provided the perfect background.

Marshall was something of an entrepreneur, and he thought moving into sports management was an excellent idea. He spent several months studying the form of the British players and, after trying and failing to sign up Nick Faldo, he decided the rest were lacking in ambition. According to Jack Newton, one of Australia's best players at the time, Marshall then attempted to persuade him to become a client. Newton declined but claims he recommended Norman. "If you're ever going to get hold of someone with raw talent, it's him," he said. Meanwhile, Thomson was busy arranging for Norman to meet Marshall in Melbourne.

At Victoria, Norman, his blond Beatles haircut falling over his eyes, was wandering along, animatedly discussing rugby and football with the Englishman when Thomson handed him a driver. "Show James how good you are," he urged as they stepped onto the eleventh tee. Norman was in his street shoes, but he casually unleashed a huge drive that bounded far past the three-hundred-yard marker. Marshall had never seen anything like it. His assessment of the young Australian then and in the ensuing months was that he was "a very rough diamond. Bit of a Jack the Lad. Totally unpolished. The sort of fellow you'd expect to find around Bondi Beach. He was a very outgoing, gregarious, rough-at-the-edges type of guy."

But he was astute enough to realize that there was a lot more to Norman when it came to the course.

"There was something about him that was very different from the English and European players that I had met," Marshall says. "I had a gut feeling that he was a winner. He was very ballsy, very tough, and he had enormous self-confidence. He was a very exciting guy to watch hitting golf balls. And he was very young. It took a lot to get Peter Thomson enthusiastic about anybody. Peter Thomson is never the kind of guy who throws bouquets around all over the place. But Peter thought he had a good chance at being very good, and I liked Greg's attitude, and I liked Greg very much when I met him. I thought it would be quite a lot of fun. I thought I could do quite a lot for him."

That evening Marshall invited Norman to dinner at the Hilton. "He was very charming," Norman remembers. "He said all the right things at the right time."

Marshall claims to have had no thought of managing Norman at all, but he did bear in mind that Ed Barner, whose management of Johnny Miller and Seve Ballesteros would eventually end in tears, was circling like the proverbial shark. Over dinner he questioned Norman closely about his goals. Norman was impressed by Marshall's worldliness, his autocratic air. Here was a man he felt he could really talk to about business. He told Marshall that he felt as if he were being blackmailed by his sponsors. Would Marshall consider helping him? Marshall shook his head. Without a contractual agreement between them, he had no right to intervene.

Norman studied him thoughtfully across the table. Mere hours had elapsed since he had gripped Marshall's hand at Victoria, and yet the glimpse he had caught of Marshall's world—a sophisticated whirl of butlers and landed gentry, first-class flights and fine dining—had left him no doubt that he wanted to be part of it. He decided to trust fate. Shyly, he told Marshall that Thomson had spoken very highly of him and asked the Englishman if he would be interested in managing him.

"Not particularly," Marshall said bluntly.

Norman was crushed. It was the last answer he had expected, and disappointment rose like bile in his throat. Marshall smiled. He liked a man with ambition. He probed Norman further about what sort of arrangement he had in mind and, at the end of the evening, agreed to think it over.

Curiously, it was not Norman's beachboy gaucheness that made Marshall hesitate. It was the awful possibility that Norman, being so young, would have meddling, overbearing stage parents. He had been through that already with Faldo. He made it brutally clear to Norman that he wanted his decision to be made independently, without any prior consultation with his family or advisers. "What I didn't want was to get involved with parents and uncles and aunts and brothers and all of that sort of stuff, because one of the problems when you manage a young player is you get a lot of parents who are on an ego trip and suddenly they're on the bandwagon: 'It's my son and I want to know what he's doing.' "

But Marshall knew intuitively he was on to a good thing. He drafted a contract in his hotel room that night and the principles were agreed with Norman the following morning. Then he told the Australian to get himself a lawyer.

The first Norman's parents knew of it was when he blithely informed them he was about to sign his life away. Their reaction was one of total shock and disbelief. As far as they were concerned, Marshall was a stranger not only to them but also to their son. One round of golf did not constitute a relationship; one meal at the Hilton was no basis for unconditional trust.

Earp rang Marshall and demanded in no uncertain terms to know his intentions. Norman's parents entreated him to think again. But his mind was made up. The fact that Marshall was a friend of both Thomson and Wolstenholme was endorsement enough for him. On February, 17, 1977, forty-eight hours after meeting the Englishman, he signed on the dotted line, "against the wishes of Charlie Earp, against the wishes of my mom and dad, and against the wishes of all my friends in Brisbane," Norman says. "They actually saw through this guy. Everybody did except me. And they all tried to talk me out of doing it."

The die was cast. Under the terms of the contract, Marshall was entitled to 25 percent of Norman's nontournament earnings, a reasonable deal by sports management standards. Within a fortnight, the $750 bonus check due to Norman was in his bank.

NERVOUS THAT HE WOULD BE ROBBED, NORMAN PACKED IT ALL INTO A BRIEFCASE AND CARRIED IT ON THE PLANE WITH HIM.

"My whole approach to management was very different to, perhaps, some, in the sense that I didn't have to make a living, so I wasn't relying on Mr. Norman being successful," Marshall says. "So I never, for example, took a penny of his prize money. Ever. My whole basis was to (a) obviously negotiate good commercial deals for him and (b) to try and get him set up mentally—just like a father with a son—steering the guy in the right direction. . . . My whole objective was to keep his feet on the ground and turn him into a winner who was able to cope with the pressures of winning and losing, and the press and life in general. Because he had led a very sheltered life."

Norman's prospects had now taken on a rose-tinted hue. The Australian Golf Writers Association had voted him the outstanding young player of 1976 and presented him with a return ticket to London, and Marshall had arranged for him to play in three events in Japan. Traveling with Wolstenholme, he shot a closing 66 in the thirty-six-hole Kuzuha International in Nagoya to win by two strokes. He was paid in cash. "I remember sitting on a bed in this hotel room with like a zillion yen all over the room," he said. "I thought I'd never need to work another day."

Nervous that he would be robbed, Norman packed it all into a briefcase and carried it on the plane with him, later depositing it in a foreign bank account at American Express in London. On one of those leaden March days when the wind blows cold enough to freeze the breath in your lungs, Norman arrived in England to start his new life. Marshall picked him up at the airport in a big black Bentley and ferried him home to Hampshire through a patchwork of green and white. When they turned up the long driveway that led to the magnificent Beaurepaire House, Norman felt a rush of euphoria. Lois, Marshall's warm, smiling wife, and the Alsatians Bruno and Celia were there to greet him. He pinched himself. If he hadn't arrived yet, he was well on the way.

Norman was frozen to the marrow. His skin stretched taut across his bones like a cold compress and his rain jacket restricted his backswing. His hands had lost all feeling. He stared miserably across the bleak moonscape of Royal St. George's, gripped and regripped the club, and contemplated another bogey. There was no doubt that he was going to miss the cut in the British PGA Championship, his first British tournament. He tried to convince himself it was because the course didn't suit him.

"I dislike the type of golf test Royal St. George's presents because I believe luck plays too great a part," he said nearly six years later. "I dislike St. Andrews and Muirfield for the same reason. I prefer to play 'target' golf on a course where I know that there is no hidden pimple in the middle of the fairway to send my ball into strangling rough."

In 1975, Severiano Ballesteros had formed exactly the same impression. "It was horrible," recalled the Spaniard who, despite winning three Opens on the links of St. Andrews and Royal Lytham, has never found a place in his heart for St. George's. "So cold, so much wind, so different from any other course I had ever known. Especially I didn't like the fact that there were no trees for my eyes to get reference. I tell you, by the time I had played one round I didn't like anything about Sandwich."

After all of Marshall's support, Norman felt embarrassed to have missed two consecutive cuts. He subjected himself to a harsh postmortem of each costly shot and set off to Blairgowrie for the Martini International determined to justify his manager's faith. There, on the heather-lined fairways, Norman found his feet. He stretched to the watery sun, flexed his golfing muscles, and played with as much joy and abandon as he ever had in Australia. After three rounds he was two strokes behind the leader, Howard Clark. He felt comfortable and confident. At the tenth on the final day, he seized his chance. He made five birdies in six holes for a course-record 66 and victory by three shots over Simon Hobday. His 277 total earned him three thousand pounds. "I've been trying to forget him ever since," says the Zimbabwean.

Ken Schofield, the executive director of the European Tour, has a vivid recollection of seeing the Australian's name next to his final-round score: 1066 (ten under par, 66)—the year of the Norman Conquest.

The media embraced him with open arms. Bored rigid with the aging European stalwarts who had not yet surrendered to the new guard, they saluted him as a surfer-boy incarnation of Nicklaus. "Dazzler Greg Storms In," cried the *Sunday Express*. The *Sunday Telegraph* described him as "the most exciting newcomer to hit the world professional scene for some considerable time. Norman catches both the eye and the imagination. With his blond hair and Nicklaus hairstyle goes a lovely looping swing and a slide into the ball that generates enormous power with no apparent effort."

Marshall was ecstatic. He rewarded Norman with a shotgun. While Norman tried it out on an assortment of unfortunate rabbits and grouse, Marshall spent days on the phone to potential sponsors. He had known the Australian for less than a month and already it was hard to imagine life without him. Norman radiated energy and a kind of irrepressible exuberance. They played golf together, went shooting together.

"He lived with me literally as a son might have done," Marshall says. "He was a fun, normal guy, sort of like a great big teddy bear. He was very kind and considerate."

From the outset Norman, Marshall, and Earp had been in agreement that Europe was the ideal proving ground for him. Norman's plan was to go to the United States when he was twenty-five and had some experience behind him. "He had a lot of growing up to do, golfwise and otherwise," Marshall remembers.

A few days after Norman's victory in the Martini International, Marshall ordered him to pack a bag. They were off to Los Angeles to talk business with Wilson, the sporting goods company. It was Norman's introduction to the thrust and parry of deal making and it left an indelible impression on him. When he returned to London, he had a three-year contract worth one hundred thousand dollars, plus bonuses.

"I fully expect Greg to be a millionaire by the time he's thirty," Marshall told reporters.

Norman reacted to his newfound wealth with unabashed glee. He embraced it, celebrated it, and reached eagerly and unashamedly for the trappings that accompanied it. Later he recalled that the contract with Wilson "paved the way to an extravagance I had never been able to enjoy previously" by making him feel secure and prosperous. He decided he simply had to have a new wardrobe. Naturally, Marshall knew just the place and had all the right connections, and before Norman could say "American Express," he was being shepherded around Harrods with the store manager at one elbow and his own manager at the other. There followed a shopping spree which—although insignificant compared to some of Norman's later indulgences—was the biggest he had ever been on at the time. Suits, sport jackets, shirts, ties, trousers, underwear, and a fine watch piled up at the checkout, and the eventual tally was a staggering four thousand pounds.

It didn't stop there. He loved the speed and superior lines of Marshall's Ferrari, and a second-hand Ferrari of his own was the next item on his agenda. Stewart Ginn, another Australian managed by Marshall, remembers Norman's infectious delight when he picked out the sleek red car and paid the salesman. "He wanted to drive it straight out the showroom," Ginn laughs. "He couldn't bear to wait two days for it to be delivered. He said, 'Give me the keys, I want to drive it right now!' "

Norman enjoyed nothing more than to put his foot flat and feel the wind in his corn-blond hair. Fined £150 for doing 112 miles per hour, he took to playing a dangerous game of hide and seek with police on the country lanes. Within months he had decided that the red Ferrari was too conspicuous and bought a silver one, which he treasured. Although he pushed it to 162 miles per hour, he was stopped only once for speeding, and the policeman asked for his autograph and let him go.

Longmuir recalls with amusement Norman's passion for his cars. Whenever they went into London's West End, Norman insisted on driving, and he had Longmuir and the Italian player Baldovino Dassu in the car one night when he went straight through a red light. "It was just turning red," recalls Longmuir, "but there was a police car behind us, and this police car was straight on our tail and pulled him over. I thought, 'Oh my God, he's going to have the book thrown at him here!'

"But Greg jumped out and he said, 'Before you say anything, if I had tried to stop at that light, I would have caused an accident.' And the policeman was sort of taken aback. He thought, 'Holy shit, who is this guy?' And let him off! It was great."

By the time Norman finished, he had spent more than one hundred thousand dollars on the Ferraris. Commenting on this spree in 1981, he told Australia's *National Times*: "That was stupid. I had the money and I thought, 'Now I'll go out and live like a king.' But I'm over that now. I've sold both Ferraris and I want more of a sedan-type car. I also went mad buying good clothes. I have shirts I've never got out of their wrappers."

His erstwhile manager remembers that period well. "He had two things that were always bubbling to the surface, that needed controlling," Marshall says. "One was that he had a phenomenal ego. I don't think I've ever met anybody with quite such a big ego, even at that age. Secondly, he was ultramaterialistic. Very impressed by money, very impressed by people who had money, and very materialistically oriented. Those, to me, were slight danger signs. I tried to get him to get life into perspective."

But Norman's perspective had already been irrevocably altered. Even now he can recall feeling "like I was King of the Hill. All of these things you get enamored with. You don't see the forest for the trees. I had all these things around me and showered on me. I felt like I was some Lord of the Manor."

While Marshall opened the door to a lifestyle Norman had only dreamed of, taking him to publicity launches and dinners with Muhammad Ali (Marshall's twin brother, John, produced the renowned Ali documentary *The Greatest*), Norman set about conquering Europe with his raw talent and uncomplicated charm. There was no side to him; what you saw was what you got. "He was very green between the ears," Newton says. "I mean, he hadn't been playing that long and he sort of burst onto the scene, had a lot of success early, and was pretty confident and brash."

But as Derek Pillage, who managed Sandy Lyle and Lee Trevino early in their careers, observed, "There was something about him that was different from anybody else, almost like a young Sean Connery."

To the British press, Norman bore more than a superficial resemblance to the Golden Bear, and they were constantly comparing them. "He looks like Nicklaus, he swings like Nicklaus, and he hits the ball as far as Nicklaus," they reported on the eve of the British Open Championship. Norman, whom Nicklaus was trying to persuade to move to America sooner rather than later, tried to play it down.

"THERE WAS SOMETHING ABOUT HIM THAT WAS DIFFERENT FROM ANYBODY ELSE, ALMOST LIKE A YOUNG SEAN CONNERY."

"Sure, it's good to get the flattering publicity and attention," he conceded. "But I don't want to be a bighead. That's my greatest fear."

Missing the cut at Turnberry went some way to ensuring that didn't happen immediately, but his game and his physique were so extraordinary that he couldn't help but attract comment. "Greg had a lot going for him," said Marshall, who was fielding endorsement offers from day one. "He was unusual-looking, he was tall, he was blond, he was an extrovert, and he generated a lot of excitement wherever he went."

But already Norman's gifts were the target of resentment. There was a perception among certain players that he was snobbish and standoffish. "He had a huge amount of style, and I think the British players looked upon him in a jealous manner," Longmuir says. "In some ways the European Tour was a little bit cliquey in those days. It was very British. And he blew them apart."

Analyzing Norman's swing, Lou Miller, the head pro at Pinehurst, North Carolina, and one of the leading teachers at the time, was astounded to hear that the Australian had only taken up golf in his late teens. "He has talent beyond those few years of experience, and once he has harnessed his tremendous power, he will be an outstanding player," he said. His only concern was that Norman's legs might occasionally be too active, causing him to "hit a big push shot to the right." For the most part, Norman's "amazing hand and eye coordination" helped him to correct any problems, but Miller worried that that facility might desert him under pressure.

Ken Brown, who first played with Norman in the Uniroyal International at Moor Park, where he finished tied for ninth, says that, while his technique wasn't nearly as good as it is now, Norman was a "very impressive hitter of the golf ball. He did hit it absolutely enormous distances and the equipment we used then wasn't very good. But each round, he'd miss two or three putts, and his short game then was just like a miniature full swing. Now he has one of the best short games in golf."

Brown warmed to the Australian immediately. "Whenever I played with him, I always thought that he took the game in a nice spirit. Although he tried his hardest, gave it 110 percent, even in the early days I thought he was a very sporting person. He took it all in his stride, all the ups and downs. He took it as a game, rather than an obsession. It wasn't life and death. As a personality, he was larger than life. He came over with James Marshall and he had the air of already being a superstar and a millionaire, even though he hadn't proved that he was a star."

Under Marshall's guidance, Norman quite literally blossomed. Marshall was firm with him, patient with him, coaxed him, and gently educated him. When Norman came home after missing a cut and wanted to sit around venting his frustration and disgustedly telling his manager he could have beaten half the field, Marshall would shut him up by telling him, "Well, you didn't. There's no point in saying [what] you might have done."

Marshall was quite protective of his young protégé, and right from the start there was a sort of distancing between Norman and the other players—even Australians he knew. He discouraged Norman from hanging around the golf club after his rounds. To Marshall, the course could be likened to an office or even a boxing ring, and long lunches and drinking sessions with players one was trying to beat were not conducive to a tough competitive attitude.

Another area he worked on with Norman was media relations, explaining to him that he couldn't just be nice to the press when it suited him. "You had to be able to be civilized to the press whether you had a good round or a bad round. I tried to get him to see that also in people, that the local caddie was just as important as the local president in his own way. I tried to sort of instill in him a sense of values, I suppose."

To anyone who had ever known Norman as a sun-kissed surfer, with hardly a worry in the world as he took his first steps in golf, the change in him was dramatic.

"Marshall gave Greg a lot of sophistication," Ramsey says. "I think Marshall almost taught Greg to hold a knife and fork. That was my feeling at the time."

Norman freely admits it. "He actually took me under his wing and taught me the finer side of life. You know, because I didn't have any refinement about me, about how to dress and how to eat at dinners and all that stuff. He taught me all that. It was wonderful. From then until now, the things he taught me all those years I use every day. So there was a lot of good that he did and a lot of bad."

There was one other person who had almost as much influence over Norman at that age as Marshall, and that was Ginn, Marshall's other client. Ginn first got to know Norman when he was paired with him for the first two rounds of the West Lakes Classic. "I thought, 'My God, this guy's unbelievable,'" says Ginn, now playing on the Japanese Tour. "As a fellow competitor, you knew he was something special. It was scary to watch him play in those days. He had no fear. He still has no fear. I'd never seen a player go at a golf ball the way he did at that time."

The week after West Lakes, Ginn and Norman met up for a beer and a meal, and they have been firm friends ever since. During Norman's first few years on the tour, they shopped, played golf, and hung out at Beaurepaire House together. "He was a lot of fun," Ginn says affectionately, "a real character." Ginn would borrow one of Norman's Ferraris and Norman would drive the other, and they would tear off to tournaments like some high-speed version of Jack Kerouac and Neal Cassady (alias Sal Paradise and Dean Moriarty) in *On the Road*, footloose and in love with life.

"Ginny taught Norman how to be Hollywood," says Mike Clayton, an Australian player, course designer, and columnist. "Ginny had the big hair and the Ferrari. Ginny wore the most outrageous clothes in the seventies. Ginny is the only guy whom you can look at in photos from the seventies and he doesn't look ridiculous. He could carry it off. . . . Greg cultivated his image pretty early on and he could pull it off, too. He had the presence to pull it off."

Ginn, who nicknamed Norman "Hollywood," described him as a quick learner when it came to style and fast living. "When he was twenty, twenty-one, he was a wild boy," he laughs. "He was mad. He was a bit crazy. He was like a wild horse—you couldn't tame him. In a lot of respects Marshall was quite good for him. He helped him out, taught him what to say and how to say it. Before Marshall came along, his nickname was 'Bomber.' One reason was how hard he used to hit the ball. He didn't care what was in the way—trees, skyscrapers. But it was also because he was a maniac in a car and he was a good joker. He loved to play pranks—he still does. He was mad."

"He had his wild moments," Jimmy Barden, a friend from Norman's youth, told Hodenfield in *Today's Golfer*. "Once we were towing Merv's boat back of my car and we got stuck in a traffic jam. So Greg says turn here, now turn here, and soon we were pulling this boat over the back nine at Virginia. I had no idea where we were going. He just kept pushing me along."

One of Norman's favorite party tricks was ripping on the hand brake while traveling at an unsafe pace. "I remember coming up the drive to the golf club at the Australian Open with him," Ginn says. "We were in a souped-up yellow Ford or something from one of the cowboys, and he locks the brakes, and the engine is screaming and smoke's pouring out, and he doesn't care. He was an idiot."

Norman always claims that, as a young man, he was an introvert. "I absolutely had to force myself to speak to people, no question about it," he told *Fore!*. "I was so shy it was almost painful. I was into myself and I was terrified to bring myself out. The only time I felt sure of myself, the only time I felt confident, was when I was on the golf course." He has a clear recollection of sitting by himself after the presentation ceremony at West Lakes, dressed in white trousers and a green shirt, knowing that he was supposed to mingle with sponsors but not knowing how. "I said to myself, 'Son, you've got to change,' " Norman remembers. " 'If you want to be the best player you can be and go on and win golf tournaments, you're going to have to learn to mingle and make conversation.' That was harder for me than working on my golf game because it went against my grain. It probably took me five years."

His mother says that he was only shy-ish. "He always says that when he won the West Lakes Classic he sat in the corner by himself having a beer, but I think that's a bit of an exaggeration. His friend was caddying for him so he was probably there."

On the tour Norman was popular with those players good enough not to be jealous of him, namely Sam Torrance, a rough, talented Scot; Michael King, universally known as Queenie; an Irishman with a talent for fun named John O'Leary; and, of course, Longmuir. There was a tiny pub behind the race course in York that was a favorite haunt of the five of them, and they spent time there whenever they were in town. "Greg used to do alot of nice things for people," Ginn says, remembering Norman's kindness toward the owners, "and one of them was always staying there. It was only a tiny place and he could have stayed anywhere he liked, but he always made a point of going back there, even when he became who he became."

But for all Norman's apparent openness and effervescence, he was intensely private. "He was a tough guy to get close to," Longmuir says. "You sort of had to get to know him." He remembers thinking it strange that Norman discouraged any conversation about his life back in Australia. "He's quite a deep person. You won't find out much about him by being with him. He won't really talk much about his past. . . . He never spoke about his family. I got the impression that his father thought he should have stayed at school or was disappointed that he became a sportsman."

Years later Norman told *Sports Illustrated* that Merv's muted response to his early achievements preyed on his mind. "Even when I started climbing the ladder, he didn't think I'd be anything," Norman said. "I had a point to prove to him, to everybody."

Today Norman believes that his first three victories were crucial to his success. "The West Lakes Classic, the Martini, and the tournament I won in Japan—my first three tournaments I won on each respective tour—were the most important for me."

In the second half of 1977, he was eighth in the Scandinavian Enterprise Open, third in the Irish Open, and racked up five top-five finishes in Australia. He also went to America to play in the Memorial Tournament in Dublin, Ohio, at the invitation of Nicklaus. When he missed the cut, he was totally distraught. Larry O'Brien, vice president of Nicklaus's Golden Bear International, recalled, "Every morning he'd get up early and go hit three hundred or more balls on the practice tee. He was so determined that this would not happen again."

The only hitch in a well-laid set of plans was the $180,000 Australian Open pro-am, to which Norman was not invited. It was a petty snub and Marshall was justifiably angry on his behalf. "Here is a guy who has made a terrific impression for Australian golf in Britain and Japan this year," he told

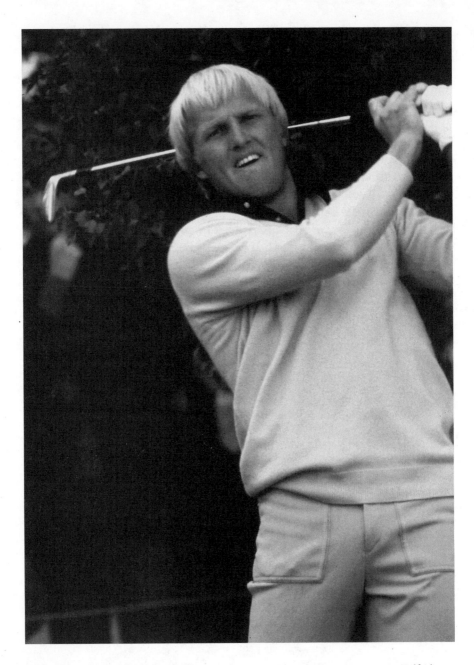

Norman, blossoming under James Marshall's direction, swings his way to success at Fulford in 1978. (© Phil Sheldon)

the press after heated confrontations with various officials. "Yet he is kicked in the backside like this." When the officials claimed there had been an oversight and allowed Norman to play, he got back at them by winning.

In retrospect, Thomson believes that Norman's first few years on the European tour were some of the happiest of his career. "I don't think there was any pressure on him at all. He was enjoying himself immensely. The 'majors,' as we call them, didn't come into his thinking. He was out there having a ball, playing golf, which he wanted to do more than anything, with plenty of social life, big flashy cars, and a lot of money flooding in. He was on top of the world."

LOVE AND WAR

"The envy brigade is very strong in golf."

Colin Snape, 1997

In the December 13, 1978, edition of the *Sun,* there is a picture of Norman with a big smile on his face and his arm around Sue Barker, the British tennis player who had been No. 3 in the world the previous year. They make an attractive couple. The headline reads, "It's Sue with Her New Beau in Tow," and Norman is reported as saying, "She's going to teach me tennis and I'll teach her golf."

For a sportsman who was routinely described as movie-star handsome and charming to boot, Norman seems to have had few, if any, serious relationships before he married. Longmuir has a dim recollection of an Australian girl, left behind during his first season, but essentially Norman was quite reserved. On the golf course he had a natural presence and a ready smile that made him seem more gregarious than he was, but away from it he preferred to race his car down the narrow country lanes, walk the dogs, or sit with his gun on the hood of Marshall's jeep in the dark grounds at Beaurepaire House, picking off rabbits in the headlights.

"When he came back from a tournament, he wasn't interested in getting into the car and driving into the city to the nightclubs," Marshall says. "He wasn't like that."

To some extent that changed when he met Barker at a golf tournament in Brisbane in November 1978. Introduced by Marshall, they liked each other on sight. When they left Australia, they left together, and Barker followed him to the World Cup in Hawaii, Mexico City, and New York before they returned to England for Christmas.

In February, Barker, who had recently split with her coach and suffered a slump on the tennis court and had also broken off her engagement to a tennis player just six weeks before she met Norman, told the *Mirror*, "It worries me that I'll be away from Greg, but we both realize that our careers are the most important thing at the moment." In the *Daily Mail* she described her relationship with Norman as "an easy thing. Not intense. We're very similar."

"The guy who said absence makes the heart grow fonder was dead right," grinned Norman. "I'd hate to see my telephone bill."

That season Norman had won four times in Australia and once in Fiji, beginning by making seven birdies and an eagle in a course-record 64 to beat Ian Stanley by three strokes in the Caltex Festival of Sydney Open in January. Over seventy-two holes he made just three bogeys. Elsewhere, he felt he had met ill fortune at every turn.

"I'm not using that as an excuse," he said in September at Pacific Harbor, the Fijian resort for which he had signed a two-year deal to represent. "It's just a totally new experience for me. I seem to have been dogged by bad luck since my two Australian victories in January. Take the Swiss Open last week. I was a shot behind playing the eighth hole, and I knew I could reach the par-five in two for an eagle chance. My shot hit a small stake fifteen yards in front of me, flew back, hit my caddie, and rebounded into deep rough. Any chance of winning went out the door right there. And that's the sort of luck I've been having."

Three days later he won the South Seas Classic on the third hole of a play-off.

Marshall remembers Norman's brief romance with Barker as a rarity in his life. "I would not say he was a lady killer in any stretch of the imagination. As I say, the Greg I knew and managed and who lived with us was very, very different from the Greg he became, but leopards don't change their spots. They can only change them superficially. I mean, there are numerous things that Greg will say about things that just plainly aren't true. For example, if you were to say to Greg, 'Did you know Sue Barker very well?' he'd brush it off and say, 'Very superficially.' But of course it's not true. He was very keen on Sue. It was Sue who finished the relationship."

In point of fact, Norman was denying that his relationship with Barker had ever been anything but the most casual of acquaintainceships by May the following year. "We were just friends," he said firmly. "It's hardly worth mentioning."

The line of traffic stretched far into the foggy distance on the mountain road that led to the New Territories. Norman and Marshall sat resignedly in the back of the limousine, staring out at the misty rain that blurred the Hong Kong skyline. They had allowed an hour to get to Fanling Golf Club, but it was taking two. Norman glanced at his watch and swore. "We're going to be lucky to make it," he said.

In three years on tour Norman had learned several useful lessons, one of them being that the first rule of travel was to be patient in situations about which he could do nothing. However, he had also become much more outspoken. Take the subject of appearance money, which was an issue very early in his career. "Players can't bitch about what the sponsor wants to do with his money," Norman said, after hearing that Bob Shearer planned to boycott the 1979 Australian PGA because David Graham was getting ten thousand dollars to play. "If the Yanks get it, certainly the Aussies should get it if they've proved themselves. I know Melbourne is Bobby's hometown, but he's won nothing really big yet. David has won the Australian Open, he has proved himself in America, and he won the World Match Play Championship."

It was the first of numerous rows in Australia over appearance fees. By 1981, Norman was paid everywhere he played, with the exception of the World Match Play, the Martini, and in the United States. His fees in his own country had rocketed to fifteen thousand dollars, although Marshall claimed he didn't receive a cent to play in the Australian Open. Significantly, Norman was one of the only players to support his arch-rival Ballesteros during the Spaniard's dispute with the European Tour Players Division that year, describing him as "the Arnold Palmer of Europe" to officials. It made no difference. Ballesteros resigned from the tour in protest over the appearance-money ban and was controversially left out of the Ryder Cup.

In Hong Kong, where Norman was appearing early in 1979 as part of his Cathay-Pacific deal, Marshall climbed out of the car and enterprisingly organized a police escort. They arrived at the club with five minutes to spare. Norman was three strokes off the lead and paired with Little Lu, the nephew of the diminutive, pork-pie-hatted Mr. Lu, who was narrowly beaten by Lee Trevino in the 1971 British Open. The gallery was large and vociferous, and when the referee awarded him a free drop from ground under repair at the ninth, they took on a mob mentality. Upset by their perceptible anger, Norman topped his next tee shot, but he held on to win with a sixteen-foot birdie putt at the last. The twenty-thousand-dollar check was the biggest of his career so far.

Five years later, when he again won the Hong Kong Open, Norman whiled away a rain-out by hitting balls out of his hotel window into the harbor far below.

WHEN HE AGAIN WON THE HONG KONG OPEN, NORMAN WHILED AWAY A RAIN-OUT BY HITTING BALLS OUT OF HIS HOTEL WINDOW INTO THE HARBOR FAR BELOW.

When the first-class passengers were called, Norman and Marshall made their way out to the plane. Norman smiled perfunctorily in the direction of the flight attendants as he headed toward his seat. Then his heart stopped, skipped a beat, started again jerkily. A strange feeling of euphoria swept over him. He fastened his seat belt and looked over at the beautiful brunette who had caught his gaze.

"I remember telling James Marshall, 'I bet you I'll marry that woman,' " Norman says. "And I had never even met her, never even said one word to her."

It was the summer of 1979. Norman and Marshall were flying from Detroit to New York after his first U.S. Open at Inverness, where he had finished forty-eighth. His disappointment vanished at a stroke when Laura Andrassy came down the aisle. Marshall cast an amused glance at his face and shook his head.

"What can I get you?" Laura asked.

"A 7-Up, please," Norman said.

Marshall jumped up.

"You sit down, honey, and I'll get the drinks," he said, and reached for Laura's tray. Ignoring her protests, he steered her briskly into his seat. "I'd like to introduce you to Gregory Norman," he said, and departed to help several open-mouthed flight attendants mix drinks for the passengers.

Norman flushed with embarrassment. He hated being called by his full name. Recovering his composure, he politely began to ask her where she was from and about her job at American Airlines. "He was shy and so was I, but we managed to get a conversation going," Laura recalled.

Laura had done several charter flights with athletes, notably the Oakland Raiders and the New York Knicks, most of whom had left a bad impression on her ("They're all kind of grubby guys."). Her first reaction when she heard Norman was a golfer was, " 'Oh, not another one of those athletes.' But he was such a gentleman. He didn't drink and he wasn't a rowdy type of guy, and I was very impressed by that."

Later in the flight she went up to the cockpit. "I said, 'Guys, I think I'm in love. There's this golfer out there named Greg Norman.' They said, 'He's pulling your leg. There's no such golfer.' They said he was giving me this story so I'd go out with him."

Fate hasn't often been kind to Norman, but it was kind to him then. The forty-minute flight was extended to eighty by air traffic controllers, and he asked Laura to have dinner with them when they reached New York. At first she was hesitant, but Norman persisted, and when they landed at midnight she agreed to meet him in Manhattan. He was checking into his hotel when she paged him. There was a fuel strike and she couldn't get a taxi. Refusing to be diverted, Norman decided to call a cab and collect her. None were available for love or money. He was standing on the empty street, cursing his luck, when a limousine pulled up and two passengers stepped out.

"When he showed up in front of my hotel in this long black limousine, I thought, 'Who in the heck is this guy?' " Laura says. By then, it was nearly 2:00 A.M. and every restaurant they tried was closing. Norman and Laura sat in the back of the limo with the lights of Manhattan flashing in and laughed until they cried. "I thought he was wonderful," says Laura, who wondered afterward whether she would ever hear from him again. "We had such a nice time. We got along just like that, immediately. He was a real gentleman. Not pushy. Very appealing, in fact."

The bill for the limousine was two hundred dollars. "You're crazy," Marshall told Norman gruffly when he put him on a plane to Bermuda the next day. Norman didn't care. He had already tried to persuade Laura to come to Britain for the British Open. "I thought, 'This guy's crazy,' " Laura said. 'I don't even know him.' " She suggested that he come to New York again instead. Norman, who had returned to Britain for a few days before leaving for Japan, arranged to spend three days there on his way back. On their first evening together, they had a moonlit dinner at the Twin Trade Towers restaurant.

"I guess that's probably when we fell in love," Laura says.

Norman did convince Laura she should come to Britain, although she suggested it be after the British Open, not before it. "The tournament is too important to you and I would only be in the way," she said, so Norman went to Royal Lytham well before the tournament started. Out in the twisting sea breezes, he mapped the soft ochre links and tall grasses and puzzled over the greens. He was disappointed when he finished eighth. That was the year that Ballesteros, the raven-haired Spanish genius, combined some of the wildest driving and most magical recovery shots—most notoriously a birdie from the car park near the sixteenth on the final day—ever seen at a British Open, to become the youngest winner this century. Norman, who felt he was in with a chance, scored a 76 that day and complained that the last round "did not treat me kindly."

The day after the Open, he drove his red Ferrari to Heathrow Airport to fetch Laura. She was only in London for four days, but they made the most of them, taking long walks through the woods at Beaurepaire House, sight-seeing at St. Paul's, Madame Tussaud's, and the Tower of London, and enjoying cozy dinners with James and Lois Marshall. They felt very comfortable with one another. The only bad moment came when Norman's Ferrari was damaged by vandals while they were at dinner one night in the West End. The bill for restoring it came to one thousand pounds.

Toward the end of the season, Norman strained his back and was out for six weeks, but he recovered in time for the Australian Open. With the exception of the majors, there was no title on earth he wanted more and, when he shot 73, 69, 73 to take the lead going into the last round, he was overjoyed.

On Sunday a duel developed between Norman and Newton. To Norman, Newton was "a character of enormous magnetism who treats the game with an outwardly casual approach, chain-smoking his way from tee to green and, when the day's work is finished, is always ready to slap a dollar on the bar and enjoy himself." That there was a little more to Newton was demonstrated by his performance at Metropolitan. Norman, who could have won with a birdie on the eighteenth, three-putted from the lower tier some twenty feet away to hand the tournament to his rival.

To this day he can remember his mind going black and his body turning ice-cold as the putt that would have left him tied for the Australian Open slipped past the hole. "The combination of disappointment and disbelief was merged into a nightmarish experience I will never forget."

Up in the stands his mother burst into tears. Newton was engulfed by jubilant well-wishers. Sportingly, Norman put an arm around him and said, "Great work, Newts," before stumbling away to the locker room, where his father and caddie were waiting. Told an hour later that he had been fined fifty dollars for failing to reappear for the prize-giving ceremony, he blew his top in the tournament director's office, claiming that nobody had come to tell him it was taking place.

"The next day the Australian papers all carried the same story: 'Norman lacks the guts to become a champion,' " he recalled in his instruction book *Shark Attack!*. " 'He missed his chance, and now he'll never win a big one.' When I saw those headlines, I was livid. I vowed to [teach] those newspapers a lesson, and the next year I did."

He took a break then and enjoyed the summer, fishing and shooting kangaroos to his heart's content. His antidote to all the activity was the occasional lie-in. "I've been known to sleep for twelve hours when I'm not playing golf," he grinned.

Because of a dispute between Marshall and the sponsors (Marshall claims it was the other way around and that, after a "dust-up with Cathay Pacific, Norman almost became persona non grata" in the region), Norman did not defend his Hong Kong Open title. Neither did he get to the Spanish Open. He and Ginn flew into Madrid from the Italian Open, unaware they needed visas, and they were put straight on a plane to London.

In the end both incidents were minor blips in a brilliant season. Norman cut a swathe across the European circuit, finishing ten shots clear of the field in the French Open, winning the Scandinavian Open and the World Match Play, and racking up more than a dozen top tens. "Each tournament you win is like going up another step," he said. "Then all of a sudden you come to major championships. . . . By the time I'm thirty or thirty-one, I'll know if I'm going to make it to number one."

At the Irish Open in August, Jackie Lee, who had followed Paul "the Singing Caddie" Stevens onto Norman's bag, turned up late for duty and was promptly sacked. Scotty Gilmour, a grizzled veteran of more than twenty years on the U.S. circuit, offered his services. He had started caddying during World War II, been evacuated to Turnberry during the Blitz, and later carried the bags of some of the best players in the game, including Tony Jacklin, Tom Weiskopf, Gary Player, and Arnold Palmer.

Norman reminded him of Raymond Floyd. "Same kind of mind as Floyd," says Gilmour, who earned £175 per week plus 5 percent for a top-twenty finish. "Completely zoned. Just cut everything off in the world. Kind of a Jekyll and Hyde on the course and sometimes in his social life . . . same type of personality as Floyd. They can be the nicest guys in the world one day and the next day they're the complete opposite." He had lots of fun with Norman in the beginning. "He was a bit crazy. Quite wild. He'd jump in a car and go a hundred miles an hour down a country lane. Reckless. I had some good laughs with him."

When Norman finally won the Australian Open at the Lakes that year, Gilmour told reporters, "I've caddied for the best and let me tell you, he's going to be the one to beat around the world. Next year, he'll be a household name."

"He's a great believer in me," said Norman, for whom victory had brought the promise of the most priceless award of all, an invitation to the Masters. "He never thinks I'm going to shoot a bad round. He's done a lot for my game."

He had been desperately disappointed when he lost the European Order of Merit by just £278 to Sandy Lyle, but it hadn't altered his lifestyle. In Australia the *National Times* reported that Norman had bought and sold property in Honolulu, London, and Queensland. His most recent purchase was a $175,000 Gold Coast house, with a pool and a jetty leading down to the sea, which Laura was helping him to decorate. When in the United States, he stayed with Laura in her Washington, D.C., apartment.

"Laura's very upset with me because I don't know how much money I've got," laughed Norman, who was heading off to Divot, his new home at Paradise Point. "I've got bank accounts here and in England and America. When I get a check, I put it in the bank in whatever country I'm in. I don't know what it adds up to."

The envelope that would influence Norman's destiny arrived at his parents' home in Brisbane early in 1981. The card inside, with its distinctive symbol—a yellow flag inside an emerald green outline of the United States—was more than an invitation. It was a passport to agony, ecstasy, and history.

Norman was delirious with excitement, promptly winning the Australian Masters by seven shots at Huntingdale and setting off to Augusta with hope in his heart. Years before, Palmer had said, "From the moment I set foot on Augusta National, my whole view of the game of golf changed. In fact, I think Augusta National actually set the tone for my entire career. It was such an immaculate place with everything done first class. And the grass was just beautiful. It was pretty awesome."

In a slightly different sense Augusta set the tone for Norman's career. As soon as he turned up Magnolia Drive, breathed in the heavenly scent of the pines, and saw the pristine white clubhouse; the pink, white, and scarlet splash of azaleas, rhododendron, and dogwood; and the snowy bunkers etched against the flawless emerald fairways, he felt the same way Palmer had. "I'll never forget how I was struck by Augusta that first year," he told *Golf Digest*. "This was what golf was meant to be, pure golf. This was the purest form of golf tournament. Everything about it was first rate. That drive up Magnolia Lane, with the clubhouse ahead, the practice ranges on either side, it just gets you in the perfect frame of mind for a tournament."

Standing on the first tee a few days later, Norman struggled to recall his earlier enthusiasm. He felt sick. Nerves gathered like termites in his stomach and gnawed away at his innards. His clubs felt like lead weights in his hands. He avoided Nicklaus's eyes, stared glumly down the fairway, and executed a stiff practice swing. When the starter announced his name, he pushed his drive woodenly down the first and walked after it with his eyes fixed firmly on the hill in front of him.

A smile tugged at Nicklaus's mouth. He put an arm around his young partner's shoulders and said quietly, "I don't know about you, but by the time we reach the top of this hill, my feet will just about be back on the ground, I'm so nervous."

"THAT DRIVE UP MAGNOLIA LANE, WITH THE CLUBHOUSE AHEAD, THE PRACTICE RANGES ON EITHER SIDE, IT JUST GETS YOU IN THE PERFECT FRAME OF MIND FOR A TOURNAMENT."

Norman had never felt so grateful to anyone in his life. Relief flooded through him, the nauseous feeling receded, and all of a sudden Augusta looked beautiful again. He felt he could focus, could think about putting his name on the leaderboard. "Take a deep breath and let's enjoy the golf," Nicklaus said encouragingly.

Norman did just that. When the round ended, he was tied for the lead with Johnny Miller, Keith Fergus, Lon Hinkle, and Curtis Strange at 69. "Just being here is probably the greatest thrill of my life," Norman told reporters.

It was the first time many of the Americans had seen Norman play, much less had the chance to speak to him, and Norman felt slightly overwhelmed by the size of the press corps. "What should I say if they ask me what I do?" he panicked.

"Oh," said Marshall airily, "tell them that you love hunting great white sharks."

In his press conference Norman, lighting up the room with his sunburnt, muscular physique and toothpaste smile, painted a picture of blissful childhood, surfing and skin diving on the Great Barrier Reef, casually remarking that he would love to have shot the sharks that ate the fish he caught. The next morning, the headline in the *Augusta Chronicle* read, "Great White Shark Leads Masters."

Nicklaus took control of the tournament in the second round, shooting a 65 that could easily have been a course record, and it left him with a four-shot lead. Norman recorded an impressive 70 and played Augusta, where experience is everything, as if his game were made for the spacious fairways and enigmatic greens. The third round developed into a duel between Nicklaus and Tom Watson, but Norman held on to record a 72 and was in third going into the final round.

Afterward, he described his six-iron to the sixteenth on Saturday as "one of the best six-irons of my life. Jack had the honor and he hit a shot in there close. Jack is Jack at Augusta. The people went nuts. I stepped up and hit a six-iron inside of him. I'll always remember that shot. I felt like King of the Hill."

Had it not been for a double bogey at the tenth on Sunday, Norman might have been able to overhaul Watson. At the seventh a perfect pitch shot earned him a birdie and moved him alongside Nicklaus at five under par. At the turn Watson was just two in front. But at the par-four tenth, Norman pulled his drive into the trees and was three under par when he emerged from them with a six. He finished fourth at five-under 283, three behind Watson and one behind Nicklaus and Miller, an extraordinary achievement for a player with so little experience on American courses—none at Augusta.

The American media greeted his arrival as rapturously as their European counterparts had four years earlier. "With his platinum-blond Prince Valiant hairdo, Norman looks more like a surfer than a golfer," wrote Herbert Warren Wind in the *New Yorker*, "but . . . [he] should do very well if he decides to campaign in this country."

"Norman's an awfully strong young player," Nicklaus agreed. "I think he will get a Green Jacket one of these days. He's also got something golf needs—charisma."

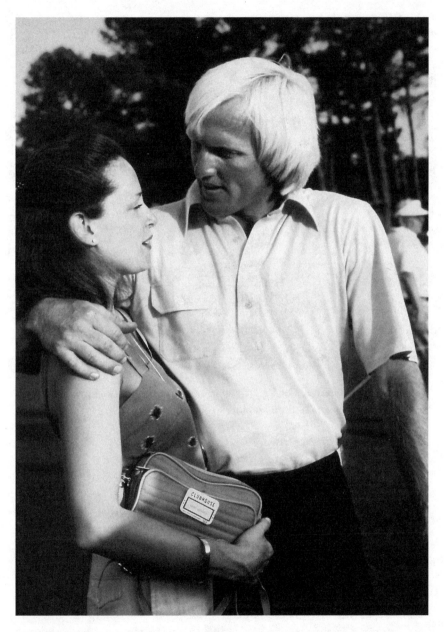

Young love: Just days before he proposed, Norman embraces Laura at Augusta.
(© Phil Sheldon)

Showman: With eventual winner Tom Watson looking on, Norman aims for success in the 1981 Masters at Augusta. (© Phil Sheldon)

"He's like a big cat, almost ferocious in his intensity," said teacher Paul Runyan. "I thought his swing looked very sound."

These accolades were all very well, but Norman, who had been close enough to the Green Jacket to almost feel its cool silk lining sliding over his shoulders, was bitterly disappointed. It's hard to imagine that he wasn't heart-sore as he drove away from Augusta, and yet it was the first of numerous occasions in his career when he appeared to put his disappointment into a locked room in his mind and move on almost instantaneously. That night he asked Laura to marry him.

"I'm the kind of guy who just lives for now," Norman said. "I can forget about everything. When I lost the Masters, I went back to the house and [Laura] and my friends were all sad. I had to cheer them up. There was nothing to be done except learn from it. I have."

The invention of Norman's Great White Shark label had a bizarre twist. Norman felt that, during the press conference where he talked about hating sharks and wanting to destroy them, a misunderstanding had arisen and the journalists gained the impression that he had actually shot a few. Since this was not the case, the inaccuracy bothered him. "When I got back to Australia later that year, I decided to put my conscience at ease," Norman recalled. He put a .303 rifle in the cabin of *Divot II*, his twenty-eight-foot oceangoing cruiser, spent several hours patrolling the coastline in Queensland and, when he spotted a dorsal fin, "buried several bullets into the thick skin of an ugly hammerhead and hoped those American golf writers understood."

As to whether the shark—massacred to lend veracity to an unpleasant embellishment—understood, he doesn't say.

His conscience clear, his dream partly realized, Norman launched into 1981 with gusto. "No one could ever accuse Greg Norman of being modest," Louis T. Stanley observed in the *Pelham Golf Yearbook*. "His self-confidence and belief in himself are tantamount to a pep talk. When he arrived in Britain this year, he mentioned as an aside that he intended to win three tournaments. Just like that. And the remarkable thing is that he almost did so."

Item one on Norman's agenda was to win another Martini at Wentworth. All week long rain slanted across the fairways of the Burma Road course, and Sunday was no different. By the time Norman reached the eighteenth, delays had stretched his final round to almost six hours. He was cold and wet, but he felt good on the greens. His mother had mailed him the putter he had vented his rage on after the Australian Open two years earlier.

Once again, his drive died where it pitched, kicking up a muddy spray. "You need an eagle to be sure of winning," his caddie told him.

Norman hesitated. He selected a one-iron, gave it everything he had, and it soared 228 yards down the fairway. It landed eighteen yards from the pin and Norman stroked it in for a three. When Bernhard Langer's birdie putt turned away from the hole, the Australian had won his third Martini with a total of 287, the only score under par.

To Norman there was no reason he couldn't win three successive events, but Faldo had other plans. The Englishman's willowy swing and methodical approach were suited to Ganton and, in the final round, when unruly galleries crowded the fairways, he swept to ten under par to win the British PGA Championship.

"Faldo always had an edge over Greg, mentally," Gilmour remembers.

It was a bittersweet triumph. Faldo and his playing partners, Ken Brown and Norman, finished forty minutes after the previous group. Faldo and Norman were fined fifty pounds each for slow play, and Brown, a frequent offender, one hundred pounds. They were outraged. "It wasn't our fault," Faldo whined. "We had a big gallery and had to wait at least thirty-six times for the fairway to be cleared. It's really upsetting. We put on a damn good show, but instead of a slap on the back we get a slap in the face."

In those days Brown was something of a rebel without a cause, a gifted player with a knack for finding trouble; and Norman, angry at his uncaring attitude, chose the interval when their penalty was being decided to take him to task over it. Norman informed Brown that unless he changed his habits, he would destroy himself on the golf tour and that other players on the tour would grow to hate playing with him.

Brown's memory of the conversation is hazy, but he does know "it would have been water off a duck's back. I was forever being chastised for something or other."

The next week Norman bounced back with an easy victory in the Dunlop Masters, taking his earnings for the year to twenty-seven thousand pounds. "Two out of three isn't bad," he grinned.

"Norman is not only a successful player," remarked the *Mirror*, "he has taken over from Severiano Ballesteros as the darling of the crowds. And unlike the Spaniard, the big, fair-haired Australian always has time for a wave and a smile, whether he has just birdied a hole or dropped a shot."

His free-wheeling, happy-go-lucky style of play had won him a huge following, particularly among women. "Greg does appeal to the girls," said his mother. "We get heaps of fan mail from women all over the world asking for pictures and autographs. But Greg only has time for two women, me and his girlfriend." Norman phoned Toini for half an hour every single day from wherever he was in the world.

"I'd be telling a lie if I didn't say I'm amazed at how well I've done so quickly," said Norman, who was in the process of signing a deal to represent the Rolls of Monmouth club and drive a Rolls Royce. "I'm feeling pretty good." He had won nineteen of the one hundred events he had played in as a pro. "I don't think I've ever played a bad round of golf, even when I first picked up the clubs at fifteen," he told *People* magazine in Australia. "It's probably true that I'm a natural, but that doesn't mean it was all easy."

He told *Woman's Day*, which featured him in a swashbuckling pose at the wheel of a speedboat, that he never dreamed of staying in anything but the best hotels. "Can't see the point in it." That, he said, was why there was so much "bitching" about him. "I know there are some people who are not very nice about me. That's understandable. I've come a long way in a short time. I've tried very hard and succeeded."

Tony Johnstone, the Zimbabwean, remembers playing with Norman at the Italian Open. "He started eagle, hole in one, and I'd never heard of him. The night before John Bland and I were looking at the noticeboard and I said, 'Who's this G. Norman?' He said, 'You've never heard of Greg Norman? He's going to be a superstar.' After two holes with him, I knew that. He shot a 64 and made it look easy."

"The secret of his success is an outsize ego," Louis T. Stanley observed cuttingly. "His belief in himself is off-putting, but it does the trick."

On July 1, 1981, Norman and Laura were married at St. Mary's Catholic Church in Old Town Alexandria, Virginia. Marshall was Norman's best man, and his parents flew in for the ceremony. Because of the time constraints— they had brought the wedding forward from September to July to coincide with Merv and Toini's trip to the U.S. Open—it was a small, intimate ceremony, with only a few of Laura's friends and her immediate family invited.

"I'm fantastically happy," Norman said.

Marshall's reaction to their marriage had been mixed. "He said he was excited, but I don't think he was excited," Laura says with a laugh, speculating that he viewed her as an interloper in the close relationship he enjoyed with Norman.

Ginn, who could see the cracks appearing in the Marshall–Norman relationship, suspects she was right. "The writing was on the wall. When Greg got married, there was someone else to help him and advise him."

HIS FREE-WHEELING, HAPPY-GO-LUCKY STYLE OF PLAY HAD WON HIM A HUGE FOLLOWING, PARTICULARLY AMONG WOMEN. "GREG DOES APPEAL TO THE GIRLS," SAID HIS MOTHER.

The couple held three receptions, one in Washington, one in England, and one in Australia, and they were planning to buy a house in the United States. "One of the wonderful things about Laura is that she hates golf," Norman said. "When I come back to the hotel after a grueling day of competition, we can relax over a meal without talking golf."

"Laura has given Greg a more level-headed approach to life," his mother concurred.

But not even Laura's influence was failsafe. The more desperate Norman became to win a major, the more pressure he put on himself, and now he grew agitated days before the British Open began at St. George's. "He was pacing up and down waiting for the gun to go off," Laura said. "I tried to tell him in a subtle way that it wasn't a race."

The previous year he had been exactly the same way at Muirfield, saying he felt "like a dog straining at a leash" days before the event started. Walking to the first tee in the first round, he felt drained. "So far the Open has not been the happiest of experiences for me, but to win it still remains my biggest ambition in golf."

At Sandwich the Open kicked off amid the usual flurry of silly-season stories. In twenty years the Americans had won the title thirteen times, but they complained that the event was prohibitively expensive. What with first-class air tickets to procure, wives and children to bring, coaches to pay, and five-star hotel accommodations to be found, only those who finished in the top fifteen broke even. On a more serious note, Lee Trevino said that the course was playing so long, the power players would do well, namely, Ballesteros, Norman, Nicklaus, Watson, and Floyd.

For Norman, at least, it was not to be. He was two behind the leaders, Nick Job and Vicente Fernandez, after an opening 72, and in the second round he crashed to a 75. There is a picture of him standing knee-deep in grass, Rupert the Bear trousers splayed, teeth gritted, his huge hands struggling to hold on to his follow-through after extracting a clump as big as a haystack from the rough.

He had peaked too early again. And in spite of the fact that he had come to the realization that he had to find "the key that unlocks Britain's seaside links," regardless of whether or not he liked them, because those were the courses on which he would ultimately be examined, he flew into a rage and refused to speak to the press.

"Greg Norman fell by the wayside with the second-round 75 and put on a display of petulance that would have done John McEnroe proud," an Australian newspaper reported. "More seriously for the future of Norman's golf, boiling temperament off the course spilled onto it the next day. Making a charge back into contention, he misjudged a drive that wound up in a fairway bunker. Cursing as he strode after it, Norman slashed at the sand all too hurriedly and had a bogey. He could not curb the tide of self-destruction and picked up more bogeys on three of the next four holes. It was a crucial time in the world's premier Open tournament and Norman blew it."

As a teenager Norman had indulged his temper freely on the golf course until the day his father walked away from him in disgust. Playing in a club match at Virginia, he had thrown a series of tantrums, finally sending a seven-iron cartwheeling down the fairway. Merv went straight home. When Norman returned, sheepish and repentant, Merv gave him a lecture that turned him white beneath his tan.

"No self-respecting golfer would think of doing what you did today," Merv raged.

"He used to get mad with himself if he didn't hit the perfect shot," Toini says. "I used to caddie for him a bit, and I'd tell him that he had to learn not to expect perfection all the time. But he always did expect perfection."

Norman, who had never thought of how his behavior might look—much less considered the effect it might have on his game—was almost in tears. He made a mental resolution never to throw a club again. "Certainly, I have a temper. Sometimes I think I graduated with straight A's in this department," he admitted years later. But in golf he learned to keep it in check.

Off the course he was less successful. Little things sent him berserk. In a classic case of road rage, in the early eighties in Britain, he chased down a car which had swerved recklessly in front of him and punched the driver in the jaw.

"He had a very quick temper," Marshall recalls, "which I spotted very early on and which I tried to get him to control. For example, he might be going through an airport and somebody would brush against him completely by accident, and Greg would almost turn around and hit the guy. He was funny like that. He had a very short fuse."

A definite flashpoint was smoking, which Norman hated. Longmuir and Queenie avoided lighting up anywhere near him because they knew it irritated him, but it could not always be avoided. One evening Norman and Longmuir went with Queenie and a couple of his wealthy Sunningdale friends to the Thatched Tavern, a low-ceilinged old pub, rich in character. The moment they sat down, the woman in their party lit up a cigarette. Discreetly, Norman opened the door to let some fresh air in. She stood up and closed it. Norman opened it again. She closed it.

"She kept making comments," Longmuir recalled. "She was moaning and bitching about Greg and Australians, and he finally snapped and he chewed her out in front of everyone. I mean, I would have tended to have suffered the smoke and thought, 'Well, I'm not going out with them again,' but Greg heard a comment made against him and sort of told her straight [what he thought of her]. It all went very quiet after that. But that's Greg. He's only being honest. He wanted some fresh air in the room."

Norman did not win again that season, but a tie for fourth place in the British PGA Championship helped him feel he was inching nearer to his goals. Thomson was skeptical. "Jack Newton's got tennis elbow, Stewart Ginn is a walking hospital case, Kel Nagle suffers from old age, and Greg Norman, our best hope, is a shadow of his former self," he wrote in the *Melbourne Age* on the eve of the Australian Open.

Looking back, Thomson claims that he only said those things "to sting him a bit, make him try a bit harder and get a bit more ferocious." Norman was determined to prove his worth, but for the second time in three years, an aggressive birdie attempt at the last when a par would have sufficed cost him his national title.

Afterward, Norman put his clubs in the cupboard, loaded provisions onto his boat, and planned the honeymoon he and his wife had not had time for during the season. Norman charted their course along the Great Barrier Reef, and they cast off in high spirits. It didn't go quite as planned. Laura was seasick, and nothing made her more nauseous than the gentle bobbing of the boat when Norman stopped to fish. He teased her gently about it, but there was nothing to be done.

Christmas more than made up for it. They relaxed in the Queensland sunshine with Norman's family, and Laura impressed her in-laws with Christmas lunch. Over the next few weeks, while barbecuing steaks, lying by the pool, and drinking beer with friends, Norman unwound. The Australian Open receded to the back of his mind. And that was how 1981 ended, on a high note.

5

THE YEAR OF LIVING DANGEROUSLY

"Greg fires everyone who gets close to him."

American golf writer, August 1997

The 'doorbangers" Norman used to call them. They arrived, unsolicited and uninvited, sometimes well-meaning but almost always intrusive, walking boldly along the soft pale sand to the Normans' front door, scaring the pelicans into the bay. They wanted autographs, they wanted advice, they wanted to chat, to look around. Soon Paradise Point became Paradise Lost. Their refuge ruined, the Normans were forced to sell.

That was how 1982 began. An atmosphere of menace hung over everything. Even a friendly fishing competition almost ended in disaster. Norman, out at Moreton Island with Cyril King and his three sons, Greg, Gary, and Steve, decided to see who could catch the biggest fish. The idea was for Cyril and Steve to fish along the coastline, while Norman and the others headed out to sea. East of Glasshouse Mountain, they dropped anchor. Absorbed in their tasks, they failed to notice a subtle change in the conditions. Waves slapped warningly at the boat. The wind picked up. Norman was opening a beer when a blue wall of water came out of nowhere, curling above them like a biblical tidal wave and crashing down on the deck.

Pandemonium ensued. Gary was hurled into the engine casing, fishing gear flew, and Norman and Greg grabbed frantically for anything that would save them from being swept overboard. Several terrifying minutes elapsed while the boat fought to right itself. When the waves died down sufficiently for them to move, they abandoned the competition without a qualm and headed shakily for the shore.

Unsurprisingly, Norman sold *Divot II* two weeks later. What happened next was symptomatic of his increasingly cavalier attitude toward expensive toys. Having invested almost immediately in a seagoing cruiser, he sold it after less than a month, deciding that it didn't make sense to be tied up unused and neglected for most of the year. He and Laura then went house hunting near Surfers Paradise and purchased a large colonial-style property on five acres of land, with four bedrooms, a separate guesthouse, and a swimming pool. One boundary fence was long enough for a five-iron shot, so Norman built a practice fairway and could hit balls all day long in the sunshine for the entertainment of the wallabies and roos.

UNABLE TO SLEEP, HE WOULD SIT ON THE BED WITH HIS HEAD IN HIS HANDS, ANALYZING THE TOURNAMENT SHOT BY SHOT, PUNISHING HIMSELF UNTIL DAWN.

Ten weeks after his last competitive stroke, Norman returned to the fray to find that the endless distractions had taken their toll on his game. Inwardly, his head spun with financial transactions. He finished a disappointing eighth in the Victorian Open won by Mike Clayton and did worse still in the Australian Masters, scoring two 73s and a 78 in the third round. He complained he couldn't concentrate. After each poor performance, he tortured himself, putting distractedly on his hotel carpet for hour upon hour. Eventually, unable to sleep, he would sit on the bed with his head in his hands, analyzing the tournament shot by shot, punishing himself until dawn.

When March came it was almost a relief to escape to the Hong Kong Open, to be alone with Laura, to be able to sit peacefully in a hotel room high above the frantic city, and feel the joy come flooding though him when she told him she was expecting their first child.

"James," Norman almost shouted down the phone to Beaurepaire House, "I've got some great news. Laura's pregnant and we're going to have a baby in October."

According to Norman, silence echoed down the line. "James?" he repeated uneasily.

"Well," said Marshall at length, "I can see this is going to throw a spanner in the works."

Norman went white with rage. In a single motion he ripped the telephone out of the wall and threw it across the room, smashing it to pieces. A gaping hole in the hotel plaster bore vivid testimony to the beginning of a vicious end. "It devastated me and it devastated my wife," Norman says. "Because we couldn't understand why he would make a statement like that."

The bailiffs came at 3:00 A.M., knocking on the door with a subpoena.

"They came then because they knew they would get him," Laura says, remembering Norman standing bleary-eyed on the front step, staring at the court summons that was all that was left of his five-year relationship with James Marshall.

It is ironic that the end came at a time when everything, at least on the surface, was perfect. Marshall's prediction about the enormity of Norman's financial success had come true. Since taking him on, Marshall had negotiated endorsements with Spalding in Australia, Slazenger internationally, Qantas (which was horrified when a loophole in the small print allowed Norman to sign with its rival Cathay Pacific), BMW in the UK, Korralybyn Golf and Country Club, Schweppes, and others. In 1981, Marshall told journalists that if Norman chose to quit playing then, he would be comfortable due to property on the Gold Coast and in London and a share portfolio which brought in an annual return of 25 percent. On the tour Norman sailed from event to event in a Rolls Royce, with the aura of a man who had already made it.

"James gave Greg this style almost of how to play the tour," Longmuir says. " 'You don't want to be like everybody else—here's a Rolls Royce.' It did have a positive effect, I'm sure, on the way he played and the way he was perceived by other players."

Perhaps because of all this, Norman was gaining in stature and confidence with each passing day. The seasons had burnished his skin and filled out his frame, and now he seemed to tower over lesser players like a Viking. He expressed opinions in a forthright, uncompromising way that left those unused to such frankness, shaken. He was his own man, and the more he took charge of his career, the more inevitable it became that it would eventually end in conflict with Marshall. "[James] wanted to be too much involved in Greg's life, I think," Longmuir observed.

It was a classic case of an irresistible force meeting an immovable object. Marshall felt that he had treated Norman like a son and made him a star, while Norman thought that although Marshall "took a personal pride in the molding of Greg Norman," he was also "possessive," and that, among other things, led to problems in their relationship. But it took the telephone call from Hong Kong to end it. "There was a lot more to that situation," Norman says, "but that was the straw that broke the camel's back."

Marshall had no recollection of the phone call. "Why would I have said that? Let's look at it logically. If I had said that Laura being pregnant might present a problem—and I don't believe I did say it—I would only have meant it would be hard for Laura with Greg traveling all the time. It's a lovely story. I find it very amusing. But it isn't true."

When Norman arrived in Britain for the new season, he and Marshall went straight from the airport to a sponsors' dinner at the Grosvenor House hotel. Afterward, Norman suggested to Marshall that they go upstairs for a quiet drink. Then he informed his manager he was leaving him.

To Marshall, it was a bolt from the blue, the very last thing on earth he expected to hear. "It came as a complete surprise." Minutes later, when the cruel words and bitter recriminations finally died on pinched lips, beneath icy gazes, Marshall got up from the table, told Norman he would be hearing from his lawyers, and walked out of his life forever.

"Just let's say that we decided that he was going to go his own way, and that was that," Marshall says tersely. "We settled out of court."

Asked how Norman felt, Marshall replied, "I don't know how he felt. I was sad that things turned out the way they had. I felt, without being dramatic—"

"Betrayed?"

"Possibly. I felt sad that somebody who had lived in my house and been treated almost like a brother behaved the way he did."

"I'm not going to get into it," Norman says. "I'll just tell you one thing about people in life. The key ingredient in life with anybody is loyalty. Most of the time people fall out with you because of lack of loyalty. . . . To me, if somebody wants to sever a relationship and says, 'Look, Greg, I need to move on, I've been offered another job' or 'I'd like to go and do this,' fine, go. We've had a great relationship; I'm happy for you to go and find another job or do something different or new. That's not showing lack of loyalty, that's just showing that you want to move on in life.

"Lack of loyalty is when someone uses you, manipulates you, does things behind your back that you find out later on. You can build up wonderful long-term relationships with loyalty. Soon as somebody crosses that loyalty line with me, I've got no time for them. Because I give so much. I'm a giver, not a taker. I'm a very generous individual with my time, my effort, my money, my emotions. My cards are on the table, and when they're on the table, everybody knows exactly where they stand."

Laura compared Marshall to a "jilted lover. . . . Greg was very hurt by what happened. We really loved James and Lois a lot. They were like family to Greg, and they became like family to me. He was Greg's best man at the wedding. So I look back on it and I feel sorry that it went the way it went, but I still have great memories of James and Lois and always will. And I'm never going to let anything come in the way of that. I think he cared about Greg so much and he felt so devastated because Greg wanted to go on his own that he could never get over that. Greg just needed a change and that was the way it was. He has no bad feelings about James whatsoever."

The change Norman wanted was the freedom to go to International Management Group, the Mark McCormack organization that has looked after the careers of everyone from Arnold Palmer to Tiger Woods. Marshall felt that IMG began trying to poach Norman within a year or two of Marshall's taking him on, and Norman was signed by Ian Todd and John Simpson, now Faldo's manager, at the British Open in July, months after leaving.

"I was always conscious that IMG was sort of hovering around, but that's something I didn't bother to think about," Marshall says. "It didn't worry me, and I have to say I had complete trust in Greg so that gave me a double reason not to worry. I'm not bitter about it. If I were to look back on what happened, I would only say that I was very disappointed that it happened the way it happened."

They have never spoken since.

"James Marshall was the guy who really started the ball rolling for Greg Norman," Gilmour says. "He was a super guy. It was his idea: 'the Shark.' He took Greg Norman and was developing him into a superstar. He managed him great, and McCormack got all the benefits."

Longmuir's recollection is that Norman was very guarded on the subject and he suspected a great deal of money changed hands. "I guessed it was hurting him. I just remember Greg being pissed off by the end of that situation."

Marshall felt equally aggrieved. He maintains that Norman got away lightly. "I know of many cases of people whom he's alienated along the way, who were very kind to him in the early days. I think money can change a lot of people, and undoubtedly it has changed Greg. The Greg Norman who is portrayed on the screen or through the press as being the great sportsman, the great loser, the really nice guy, the down-to-earth, kind, straightforward, honest person, well, there's another side to Greg; and I think over the years people who know him have seen that side. The Greg I like to remember was the Greg that I managed for five years and had a great time with, and was great fun to be with. I prefer that Greg to the Greg who went to IMG and took on another sort of guise."

On June 2 the split was announced in the British papers. "We have parted on good terms," Norman said, and then he tried to turn his attention to his golf game. But by now it was clear that he was experiencing his first real slump. The principal cause of it was his putting (statistics show that he was second in driving distance from the tee, seventh in driving accuracy, second in greens in regulation, and out of the top twelve when it came to putting), but a sharp decline in confidence didn't help.

He hit rock bottom at the Martini. In the final round at Lindrick, he hooked his tee shot into the trees at the seventeenth and racked up an impressive collection of penalties for a fourteen. The gallery thought it was

Norman, nicknamed "Hollywood" by his friends, shows off the strength and power that led Jack Nicklaus to describe him as "a durable athlete." This is at the 1982 Martini. (© Phil Sheldon)

hilarious. Norman, who eventually finished with an 82, nineteen strokes behind Bernard Gallacher, found it difficult to believe his game could get any worse. "I felt desperate about my situation and, for the first time in my career, desperate about the problems in my game," he recalled later.

"Golf's chief pommie-basher this week celebrates an anniversary he would rather forget," sneered the *News of the World.* "It's exactly a year since Aussi Greg's last win. . . ." There followed a cheerful cataloguing of Norman's recent ills: his surgery for piles, the "huge" abscess in his mouth, his breakup with Marshall, and, last but not least, the fourteen he notched up at the Martini. Norman, who had played just seven events since November 1, an average of one event per month, acknowledged that his biggest problem was lack of competition.

Elsewhere, Laura was asked if it concerned her that so many women followed Norman on the course. "I trust him," she answered simply. "And do you know something else, I'm so pleased other women find him attractive. It means all of us are right. But the difference is, he's all mine."

It was Laura who finally came up with a solution to Norman's woes, suggesting he call Dr. Rudi Webster, a "mental skills coach" he had met the previous year. Webster believed that ridding the mind of disruptive influences was critical to success on the sports field, and he had worked wonders with the West Indies cricket team.

"I TRUST HIM,"

SHE ANSWERED

One telephone conversation turned Norman's year around. Counseled by Dr. Webster, Norman realized that his mind and how he controlled it were as important as any shot, and that he should never think of golf in terms of numbers but in terms of hitting the ball. Years later, when Webster interviewed him for his book *Winning Ways*, he asked Norman if he ever had problems concentrating. Norman confessed he did. "When the pressure becomes too great or if I get tired mentally, my concentration goes. My mind often wanders at crucial times. If I've parred an easy par-five instead of getting a birdie, I say to myself, 'Damn it, you should have birdied that hole.' "

SIMPLY. "AND . . .

I'M SO PLEASED

OTHER WOMEN

FIND HIM

ATTRACTIVE. IT

MEANS ALL OF US

ARE RIGHT. BUT

THE DIFFERENCE

IS, HE'S ALL

MINE."

He told Webster that he tried to focus by thinking "rhythm, get good rhythm" over the ball. "Once I put that thought in my mind, everything else is blocked out. It is like putting a protective around my head to keep out distractions."

"When you do this you make a common mistake," Webster wrote. "You leave your concentration in the past and you forget the present. The same thing will happen if you project it too far into the future. Remember, the point of power is the present."

After an hour on the phone during his original conversation with Webster, Norman felt his confidence seeping back. Laura thought there was more to it. "You're not working hard enough at the game," she told him frankly.

Thirteen days later Norman shot a record-tying 65 to take a three-stroke lead into the final round of the Dunlop Masters at St. Pierre. "It could have been a 61," said Norman, who had followed Laura's advice by hitting thousands of short-iron shots and putts at Wentworth during his week off. "I missed four putts inside seven feet." The following day, he won by eight strokes over Langer with another 65.

All the while the Marshall situation gnawed at Norman's mind. No sooner had he made up his mind to try to qualify for the U.S. Open—the USGA had not seen fit to invite him—and inspect the house they were buying in Florida at the same time, than he was forced to cancel because of a business meeting/courtroom date that couldn't be postponed.

Throughout the legal "to-ing" and "fro-ing" of that season, Norman continued to perform, winning the State Express Classic the week before the British Open. During the tournament, he spotted a plaque at the Belfry showing that Ballesteros had driven the green at the 292-yard tenth, and he took great delight in not only driving the green but holing a sixty-footer for a two. Laura had not seen him win since they married, and there were tears in her eyes when he hugged her and said, "That was for you."

At Troon, Norman shot a 65 in practice with Nicklaus, Weiskopf, and Graham to win all side bets but couldn't reproduce that scoring in the tournament. Rounds of 73, 75, 76, and 72 left him a distant twenty-seventh. Across the Atlantic, Norman fared better, finishing in the top twelve in the Canadian Open despite being left in the lurch by his caddie. Norman was cross then, but he was madder still when he reached the PGA Championship in Tulsa to find no Gilmour and no word from Gilmour.

Desperate to win his first major, Norman opened with a 66 and, after two rounds, was only three strokes behind Floyd. Playing with Floyd on the final day, he arrived at the eighteenth knowing he needed a birdie to have a chance of finishing second. Firing at the flagstick with a three-iron, Norman watched as the ball pitched just short and bounded over the green into deep grass. His recovery chip limped onto the putting surface, finishing twenty-five feet from the flag. His putt hit the hole but stayed out to give him a share of fifth place. Floyd took six and still won by three shots.

At the Irish Open the next week, Gilmour was back in service, but Norman declared himself unsatisfied with his caddie's explanation for his absence, and they parted company. Gilmour claims it was the excuse Norman needed to get rid of him and take on Pete Coleman, Ballesteros's caddie. Coleman says that Norman had been trying to lure him away from Seve ever since he worked for him during a week off in the 1980 French Open at St. Cloud, where they won by ten strokes.

"I didn't turn up in Tulsa, the reason being that he promised to pay for my flight and never did," Gilmour says sourly. He claims that Norman gave him only one air ticket ever, and that was for a flight to Australia, donated by Cathay Pacific, his sponsor.

Back in London the Normans were robbed of fifteen thousand pounds' worth of jewelry, cash, and credit cards by a gang of call girls at the Hyde Park Hotel. Norman had half-woken as they rifled through his belongings and, unable to focus in the darkness, mumbled in sleepy protest, "Laura, what are you doing?"

NORMAN FELT AN ICY SURGE OF ANGER AND DISMAY AS IT DAWNED ON HIM THEY HAD BEEN ROBBED.

"Go back to sleep," a woman's voice calmly told him.

When he teased Laura about her midnight adventures the next morning, she stared at him in surprise. "I never stirred," she said, and Norman felt an icy surge of anger and dismay as it dawned on him they had been robbed.

As detectives scurried about the room with fingerprint powder, Laura shuddered. "It's horrible to think they were creeping about the room as we slept," she said.

On the eve of the Hennessy Cognac Cup in September, Norman received a phone call from Laura, now eight months pregnant. She was alone at their new home in Orlando, and she felt as bad as she could possibly feel. "Another call like that and I'll be on the next plane home," fretted Norman, captain of the Rest of the World side.

Both he and Laura were keen for the baby to be born in Orlando, close to Laura's parents, and Norman had devised a complicated schedule of flights to ensure that he would be at his wife's side for the birth. He was quite prepared to quit midtournament if necessary. During September and October, he crisscrossed the Atlantic six times in four weeks. "It's costing me two thousand pounds a week, but it's worth every penny," said Norman, told to expect the baby on October 13.

In between, he lost the European Open when an earthworm popped out of the grass behind his ball in the split second before he was due to launch his tee shot at the seventh. Adjusting the club minutely in midswing, so as not to send the worm into the next world, Norman ended in a bank of heather and gorse. He never recovered.

On October 5 he flew to England for a televised match with Jan Stephenson, Beth Daniel, and Langer at Woburn. He was practicing prior to the 9:30 A.M. start, when he was summoned to the clubhouse for a phone call. Norman panicked. His first thought was that something had gone wrong, that Laura had miscarried or was hurt. Laura told him that she was in the hospital and in final labor. Norman was shaken to the core. He walked to the tee, his mind in turmoil. "I'm just about to become a father," he said.

There was no way he could concentrate. The cameras were rolling and he could not leave immediately, but a radio link to the clubhouse gave him a progress report every half hour from the Orlando hospital, and when he returned to his hotel, he was told he could speak to Laura at 6:00 P.M.

"Darling, we have a baby daughter," was the first thing she said.

Norman and Langer were beaten, 4–2, in the series by the women the next day, and Norman was at Heathrow Airport thirty minutes after holing out on the eighteenth green. He flew the Concorde to New York, connected to Orlando almost immediately, and was with his wife and daughter, Morgan-Leigh, just nine hours after leaving Woburn. Lawrence Levy, a chain-smoking extrovert and his much-loved British photographer friend, became Morgan-Leigh's godfather.

In the weeks that followed, while he waited for the medical clearance needed to take his daughter to Australia, Norman negotiated appearance money with the AGU. After some debate he agreed to play the Australian Open without an appearance fee but insisted on being paid for two other events.

Arriving back home he caused a storm of controversy by publicly condemning Marsh for playing in the Dunlop Phoenix in Japan instead of supporting the Australian Open. A year later Norman did the exact same thing, for which Marsh got back at him. In a barbed statement Marsh said that Australian golf fans knew that, barring date clashes and sponsor pressure, he would "continue to play in Australia without making appearance money demands, an attitude which Greg Norman does not hold despite his professed concern for the fans and Australian golf."

All through that long, tense Australian summer, Longmuir stayed with Norman and Laura in the calm timber house on the Gold Coast, where kookaburras and rainbow parakeets whirled through the trees and danced along the perimeter fence. Norman had him out mowing the practice area, a four-hour exercise, and they tinkered with clubs in the workshop and hit balls with bare torsos under a canopy of blue sky. They were never still. Even Coleman, who stayed with Norman briefly, was assigned to paint the snooker room.

"Greg's one of these guys who's a workaholic," Longmuir says. "He wakes up early and he's got to be active. He's not the sort of person that can sit down and relax very easily. You very rarely see him sitting down. And on that particular trip, if we weren't playing in a tournament and he wasn't showing me something in the car—the countryside or the golf courses or the coastline—if we weren't working in the garden or hitting balls, then we were in the snooker room, playing snooker."

In friendly matches on his table at home, Norman was as competitive as he was on the golf course. Longmuir, who had thought of himself as fairly handy with a cue, was crushed with relentless efficiency during any spare minute of his stay. He was used to it. Norman had used him as a practice opponent on the eve of the World Match Play. They had played for fifty pounds, for which Norman fought as hard as he would when the real competition started. On the seventeenth Longmuir hit his second shot stone dead, only for Norman to hole a putt from across the green to level the match. At the last they both reached the green in two. Longmuir sank a thirty-footer for a three, and Norman, carefully scrutinizing the line, followed him in triumphantly from twenty feet.

"I could not beat him, even on my best day," Longmuir says ruefully. "He'd put a lot of emphasis on a match like that. He'd sort of walk away from it feeling good."

That November, flying along the palm-fringed white beaches of Surfers Paradise with Norman, Longmuir thought that he had seldom been happier. There was an easy familiarity about the Norman household, with its beautiful but unfussy decor, that was conducive to homeyness. "There was always a really comfortable atmosphere," Longmuir said. "There was a big kitchen and that's where you lived your life. A little bit old-fashioned, I suppose. You didn't feel as though you had to dress up for dinner. I felt as though I could have walked down in my underwear and just sat down on the settee and put my feet up. It was a very livable home."

"I'D GET HOLD OF A WEDGE AND SAY, 'THAT'S FANTASTIC,' AND HE'D SAY, 'TAKE IT. IF YOU LIKE IT, TAKE IT.' HE WAS INCREDIBLY GENEROUS."

It had come as an enormous shock to Longmuir when the Australian decided to get married the previous year. "Here Greg was in the prime of his life, in terms of his condition and golf, and he had sort of latched himself up," he recalls. "I didn't think he would ever settle down that early on." Now he began to see things rather differently. "Looking back at it, for Greg, it was the stability he definitely needed at that time in his life. He would have been a wandering nomad without it. He probably would have kept on being successful because his talent was so tremendous, but his condition would have gone. He probably would have fizzled out. Laura gave him the sort of tunnel vision to success. She gave him a reason to do well, and then he began to win the big tournaments. He became a complete player when he met Laura. He was pretty wild. She quieted him down."

For the duration of his stay, Longmuir felt that Norman went out of his way to make him feel welcome and ensure he had a good time. "He used to take me up to the loft and it was full of golf equipment. I'd get hold of a wedge and say, 'That's fantastic,' and he'd say, 'Take it. If you like it, take it.' He was incredibly generous. If we went out to dinner he would always pick up the bill, always, or try to do it. Later on, when I stayed with him at Bay Hill in America, I'd go down and use the golf facilities there and he'd say,

'Anything you want, put it on my tab.' You just couldn't put your hand in your pocket. He'd give me the keys to the car. It was like, what was his was mine while I was staying there, which is another side of Greg Norman I don't think people really know."

Curiously enough, it was Norman's generosity that sparked his next explosion. Away from Surfers Paradise things had been going rather less well. Norman and Coleman were not hitting it off nearly as happily as they had done in France. "We had a stormy relationship . . . so it's not hard to remember," the caddie says wryly. "Basically, we never got on. We were both sort of domineering people, I suppose."

The problem started when Coleman gave an interview to Ramsey, who asked him how Norman compared to Ballesteros.

"Seve's a better player, but Greg's a better payer," Coleman joked.

Norman was furious. He confronted Coleman as soon as he saw it. "Nice piece in the paper," he said sarcastically.

"I said, 'Well, that's the way I see it,' " Coleman recalled. "I didn't say, 'It's not true,' because it was true. But it wasn't what he wanted to hear."

Norman's first real encounter with Ballesteros had been at the 1977 World Cup in Palm Springs, the year the Spanish team won. When the tournament was over, Norman and Shearer had decided to pay a visit to a local nightclub. There, in the half-light, propped up against the bar, was Ballesteros, smoking moodily and nursing a drink. Norman felt disappointed in him. To him, a champion athlete like the Spaniard should have had more self-discipline. "Hell, that's not right, a twenty-year-old boy smoking and drinking like that," he said to Shearer.

He had already formed the opinion that Ballesteros's swing put too much strain on his back and was too uncontrolled to make him one of the world's best players. Obviously, that opinion was revised pretty rapidly, but his assessment of the Spaniard's character remained unchanged for a long time. Norman insists that it was four years before they exchanged a single word. When Ballesteros addressed him at the 1980 World Match Play, wishing him good luck as he laced up his golf shoes in the locker room prior to meeting Faldo in the quarterfinals, the Australian nearly fell off the bench. "He remained aloof and distant as far as I was concerned," Norman said. "I thought it was strange behavior."

Coleman says that Ballesteros's taciturnity was nothing unusual and certainly wasn't directed at Norman in any malevolent way. "Seve would blank most everybody. Seve, unless it was a Spaniard, wouldn't converse with anybody."

"In those days there was no question that the star of the European Tour was Seve," Marshall says, "and I think Greg was very jealous of him. He used to say, 'Oh, Seve never says, "Good shot," when you play with him,' and, 'I could have beaten him.' And I'd say, 'Hey, if you feel like that, go out and beat him.' You've got to bear in mind that in those days Seve didn't speak much English and was a young guy and a foreigner. I think Seve handled himself extremely well. Seve was always very courteous, but I think in the early days he was a bit of a bugbear to Greg and they certainly weren't chums. Seve had very little in common with Greg."

Norman claimed that it was in fact Ballesteros who was jealous and said that, during what he described as the four-year "ice-age" between them, "I had no doubt that he was practicing a type of long-term gamesmanship on me. . . . He obviously recognized me as a threat to the supremacy he had established in Europe."

Coleman laughs. "Seve always thought he was number one. He might not have liked the flashy way that Greg used to carry on, but I don't think he was worried about being second to Greg Norman."

Nonetheless, as Coleman observed to Ramsey, if there was one area that Norman consistently upstaged the Spaniard, it was his generosity toward the people around him. Ballesteros is notoriously frugal, and nobody has suffered the consequences more than his caddies. When Ballesteros finished runner-up in the 1976 British Open, his caddie received the princely sum of £250 for the tournament. When Coleman caddied for him in the late seventies, he was paid the minimum wage of £120, plus 5 percent for a top-twenty finish—2 percent less than the average.

"At the time, [Greg paid] nearly twice what anybody else was paying," Coleman remembers. "Plus, I had to look after his Rolls Royce when he was in England. I used to turn up at the local pub in it. His percentage was also 10 percent, whereas a lot of the guys only paid 5 percent."

The drawback was the verbal abuse Norman delivered on the course. "People like that are basically never wrong," said Coleman, citing a time when he spent two days before a tournament preparing yardages for Norman and then had the Australian turn on him when an iron shot pitched by the flag and bounded through the green.

"Wrong yardage," snapped Norman.

"I said, 'One thing that wasn't was a wrong yardage. It might have been the wrong club, but it wasn't the wrong yardage.' But he kept on and on, and that belittles you when you're trying so hard to get the right yardage."

As much as Coleman admired Norman's game, his ability to "kill the course with his driver," there was only so much he could take. He stayed a couple more weeks and then returned to England to work for Langer.

Two days before the start of the Australian Open in Sydney, Longmuir went to Greg and Laura's hotel room for a drink before the three of them attended a function. He knocked on the door. It flew open and Laura, panic-stricken and emotional, cried, "Thank God, you're here, Bill!" She grabbed his arm. "Greg's on the floor."

Longmuir rushed into the room to find Norman writhing on the carpet, as white as a sheet. "I thought, 'God, he's dying,' " remembers Longmuir. The hotel doctor had been called, but it was clear that Norman needed to get to a hospital urgently.

In those days Norman was much bigger than he is now. Muscles bunched on gladiator arms and across his broad chest, and there were the beginnings of a beer belly. He hung like a dead weight across Longmuir's shoulders as the Englishman, bent double and staggering under his bulk, battled to lift him.

"I physically carried him downstairs," Longmuir said. "That's how I know how big he is. What a job I had. He couldn't move, he was in so much pain. I've never seen anyone in so much pain. I put him in the back of a taxi and when we got to the hospital and they said, 'What's wrong?' he sort of blurted out, 'Give me something for this f——ing pain,' in typical Greg fashion, just demanding that they make it all right."

At 12:30 the following afternoon Norman underwent a cystoscopy to remove a kidney stone at the Masonic Hospital in Ashfield. When he came around, he was absolutely adamant that he wasn't withdrawn from the tournament. If he could walk he wanted to play. Reporters phoning the hospital were told by Laura that Norman, who had been diagnosed with a urinary tract infection several weeks earlier, had had a small stone removed. "It was a damn big one!" shouted Norman from his bed.

> **REPORTERS PHONING THE HOSPITAL WERE TOLD BY LAURA THAT NORMAN . . . HAD HAD A SMALL STONE REMOVED. "IT WAS A DAMN BIG ONE!" SHOUTED NORMAN FROM HIS BED.**

At the sixteenth hole in the first round of the Australian Open, Norman withdrew from the tournament. His face was a sickly yellow, his body wracked with pain. Doctors watching his progress on television said they could see his legs shaking. It was blowing a gale. Norman felt weak and nauseous as he struggled to twelve over par, but he forced himself on, taking frequent rests on the shooting stick Coleman carried. His parents were watching and he didn't want to disappoint them.

In the end he had to admit defeat. It was not the way he would have chosen to end that tumultuous season, but he had a lot to be proud of. He had won the Order of Merit in Europe in only eleven appearances, earning £66,405.71 and beating Sandy Lyle and Sam Torrance, who had each played twenty-three events.

6

STORM WARNING

"I find the practice fairways around the British Tour very lonely places, because quite often I am the only one there."

Greg Norman, 1983

The first indication that something was horribly, perhaps irremediably, wrong was the wall of silence. Norman walked onto the putting green at Royal Birkdale on the eve of the Open, greeted a couple of players cheerily, and was startled when they pretended they hadn't heard him and turned away. For a minute he thought they were kidding. He hadn't seen them since having cartilage surgery on his left knee in May, and he limped after them with a teasing comment on his lips. A wave of hostility stopped him dead. Several of the players walked off the green, leaving Norman embarrassed and alone. Then came the final indignity. A man he had counted as a friend shouted over his shoulder, "You should be locked up for what you did!"

There had been no indication of what was to come. After a seemingly endless stream of ailments—"Growing pains," he laughed—Norman had recovered all his old bounce and exuberance by 1983. He swept to victory in the Australian Masters at Huntingdale with a final-round 66, won the

Hong Kong Open by three, and had it not been for an "absurdly rushed putt" in the play-off against Mike Nicolette in the Bay Hill Classic, he would have triumphed in his first American event.

Peter Dobereiner, the late *Observer* correspondent, remembered being unsure how to approach him afterward. "My trepidation was groundless. Norman sought me out and said, 'Come and look at something.' That something was a blood-red Ferrari that had just been delivered, an event of much greater importance in Norman's mind than losing a play-off."

"I'VE ALWAYS LOVED THE IN- TENSE PRESSURE OF THE LAST MOMENTS OF A TOURNAMENT."

Earlier in the year Norman had overheard a conversation between two test cricketers that had convinced him (momentarily) that his relish for the spectacular option—huge, lashed drives that drew gasps from the crowd, and do-or-die five-irons—had sometimes proved expensive in major championships, particularly with regard to the 1981 Masters and the British PGA Championship the previous season.

"What part of batting do you enjoy most?" one cricketer had asked the other.

"Hitting fours and sixes."

"How much of the time do you do that?"

"About 10 percent."

"So you don't really enjoy the other 90 percent?"

"I never thought of it like that."

Norman hadn't thought of it like that either. He realized he had to come to terms with a more businesslike way of putting a score together—or pay the price. But that was easier said than done. He wasn't yet ready to relinquish the sweet high that accompanied a high-risk shot delivered safely to the pin. He lived for the tingling rush of adrenaline and the flush of pride. "I've always loved the intense pressure of the last moments of a tournament," he said. "You know, when anybody can win it. The money, the cars, and the recognition are nice, but that's not why I'm in this game. It's for those rare moments when I'm on that knife edge. There's no feeling like it."

Despite the fact that he did not experience it at The Players Championship at Sawgrass, where he was sixty-third, or at Augusta, where he was thirtieth, his smile flashed easily that spring. Married life agreed with him.

Possibly expecting the reverse, he found that Laura and his young daughter had a calming effect on him when they traveled together, and now he took them with him whenever he could.

"I remember him telling me, 'You have to understand, if we get married, golf will still be my most important thing in the world,'" Laura says. "I didn't really think about it then because I wasn't really thinking about marriage. We were just having a great time. But as soon as we got married he changed. His focus was toward me, and then when we had children, his focus was toward his family. So it was nothing I had to work on him to do. He didn't know anything else when he met me. He knew golf; that was his focus."

It was a steaming July. In April, Norman had wrenched his knee playing with Morgan-Leigh, aggravating an old football injury, and had been out of competition for two months at an estimated cost of up to seventy thousand pounds in lost prize and appearance money when he returned to Europe for the British Open. After one day in the sunshine, practicing with Laura and Morgan-Leigh, his big yellow Rolls Royce nearby at Sunningdale, he walked straight into a storm of controversy. But it wasn't, as might have been expected, the State Express Classic that caused the furor (Norman had refused to defend his title after sponsors refused to pay him six thousand pounds in appearance money). Rather, it was the publication of his book *My Story*.

The problem with autobiographies is that it's difficult to tell whether the tone used in them is that of the subject or the ghostwriter. In *My Story*, Norman, through his Australian ghostwriter Don Lawrence, comes across as smug and full of himself. Anyone and everything not meeting his high standards is laid to waste. Newton is attacked for his playboy lifestyle. Jerry Pate is someone who throws himself into ponds to celebrate victories "because those wins aren't very frequent." And Ken Brown is "a tragic figure in the game." Sacred cows, including Royal St. George's and virtually the entire British circuit, are slaughtered without compunction.

"So many talented golfers on the British Tour have not got the drive, have not got the guts or that inner power that is needed to go on and win when victory is in sight," rued Norman, who said that only Lyle and Faldo were exceptions to this rule. "The desire is there, but the raw courage required to turn that desire into a reality is sadly missing. There are too many good-time players on the British Tour who would be better off spending their spare time on the practice fairway, honing their skills to the point where they can stand up under the pressures that winning a golf tournament demands. Nobody can do it for them. They have to do it themselves."

It would be an understatement to say that his comments were met with outrage. For weeks there was hardly a golf article in Britain that did not include the words "gutless Poms," and all the nationalism and pent-up vitriol at the disposal of both media and players were heaped on Norman's head. But nothing hurt him more than the reactions of those people closest to him. It is said that there's no worse enemy than a former friend, and in the cases of Torrance and John O'Leary, Norman learned the truth of that. By all accounts they were ready to hit him.

Brian Barnes, the former Ryder Cup player, took exception to Norman's remarks about being surprised to see Ballesteros smoking and drinking after the 1977 World Cup. "Who is Greg trying to kid? Does he think he is a monk?" Barnes raged. "All this is sheer bloody nonsense." Norman, he said, had "become a bit too big for his boots, especially since he has not won a major tournament."

"To be honest with you, a lot of the pros wouldn't speak to him over that," Longmuir says. "But when you knew Greg Norman, you knew why he was saying it. He felt that the British pros were lazy in terms of not going to play the world circuit. I always thought that Sam Torrance and Howard Clark should have been full-time U.S. tour players. They didn't want to do that. Fair enough, but to become a great player, you have to take that step, and I think that was the point he was trying to make."

Norman was genuinely bewildered. He had excepted Lyle and Faldo from his criticism, and he couldn't understand why the rest couldn't take it in the spirit it was meant, as a gentle spur to encourage them on to greater heights. "A couple of guys, who I thought were good friends of mine, have walked right past me without saying a word," Norman said. "What's the matter with them? I just wrote the truth as I saw it. If they don't like it, they should tell me to my face."

He was completely unrepentant. He admitted that his golf hadn't been the same since the operation and that his short game had suffered, but he felt that he'd rather tee off at Royal Birkdale playing his average game than peak too early. "I'm here for one thing, to win the Open," he said. He eventually finished tied for nineteenth.

Schofield describes the whole "gutless Poms" episode as a storm in a teacup, but the effects were much more far-reaching than that phrase implies. Oddly, it was only Brown, whom Norman singled out as a classic example of the poor attitude and wasted talent he was referring to, who thought the Shark's criticism was well founded.

"At the time the British players, and to some extent the Europeans, hadn't been brave enough to go to America, and unless you commit yourself to doing that, you're never going to be a world beater," says Brown, now a respected television commentator. "That was what he was saying and there was some justification for it. You'd have to say we did have a track record of not finishing the job off."

Reminded of the time Norman lectured him on his attitude at Ganton, Brown laughs. "I would say that there was probably some justification for that as well. I never really did believe in myself."

If Brown's response had been the norm rather than the rare exception, things might have turned out better than they did. But of Norman's friends, only Longmuir and Queenie stayed loyal. "John O'Leary, particularly, took it upon himself to put Greg down, and you know you can't ever cross Greg that way," Longmuir said. "You're going to lose a friend for life. It got to a point where it had all sort of blown over for a bit and we were playing in York at the B&H International. I was staying with Greg that week, and we were in a restaurant. Sam and John O'Leary were on the other side of the restaurant, and they sent a bottle of wine over to Greg. This was the sort of olive branch to make up. But the damage had been done by then because John O'Leary had made a comment that was out of line. And it was typical Greg, because he told the waiter to tell them to shove it up their arse. It was very funny the way it happened. I sort of grinned and thought, 'God, what's going to happen next?' I know Greg will still speak to Sam and John, but it left a severe dent in their relationship."

It is possible that Norman does speak to Torrance and O'Leary, but it seems doubtful they are bosom buddies. So sensitive is the issue of Norman's criticism, even fourteen years later, that when Torrance was questioned about it for this book, he literally froze. "There is absolutely no way on earth that I would ever talk about that," he snapped. "No comment," he reiterated darkly and then, muttering expletives, he wheeled and walked away.

Looking back, Norman says of his remarks in *My Story*: "It was only what I saw at the time. I probably regret saying it because it affected some of the relationships I had, but you know I said it. I've always spoken the truth and maybe some of those guys reacted to the truth." He claims, "I never wanted to do that book anyway. I was against it; I fought it; but the deal was done before I knew anything about it."

Marshall, who organized the deal, dismisses that as "a lie. The book was done with his compliance. I said to Greg, 'It's far too early for you to do it,' but Greg didn't think it would be too soon. He thought it would be great. . . . And he was involved in it from start to finish."

That tournament at Fulford was the last time Longmuir and Norman ever stayed together in Britain. Frustrated and disillusioned, Norman announced at the B&H that he was quitting Europe "for personal reasons. . . . Next year you'll see me just for the [British] Open," he said. "The rest of the time I'll be on the U.S. Tour. I'm finished."

He was forty-fifth on the Order of Merit at the time and nursing a shoulder injury. "They say things come in threes, so I hope things are going to change now," Norman said. "It's been a pretty miserable season so far."

At the European Open, where he finished fifth, Norman gave Longmuir a bag full of brand new golf grips and other belongings, leaving the Scotsman with the distinct impression that he was going for good. An atmosphere of finality pervaded the whole week. It went without saying that there would always be a bond between them, but the fun and vitality Norman had brought to both golf and their relationship left Longmuir feeling empty.

"He'll always be a friend," Longmuir said sincerely. "I'll always feel comfortable with him because I know where he's coming from. You read a lot about Greg being arrogant and unfriendly, but when you understand who he is, you understand where he's coming from. He's just being himself. Success hasn't changed him. He's always enjoyed his money and he's enjoyed being generous to people."

Benevolence is a persistent theme in Norman's life except in one notable case—that of his erstwhile caddie, Scotty Gilmour. All Norman's other employees, from Coleman on, are unanimous in their praise of him as an exceptionally good payer. Gilmour appears to have encountered him before he became one.

In Gilmour's version of the events that led to their split, he had agreed to return to work for Norman at the beginning of the 1983 season on the condition that the Shark set right his principal grievance—his failure to reimburse Gilmour for at least some of his flights and hotels. But as the months ticked by and Gilmour's wages were once again negated by his expenses, resentment began to simmer in the dour Briton's breast. At the PGA Championship at Riviera, it surfaced with a vengeance.

The tournament had not gone well. Subconsciously, Norman was still favoring his injured knee and he finished well down the field, in forty-second place. "He gave me a check and just vanished," Gilmour recalled. "He was just at the point of going mad. He used to have a terrible temper. I looked at the check and it was for £175."

Standing beside the putting green, Gilmour's face fell. He had no way of paying either his hotel bill or his flight to Glasgow for the tournament the following week. Upon hearing his plight, a wealthy businessman came to his rescue, but Gilmour had had enough. When he arrived in Scotland for the next event, he marched up to Norman and confronted him. "Greg," he pleaded, "you've got to square up with me for the flights for this year. I'm broke. I don't have a penny."

Norman's face hardened. "Tom Watson says he doesn't pay for his caddie's flights, and I don't think I should either," he argued.

"So that was us finished," Gilmour said flatly. "That was the day we finished."

The relationships between golfers and caddies—particularly the intense bonds that form at the highest level—are a lot like marriages. Divorce can be very acrimonious. The relentless pace of the professional circuit and the stress of competition mean that caddies are common casualties, but there are always two sides to every story.

Marshall's experience was that Norman "behaved terribly with caddies. I don't think Greg has been very good about remembering those people who helped him on the way up. Say he was staying [at my house] and I said to him, 'You know, the local guy at the golf club would just love

87

you to come and say hi.' Greg wouldn't do that. But if I said to him, 'Lord Bathurst, who owns Gloucestershire, would be very interested in having you come to dinner,' he would be there like a shot, and I think that is one of the things that people possibly resent."

"I DON'T GIVE A DAMN ABOUT THE AUSTRALIAN OPEN ANYMORE," NORMAN SAID SULLENLY AT THE NEW SOUTH WALES OPEN.

Gilmour takes the same view: "I'm a little bitter about it. He treated me pretty bad and I was pretty loyal to him."

To Gilmour, the final straw was when he wished Norman a Happy New Year in Dubai in 1997 and asked about his family, and Norman failed to do the same in return. "He didn't say, 'How's your wife?' and my wife traveled with me everywhere. My wife and Laura got along great. She used to baby-sit Morgan. But that's what kind of guy he is. I was more than a caddie, I was a friend. It's Greg's fault that he doesn't have any friends. He's stamped on a lot of people. He's stamped on people all his life. I don't feel sorry for him. He's brought it all on himself. He's got a wonderful life, he's got all the money in the world, but I wonder if he's really a happy guy."

From each fresh crisis Norman emerged stronger and more determined. He overcame Ballesteros in a semifinal of the World Match Play, after the Spaniard suggested he get through the ball more with his right hand when he was putting, and he beat Faldo 3 & 2 in the final. Andy Prodger, Faldo's caddie at the time, remembers it as one of the few occasions they met that Norman did not allow himself to get agitated by the Englishman's deadly slowness. There was no love lost between them. "Complete opposites," Prodger says. "An introvert and an extrovert."

Two weeks later Norman won the Cannes Open. He flew back to Australia and into a row with the AGU. They were refusing to pay him an appearance fee to play in the Australian Open, although they did not draw the line at paying Nick Price, Jim Thorpe, and one or two other relatively nondescript foreign players.

"I don't give a damn about the Australian Open anymore," Norman said sullenly at the New South Wales Open. He threatened to boycott his national open for the next four years and had already entered the Dunlop Phoenix, held concurrently in Japan. "I don't hold it against Nick and Jim for getting appearance money. Good luck to them. I just can't work out what the AGU have got against me. I'm getting paid my normal fee, about eight thousand pounds to play this week, and I'm getting it next week at Tweed Heads."

To prove his point, he won the tournament. "They can't stop him," Graham, the 1981 U.S. Open champion, said after losing a sudden-death play-off to Norman at Concord. It was Norman's fourth victory in five events.

Soon afterward, Norman announced that he was selling his house on the Gold Coast so he could buy a bigger property in America. He was on the brink of signing a three-year, half-million-dollar deal with Spalding, the largest contract ever procured by an Australian sportsman and only the fourth largest by a golfer. Out of a season of chaos Norman had manipulated a triumphant departure.

When Norman left Marshall he put himself into the hands of Hughes Norton, the suave, astute head of IMG's golf division. Norton had managed a string of top players, including Lanny Wadkins, and had a reputation as a brilliant wheeler-dealer, as cunning as he was charming. Norton had been in dialogue with the Australian for several years before he left Marshall and was thrilled to be masterminding his advance into the New World.

"I thought he was the most attractive, charismatic, talented player I'd ever seen, perhaps since Arnold Palmer," Norton says. "He had a lot of the same characteristics—not only gifted but with great desire to work hard and improve. He had everything, absolutely everything. To me, you couldn't have created a better persona: Australian, which certainly Americans love; blond, which is always appealing; long-hitting, powerful, gutsy. The whole nine yards. He was the total package, ten out of ten."

Norman, who had been tempted to leave Europe in 1982, was convinced that his timing was perfect. "The best thing I ever did was holding out that extra year and playing different courses. Just take Sunningdale, Wentworth, Royal Birkdale, and St. Andrews. . . . Every week is a new adventure. I've always been a believer that anyone coming from overseas should play at least two tours. Once you've got your blooding, then you go to the States. Because you've got to keep going forward all the time in the States. One average round in the States and you get lapped by about twenty guys."

With Norton watching over him, Norman launched his assault on the PGA Tour. He had begun the year by winning the Australian Masters, with what Graham described as "the most awesome exhibition of driving a golf ball I've ever seen. Absolutely phenomenal." But when the Florida swing and Augusta came and went with only a missed cut at the TPC and a twenty-fifth place at the Masters to show for it, his confidence waned dramatically. None of the old keys helped. His swing slipped out of sync, his short game grew ragged at the edges, and his putts rimmed out.

Norman had been in the United States for what seemed all of five minutes, but already there was a small contingent pleased to see him struggle. Playing at Atlanta Country Club, Norman had just hit the par-five eleventh in two when an American star, who had required three shots, walked over to him and said, "Son, you're not good enough to play over here. You just pack your ass up and go home." Norman felt his blood boil. "Welcome to America," he thought to himself.

In the last round of the Memorial, Norman shot a 73 to finish ten over par. Desperate to stop the slide, he phoned Charlie Earp in Australia and entreated him to fly to the United States as soon as possible. Earp told him to extend his backswing and hold on until he got there. A week later Norman won the Kemper Open. He opened with a 68, was seven strokes ahead of the field after three rounds at windswept Congressional, and eventually won by five in a show-stopping display of controlled aggression and effortless style.

"We won seventy-two thousand dollars minus what I spent shopping all week," Laura laughed. When Earp flew in a day or so later, the check was still pinned to the fridge door, more than ten times what Norman had earned for his victory in the West Lakes Classic.

All of America was waking up to the arrival of a new superstar. After just three years of trying, Norman was an overnight success. His power game, movie-star orthodontistry, and ability to convey moneyed sophistication and wholesome Aussi friendliness simultaneously gave him the kind of popular appeal only Palmer had ever generated. Longmuir remembers going out to an Italian restaurant in Orlando with him and being taken aback by the scale of attention and affection he received from the notoriously parochial locals dining there.

"He's as unselfconscious as a puppy with a ball of yarn," wrote Jim Murray, the renowned sports columnist. "He's flashy. He's got this shock of platinum hair that makes him look like Jean Harlow from a distance. When he smiles, which is a lot, his teeth light up like a keyboard. He could give Liberace lessons in glitz. Best of all, he looks like what you think a world-class athlete should look like. The way you'd like to look if you made your living in sports. If you think this is common, you don't know golf. They've got guys in this game who can't see without glasses. They've got some who can't see too well with glasses. They've got guys who look like department store Santa Clauses and guys who look as if you could mail them home or clean cannons with them. Not our Greg. Greg Norman looks as if he was made by Michelangelo. He's got this wide, sloping shoulder of the practiced surfer. He has no rear end to speak of and so little waistline you wonder how his pants stay up. He could pass for a light-heavyweight boxer in any bar in the world."

"The thing that impressed me the most is that he had a certain air, a positiveness, an aggressiveness on the golf course," says Nick Price, the Zimbabwean player who lived near Norman in Florida and would become one of his closest friends. "He just had *superstar* written all over him, even in those days. He had that debonair attitude."

With Earp at his side, Norman had every reason to be debonair. "I caddied for him in 1984 in the United States Open, which we should have won," Earp says ruefully. "Should have."

The strain shows as Norman and his famous teacher, Charlie Earp, head down the stretch, with Fuzzy Zoeller in their sights at the 1984 U.S. Open at Winged Foot.
(© Phil Sheldon)

For a moment, Greg Norman's mind was a blank. He could not recall the packed galleries and narrow greens of Winged Foot, could not recall the nearness of his dream. With less than a month to go before the 1997 PGA Championship would return to Winged Foot, the scene of his duel against Fuzzy Zoeller in 1984, he could remember almost nothing about the tournament. "Eighty-four?" he asked slowly. "You remind me."

"Well, starting with the closing holes of the final round—"

"Of?"

"The U.S. Open in 1984."

"What was that? That was—"

"You made some incredible birdies to get into the play-off..."

Silence.

"The one with Fuzzy Zoeller," interjected Bart Collins, president of Norman's company Great White Shark Enterprises.

The slow light of recognition dawned across Norman's face. "Oh, with Fuzzy. Yeah, I remember vaguely." He pushed his sleeves up over his wiry brown arms. "What you've got to understand about me is I'm not a statistician," he said. "I remember things, but I don't remember them in detail because there's things that you need to put out of your head. So I put 'em out of my head. Because I don't think it's necessary to have all that stuff in there all the time. One of my greatest strengths is my mind—always has been. I can remember chipping out sideways on seventeen and hitting a shot in there about ten or six feet and making the putt. I can remember the eighteenth hole. I can remember the first hole of the play-off. And that's it, really."

THE SLOW LIGHT OF RECOGNITION DAWNED ACROSS NORMAN'S FACE. "OH, WITH FUZZY. YEAH, I REMEMBER VAGUELY."

Nineteen eighty-four was the year that Ballesteros called Winged Foot and the U.S. Open "the toughest golf course I have ever played and the toughest tournament to win." The USGA had taken care not to make it as cruel as it was when Hale Irwin won in 1974, but it was cruel enough. After two 68s, Irwin was the leader once again, with Fuzzy Zoeller and Norman contending, and a 69 helped Irwin hold on for the third successive day. Zoeller was a stroke behind at 206, with Norman at 207.

On the final day the atmosphere was tense and electric. The gallery ran amok, breaking through flimsy barriers and rushing down fairways as the thirty-nine-year-old Irwin collapsed with an outward 40 and inward 39, leaving Norman and Zoeller battling head to head. Blood-curdling roars split the air at inopportune moments. Age wasn't the only thing affecting players' nerves. The Australian, who hit fifty-three greens in seventy-two holes at Winged Foot, the most of any man in the field, chose the closing holes to miss them, his loose iron shots wandering away from their targets at the fifteenth, sixteenth, and seventeenth. And every single time, he made a miracle save.

"Anyone who thinks Greg Norman's a choker only has to watch the last three holes at Winged Foot," says Clayton. "That was unbelievable golf."

At the eighteenth hole Norman, his hair snowy white in the light, took out a six-iron. He swallowed hard. For the first time in his life, he was petri-fied of hitting a shot, scared stiff that he couldn't pull it off, scared stiff of the consequences. "It was as if that final green was a dark room and I was a little boy, afraid to open the door," he con-fessed later. He made an uncertain backswing and blocked the ball straight right into a grand-stand set well back from the green. His heart in his mouth, he stared after it. He had spent half his young life preparing for this moment, and now that it was here he felt he was choking. "I have never choked on a shot since then," he said in 1987. With Zoeller putting out on the seven-teenth, he needed a birdie to be sure of winning or forcing a play-off, and now that chance was gone. The best he could hope for was a par. Norman dropped without penalty and lofted the ball toward the gallery banked behind the green. It flew across the putting surface and came to rest in the thick collar on the far side, forty feet from the pin.

"IT WAS AS IF THAT FINAL GREEN WAS A DARK ROOM AND I WAS A LITTLE BOY, AFRAID TO OPEN THE DOOR," HE CONFESSED LATER.

In 1929, Bobby Jones had faced almost the same line on the rolling glassy surface of Winged Foot's final green. The twelve-footer he holed, a curling clutch putt that forced a tie with Al Espinosa and then victory in the play-off, became a landmark in American golf history, such was its impor-tance and degree of difficulty. Now Norman had a similar putt, only a good deal longer. He selected a small, worn patch midway to the hole and aimed five feet left. He struck the putt perfectly. In the charged silence, he held his breath as the ball trundled across the green, crossed the brown patch, struck the flagstick, and popped in the hole.

In years to come that forty-foot putt and all that it implied will be held up alongside Watson's chip at Pebble Beach as one of the most precious U.S. Open moments, and Norman felt the full impact of it. He rushed around the green in paroxysms of delight, leaping and laughing and holding his putter high.

Zoeller, standing on the fairway, mistakenly thought he had made a birdie. Reaching into his orange bag, he took out a white towel, and in one of the finest acts of sportsmanship golf has seen, waved it in gracious surrender. "I said to my caddie, 'This guy's going to beat us,' " he recalls. Gamely, he held on for a tie.

Norman grinned at him sheepishly when he came off the course. "I said to him, 'What are you trying to do to me—give me gray hairs?' " Zoeller says with a laugh. "But what a great putt under the circumstances, oh, what a great putt. TV doesn't do him justice because it doesn't show the slope of that green."

Norman was so emotional he could hardly speak. "I could not put into words the feeling I had when I made that putt at the last," he managed. He had trailed Zoeller by four shots after six holes and three after twelve. "One of those greatest feelings in the world. Golf is very hard to explain. I could feel it in my hands. I knew I was going to make it. I just knew."

Back home in Australia, they were stopping the presses to record his brilliant 69. "Fearless Greg Forces Play-Off," cried the Adelaide paper the *News*. After so many disappointments, the Shark's time had finally come.

On Monday morning Norman, Norton, and Laura drove up to the clubhouse for the play-off. Workmen spilled through the trees, tanned and sweaty, tearing down tents, grandstands, and signs, dismantling the fairground paraphernalia of tournament golf. Norton watched worriedly as Norman climbed listlessly out of the car.

"I feel like I'm going to a pro-am," Norman said slowly.

"There was a sense of letdown," Norton recalls. "It's like there wasn't the excitement of Sunday, and a bit of the magic was gone."

Norman remembers almost nothing about the last day, except "waking up Monday morning with nothing in me. Just flat. I've had that a couple of times in my career, where I've woken up the next day just dead. Nothing in you. You know, your emotion's gone, your adrenaline's gone, and boom. It's pretty hard to recoup it all and that's how I was that Monday morning. . . . Fuzzy never slept

Ecstatic, Norman rushes across the seventy-second green after a brilliant putt ties him with Fuzzy Zoeller and forces a play-off at Winged Foot. (© Phil Sheldon)

a wink, so he had his adrenaline to play with that day. I had a great night's sleep so my body went flat. We've all felt that way. It's just one of those things. Maybe I'd be able to do it differently nowadays, but in those days I couldn't. I couldn't turn it back on."

Zoeller waited on the first tee, whistling and wisecracking, as contented as a cat on a sun lounger despite the fact that he had been awake until 3:00 A.M., chain-smoking. He plucked out a telephone when Norman walked up. "Make your last call," he said to the Shark, much to the delight of the gallery.

Norman smiled unhappily. He was pale and drained after the effort of Sunday. Like Norton, Earp felt a twinge of worry as he hoisted Norman's bag onto his shoulder and followed him up the fairway.

"He didn't get the breaks," Earp says now. "Fuzzy got the breaks early. He's hit it wide on the first tee at Winged Foot. Another six foot and he'd have been dead. Greg's hit a great drive and knocked it on. They both birdied. The second hole, we'd been hitting a one-iron all week, but he wanted to hit the driver. I said to him, 'What the hell do you want to hit a driver for?' But that's what Greg wanted to do. He felt confident about it. And he blocked it. Got it behind a tree. Fuzzy hit it down the middle and knocked it on the green, well past the hole. Greg was on in three and Fuzzy knocked it in from sixty-five feet. I said to him, 'What did you do that for?' He said, 'I was only trying to hit it close.' Greg took six. On the third hole, Fuzzy's had a big block, Greg's knocked it on the front edge and taken three to get down. And that's how the round went from then on."

"LET'S GO, SHARK," A FAN CRIED ENCOURAGINGLY. NORMAN GAVE HIM A BLEAK STARE. "WHERE ARE WE GOING?" HE ASKED.

After six holes, it was as good as over. "Let's go, Shark," a fan cried encouragingly. Norman gave him a bleak stare. "Where are we going?" he asked.

"Everybody says the long putt on two was the turning point," Zoeller says, remembering that they managed to chat and share a few laughs on the way around. "But really I think the turning point was number eight. I had a three-shot lead and I hit it in to about ten feet. Greg made another bogey and that gave me an extra two shots. It was all downhill from there."

After nine holes Zoeller was five strokes ahead; after sixteen the gap was nine. Twice they were slowed down to ensure that television, which only came on at 3:00, managed to catch the closing holes, once for twenty minutes. On the eighteenth Norman took out a white towel and waved it sadly in surrender, just as his opponent had done the previous day. He scored a 75 against Zoeller's superb 67, handing the easygoing American the biggest margin of victory ever recorded in an eighteen-hole major play-off. They walked off the green arm in arm. "Fuzzy, Fuzzy, Fuzzy," chanted the fans.

"He had one of those days when nothing went well," Zoeller says of Norman. He put it down to the ebb and flow of momentum. "It wouldn't have made any difference who I was playing that week. I was on. I really had no fear at all. I was just out to do my job, and I felt comfortable on that golf course, and that was a big plus."

The fact that Norman has blocked the experiences of the 1984 U.S. Open from his mind so completely that he cannot remember a single detail of the tournament, beyond the empty feeling with which he woke on Monday morning, says a lot about the suffering it caused him. Yet he bounced back with the resilience that was to become his trademark. Two weeks after leaving Winged Foot, he won the Canadian Open, shooting a 67 for a ten-under-par total that left him two shots ahead of Nicklaus.

"This was special because my wife called me this morning to remind me it was our wedding anniversary," Norman grinned. "She said the trophy would be just fine for a present, so that was my goal for the day."

When Norman lost a play-off for the Western Open, was sixth in the Open at St. Andrews, and won the Australian PGA championship by eight strokes to end the year in third place on the world rankings, *Golf Digest* ran an article under the headline "Will Greg Norman Reach Superstardom?" In it, Dobereiner was prepared to wager that Norman would win at least one major, but beyond that he preferred to hedge his bets. "Those who know him best are equally ambivalent about his potential . . . Peter Thomson . . . has serious reservations about Greg Norman's capacity to go all the way in golf. Jack Newton refers to him as 'the Great White Fishfinger.' Graham Marsh, on the other hand, believes that Norman will improve further and become a truly dominant figure. . . . It is enough to know of the rich rewards to be had watching Norman's progress, win or lose."

7

THE SATURDAY SLAM

"Life isn't fair, but golf is ridiculous."

Jim Murray on Norman's year, 1986

When the driver of the boat reached Norman, sweeping around in a frantic curl of foam, he thought he had broken his neck. The Shark floated limply in his life jacket, his head at an unnatural angle. His face looked as if it had been savaged by wild boars.

Not ten minutes earlier Laura Norman had been sitting peacefully in a chair looking down their Orlando garden at the scene that followed the christening of Gregory Michael, their three-week-old son. The sun was setting and a few couples still lingered over their champagne. Out on the lake Norman and Laura's brothers, Richard and Jay Jr., were water-skiing. Clinging to the back of a banana boat, a kind of long rubber tube, they bounded over the rippled jade surface. When the boat began to flip, Norman instinctively let go of the rope. Jay didn't. He smashed into Norman, hitting the Australian's face with his foot and knocking him unconscious.

"I was hysterical," Laura says, remembering them carrying her husband, dripping with blood, more dead than alive, into the tranquil christening scene. "He kept saying to everybody, 'Calm her down, calm her down!' But he had this towel up against his face and every time he took the towel away there were no teeth and it was all bloody and it was awful. That's the most afraid I've ever been for Greg."

Richard Andrassy, the chief pediatric surgeon at the Children's Hospital in Houston, rushed Norman to the hospital, where he underwent a four-hour operation, received some thirty stitches, and lost three teeth. Splinters of the teeth were impacted into his jawbone.

On October 17, less than three weeks later, he teed up in the inaugural Dunhill Cup at St. Andrews. Ramsey had telephoned his house days before the event and found him full of the joys of spring. "I tell you, I'll come out of this looking better than ever," joked Norman, who was having plastic surgery the following morning. "It just hurts like hell to laugh. I look like Muhammad Ali hit me six times in the mouth."

David Graham, one of his Australian teammates in the event, hoped that the accident might knock a little sense into Norman. "He indulges in dangerous hobbies that could end a million-dollar career," Graham said.

"Rubbish," Norman said dismissively. "This wasn't my fault."

Neither was the headline that greeted his return: "Norman Enters Golf Feud." To be fair, he was only a bystander in a blazing row between his teammates. Graham Marsh had publicly condemned David Graham for accepting what he considered to be excessive appearance money to play in the Queensland Open. "Fortunately, this competition pits individual golfers against each other, head to head, and we will be playing separately and not strictly as a team," Norman said. "Otherwise, well, I don't know what would have happened."

"Graham Marsh may be hearing from my lawyer," Graham told the *Edinburgh Evening News* on the eve of the match.

"I believe David Graham is looking for me," Marsh snarled. "All I can say is that it's a good job we're playing as individuals this week, not as partners."

Five days later Australia beat the United States, 3-0, in the final.

By 1986, Norman's relish for danger, both on and off the course, was seen as a contributing factor to one of the game's biggest mysteries: the glaring hole in his record. The man who had everything—the perfect family, the perfect house, the perfect swing, the perfect image—did not have a major victory, the universal yardstick for separating the legends from the also-rans. If, in the case of Norman, there was added pressure, it was the price tag of his association with Nicklaus and of his own larger-than-life persona and giant-killing game. "I am very conscious that I have never won a major title," he said in 1983, "and until I do I will not believe that I have successfully brought together [the] ingredients for greatness."

Nowadays Norman claims that he wasn't remotely surprised when year after year went by without a major victory. "There are times when you've got to realize that you're not the only pearl in the oyster shell," he says. "There are a lot of good oysters out there with even better pearls. It's not a given." But a glance at his record in the Masters shows that he probably cared too much. After finishing fourth in 1981 with outstanding scores for an Augusta rookie—69, 70, 72, 72—he returned the next year and shot 73, 75, 73, 79 to tie for thirty-sixth place. In 1983 another closing 79 relegated him to thirtieth place; in '84 he was twenty-fifth; and in '85 he sank to forty-seventh after finishing 75, 78.

Thomson believes that Norman's problems were twofold: His swing was flawed, and he was weighed down by the burden of expectation. "Clearly, he hit a couple of hurdles with his game. It was disappointing because I think he got on the wrong trail for a while with his technique, which is the modern thing that befalls all these young players, and that held him back for a long time. I think the expectations and the 'troubles,' if you want to call them that, came after he got all these endorsements for all sorts of wild money on the promise that he was going to win a major. He was sold by James Marshall and then after that by IMG on what he was going to win. Well, logically, when he wasn't actually winning, there were queries: 'Will he fulfill his promise?' et cetera. That's when the expectations came."

Few men have worked harder or longer to live up to those expectations, but nothing Norman did was ever enough. Year after year he scooped up half the prizes offered in Australia, and yet when he had a relatively poor season, he was mocked.

Jack Newton believed that Norman's biggest weakness was his short irons. "When he was really firing, I genuinely thought he had 10 to 15 percent improvement left in him. For a great player, his eight-iron, nine-iron, and wedge were pretty ordinary. I mean, he could miss a green with a wedge."

Norton admits to growing more and more bewildered as the years passed without his client's winning a major. "I literally thought he would win a major a year. People talk about Augusta being made for Tiger. You know, it's a 68-par golf course for him and he's four under par on the first tee. That's what people always said was true with Greg. I thought Augusta he would win multiple times. Because of his heritage in Europe, I thought he would win the British Open multiple times. I felt strongest about those two, but even the U.S. Open and the PGA . . . If you had asked me to write it down, I would have said . . . he could be the fifth guy to win them all."

> **"PEOPLE TALK ABOUT AUGUSTA BEING MADE FOR TIGER. . . . THAT'S WHAT PEOPLE ALWAYS SAID WAS TRUE WITH GREG. I THOUGHT AUGUSTA HE WOULD WIN MULTIPLE TIMES."**

When Norman turned off Washington Road into Augusta that spring of 1986, he believed it himself. After a year in the shadow of what he thought was an Asiatic virus, with pneumonia-like symptoms, but which turned out to be an allergy to certain grasses, he felt as good as he had felt for as long as he could remember—strong, vital, and in control of his game. After a first-round 70, his best opening score since 1981, he felt even better. He followed it with a solid 72, and then a sweet 68 gave him the third-round lead at 210. Price (who had broken the course record with a 63 on Saturday), Langer, Ballesteros, Donnie Hammond, Watson, Kite, and Tommy Nakajima were all within two shots of him, and Nicklaus was four strokes back. Confident and excited, Norman drove off into the night to prepare himself for another dance with destiny.

"You still have to respect the old girl," he had said of Augusta National in the interview room. "When the pressure's on, you still have to be careful."

It's the noise that people remember, the wall of sound ricocheting around the scarlet amphitheater of dogwood in Amen Corner and rising like an anthem above the Cathedral in the Pines. It was the sound of Nicklaus charging. The Olden Bear, roused from a long, dispirited sleep by a newspaper article that said he was washed up at forty-six, had come to rain on Norman's parade.

102

Examined in hindsight, almost all majors have a sense of inevitability. Form, desire, and luck become a potent alchemy that seem to come to one player's aid more frequently than the rest when the tournament is viewed as a whole. Not until the final hole on Sunday did it become clear that Nicklaus was the chosen one at Augusta. Like Norman, Ballesteros had thought it was to be him. After eagling twice he was leading the tournament standing on the fifteenth fairway, absorbed in the honorable purpose of fulfilling a deathbed promise to his father. On the hole ahead he heard the gallery roar as Nicklaus almost made a hole in one. Rattled, he put a short, ugly swing on a four-iron. He watched the ball tip toward the water. He stood stunned on the fairway as a spreading ring of ripples sent a knife into his heart.

Norman had suffered a similar nightmare at the tenth, where he double-bogeyed. He had four-putted there on Friday. Afterward, he would say it was the only hole he disliked at the Masters. "I'm infatuated with this course," he admitted. "But every good-looking woman has a blemish, and in the case of Augusta it's the tenth."

That morning Steve, Nicklaus's son, had called his father and asked him what he thought it would take to win. "Well," said the Bear, "66 will tie and 65 will win." Steve told him to go ahead and do it. But Nicklaus started slowly. He was five strokes behind when a birdie putt dropped on the ninth and four behind when his twenty-five-foot birdie at the tenth was matched by the eagles of Kite and Ballesteros. Then Nicklaus made the bogey that really kick-started his round. He birdied the thirteenth and eagled the fifteenth after a 298-yard drive. When he hit it to three feet on the short sixteenth, he was blinking back the tears.

Norman heard the roar. The cacophony that day made the 1984 U.S. Open at Winged Foot "feel like playing through a graveyard" in comparison. "I remember I was on the fourteenth hole with Nicky Price, and we had maybe fifty people behind the fourteenth green," Norman recalls. "We looked at each other and said, 'Let's show these people we're not out of the tournament yet.' And I proceeded to birdie four holes in a row."

Inside the clubhouse Nicklaus waited with his son Jackie, his caddie. He was still one up when Kite missed a twelve-footer on eighteen and Norman hooked his drive on the seventeenth. The ball rolled under two tall pines near the seventh green. Faced with a 160-yard shot under the branches and onto the glassy green, Norman decided to play what he described as a "low-percentage, superaggressive" punch with a nine-iron. It bounded onto the green and ran to fifteen feet for an incredible birdie three. "I was sitting watching on TV as Norman kept making birdies," said Nicklaus, who had come home in 30, "so when I came to the last putt, I said, 'Maybe I'll stand up.'"

"I was really excited for him," recalls Price, who had played steadily without making any real gains.

Norman was walking to the last tee telling himself, "One more birdie and you're the Masters champion." On the tee he reached for the driver. Pete Bender, his new caddie, stopped him. "Take the three-wood and put it in a good position," he told Norman, "then we'll attack." What Bender didn't count on was that, having hit a sensible three-wood up the fairway, Norman would not follow that strategy to completion by going for par and hoping for a three, but would be more obsessed than ever with getting a birdie. Looking up at the colorful crescent of spectators behind the green, Norman had only one thought in his mind and it was not the par that would tie him with Nicklaus. He took out his four-iron. It was the four-iron that had contributed handsomely to the double bogey on ten, veering off into the crowd from beneath a pine tree.

"GREG WANTED FIVE STRAIGHT BIRDIES," BENDER SAID SOURLY. **"HE WANTED TO MAKE HISTORY. HE WASN'T GOING TO GO FOR THE MIDDLE OF THE GREEN."**

"There are certain situations that you get into," says Price, "where you might, for example, not be hitting your sand wedge that well. You might have hit one all day and you've duffed it. And you'll try like hell to avoid using it again. That's not a choke, it's just that you're not comfortable with it. But invariably you end up needing it, and it always seems to come at inopportune moments, under pressure."

Unfortunately for Norman, the inopportune time was the seventy-second hole of the Masters. "I should have hit a hard five," Norman says in retrospect. "I think I had 187 yards, if my memory's right, up the hill."

He never made it up the hill. Instead, he spun out on it, slicing it fifty yards right into the gallery and making bogey to hand Nicklaus a sixth Green Jacket. "I was trying to hit it too hard," Norman said ruefully. "I was going for the flag. I was going for the birdie and the win. It was the first time all week I let my ego get the best of me."

"Greg wanted five straight birdies," Bender said sourly. "He wanted to make history. He wasn't going to go for the middle of the green."

"He was on such a high after the birdies," Price says, "and you normally do hit a bad shot after a string of birdies. His just came at the wrong time. I really believe that. And he just put a bad swing on it, a little quick maybe, or overaggressive. He was so fired up. There's no way in a million years that that was a choke like people wrote. I don't think anybody was more disappointed than he was. He could have been more conservative, but that's not his nature, and that's what people find appealing about him, like they did with Arnold Palmer. That's why they want to watch him, because they know he's going to give it his all. That's just the state of the union with Greg. I think it would be a mistake for him to try and change."

He firmly believes that it was the double bogey at the tenth, rather than the four-iron shot at the eighteenth on which everyone focused, that cost Norman the title.

"The one criticism I've always had of Greg's game is his course management," Newton says. "I think he's without a doubt the best player in the world. He's an aggressive bloke and he plays aggressively, but the one thing he hasn't learned to do, in the Masters for example, is find the line [between aggression] and undue risk. Playing very low-percentage shots under the gun you might play and get away with in the first three rounds, but, in the last round of a major, that ain't gonna work."

"I always compare him to Nicklaus because I played a lot with Jack," says Newton, who was runner-up to Watson in the 1975 Open at Carnoustie. "I'm sure that Greg hits the ball as well as Jack, maybe even better. I think Greg's the best driver I've ever seen—the longest and the straightest. But Jack's mental approach and his course management are just incredible. I've seen Greg do things and I'd think to myself, 'Jack would never do that.' Comparing him to the greatest player that ever lived is maybe unfair, but when you've played a lot with a guy like [Greg] and you see what he does and how he approaches a tournament like that, under the gun, in the later stages, Nicklaus is a mile in front."

In *Shark Attack!* Norman describes Nicklaus as "the best strategist I've ever seen," but he adds that "his overall game management is a shade on the conservative side." Norman's was the opposite. He also talks a lot about "ego golf" and admits that he occasionally hits an ego shot or two himself. "But those are bad shots," Norman tells his readers sternly, "even when they are

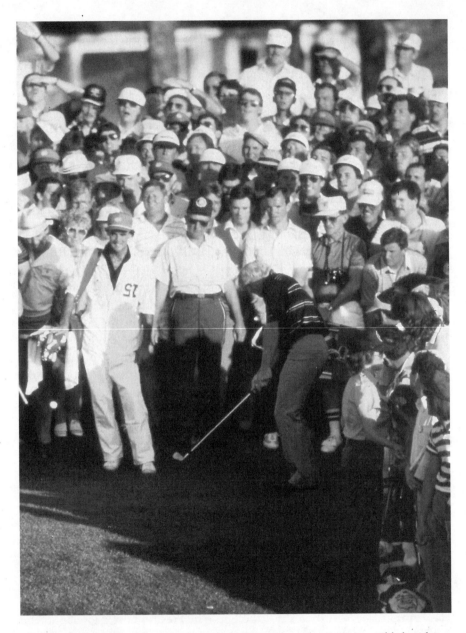

Norman chips from the gallery after hitting a four-iron right at the seventy-second hole to lose the 1986 Masters to Jack Nicklaus. (© Phil Sheldon)

played perfectly. . . . Everyone makes an ego mistake once in a while, but only a foolish player does it often. Such a golfer bases his shots not on wise course management but on self-delusion and wishful thinking."

In the Masters press room Norman shrugged off the single shot that separated him from his cherished ambition, shrugged off his flawed decision-making on the final hole, and graciously acknowledged Nicklaus's triumph. "Maybe he deserved it after what Watson did to him," he said, referring to Watson's miraculous chip-in from the rough on the penultimate hole at Pebble Beach in the 1982 U.S. Open. "What can you say?" he added. "He owns this place, basically. . . . But one of these days I'm going to break his record of six Masters anyway."

Years later Norman told *Golf Digest* that he had learned sportsmanship from Nicklaus—"I guess when you follow somebody's career, which I have really done, you learn a bit of his trade. But I have never been a sore loser. I never pouted even when I was a kid if I got beaten. I get frustrated with myself when I hit a bad shot, but if somebody else beats me, he deserves to win. I've seen the way Jack handles defeat and I've thought to myself many times, 'What would Jack have done if he were in my body right now?' It can be very difficult to walk out and put your arm around a guy and say, 'Hey, you know, what the heck, you beat me.' But it doesn't do you any harm at all, and you don't want your kids to hear that their dad was a real pain in the neck."

But while Norman was outwardly sanguine, inside he was gutted. Laura, who was accustomed to seeing him throw off defeats as if they were nothing, saw the pain etched into his face. "But after the tournament was finished, he was over it," she said. "That night we had some friends come by our house and we had a great time."

"I guess what makes me maddest is that everybody remembers my bogey at the last and not the four birdies to get there," Norman said. He couldn't understand why he should be the one singled out for criticism when it was Ballesteros who effectively threw away the tournament at the fifteenth.

"People forget all that, you see," he told the Golf Channel in 1997. "People target one individual and they think everything happened to him."

But in the end Norman, the heir apparent to Nicklaus—the most perfect golfer on earth, the consummate athlete who won one out of every five tournaments he entered worldwide and twenty out of a possible ninety-six majors—was held up alongside the Golden Bear and found wanting. Ballesteros had pull-hooked his ball into the water and Norman "slid that four-iron into the customers on eighteen," as Murray put it in the L.A. *Times*. "You never used to see Jack Nicklaus do that," Murray said. "At least, none of us ever remember it. . . . You had to beat Jack Nicklaus. He didn't do it for you."

Something was driving Norman forward, forcing him to reach deeper and deeper, and work harder and harder. It was a feeling he had, intangible at first, but then so close he could almost touch it with his fingertips. He could sense it long before he won the Las Vegas Invitational in May, shooting 73, 63, 68, 64, 65 to leave the field trailing by seven shots, and even before he won the Kemper Open at Congressional in June, beating Larry Mize, an unassuming journeyman from Georgia, on the sixth hole of a play-off. Three weeks later a third-round 62 helped him into second place in the Canadian Open. He had also come close to attaining golf's dream score, 59, at Bay Hill, lipping out for birdies at each of the last four holes.

"When it is my time to win [a major] I will win one," he told his mother. "I know I'm going to win."

Away from the course, he was blissfully content. In February the previous year, he and Laura had packed a bottle of Dom Perignon in a picnic basket and carried it down to the water's edge in Orlando to celebrate their purchase of a gorgeous piece of land. Originally owned by a property developer friend of Norman's, it was set on a peninsula across from Arnold Palmer's Bay Hill Club. That day the Normans sketched their dream house in the sand, a wedge-shaped building that would make the most of the view while protecting their privacy.

Initially, Laura had been dead set against their living on the water. "I had to fight him about it," she remembered. "Greg grew up on the water in Australia, so he was used to it. I had nightmares about my children drowning in the lakes. I know I was just paranoid, so we talked it over. Finally, I gave in and I'm happy now that I did."

When the house was completed, it was a 7,200-square-foot, two-story building, with a glass front overlooking the lake and the boathouse, and a virtually windowless back. They named it Oak Pointe after the beautiful old tree Laura refused to have removed from the garden, and they hung the U.S. and Australian flags on two flagpoles. Norman's office and workshop, where he tinkered with his clubs and cars, played pool, and conducted business, faced the swimming pool.

"He calls it business," Laura told *Golf* with a laugh, "but mostly he talks to people all over the world about cars. Actually, Greg's office is where we spend most of our time when he is home. I take the children and a few of their toys in there and we watch TV and watch people ride by on the lake or just enjoy one another when he's not sitting there behind the desk with the phone in one ear."

Norman had taken to fatherhood with an ease and enjoyment that astounded his friends. At Bay Hill he made a point of rising early every morning he was home and eating breakfast with Laura and Morgan-Leigh, walking his golden retriever puppy, and then taking his daughter down to the range with him. "He's been great with the kids," Longmuir says. In his free time he went fishing and diving with Nick Price, who lived nearby. "That's when our friendship really strengthened," Price says.

Chris Hodenfield, who spent a week at Norman's home in 1987 for a magazine piece, remembers him as "a hearty glad hander in all public situations. He paid for every beer in sight. The rocketing trajectory of the early 1980s seemed to be all his, and he walked through them as if he was basking in a sunlit ticker-tape parade."

Norman's biggest joy remained his cars. In the garage he kept a Rolls Royce Corniche convertible and a Ferrari, with Aussi 2 and Shark 1 on the plates, while the jeep, and the Jet Ski he'd bought on an impulse and already pulled a shoulder muscle using, lived outside. All his cars were fitted with radar detectors. "I've always been a car perv," Norman grinned. "I always had an ambition to have cars that stick out. The first car I ever had, I had to make flash. Guess I've always been that way, although I wish I wasn't because I spend so much money on cars. It makes me happy. Okay, so I might spend sixty to seventy thousand dollars on a car, but I never lose money."

"ACTUALLY, GREG'S OFFICE IS WHERE WE SPEND MOST OF OUR TIME WHEN HE IS HOME. I TAKE THE CHILDREN AND A FEW OF THEIR TOYS IN THERE . . ."

For the most part his relationship with America was a profitable and harmonious one. His pop-star status was such that magazines carried little lists of his likes and dislikes. Shark favorites included Japanese food, Clint Eastwood, Eddie Murphy, beer, the author Robert Ludlum, watching NFL football on TV, a variety of music from Mozart to Lionel Richie, Nicklaus, and playing Royal Melbourne and Augusta. He liked the United States because "if you're a winner here, you can earn $150,000 in a week. Win two like that and you've got $300,000. I can live on that."

At the start of the 1984 season, Norman had engaged Pete Bender, a young Californian, to caddie for him. Bender had caddied for Frank Beard, Jerry Heard, and Lanny Wadkins, but he was with Nicklaus when Norman met him during a practice round at the Masters the previous year. Norman had him doubled up with laughter that day, and when he offered the caddie a job later that season—an approach that would become a habit—Bender left Nicklaus.

At first Bender wondered if he had made a mistake. Nicklaus won the Masters and Norman shared second place with Kite. But by the time they reached the U.S. Open at Shinnecock Hills in Long Island, New York, Norman was playing the golf of his life. Bender remembers that he was "driving superbly, hitting good irons, chipping well, and his putting was great. I didn't think we could go wrong."

In the early years of Norman's career, he was a streaky putter. As a boy he had spent so much time hitting balls that his putting was neglected and left a void in his game when he turned pro. "He was such a great driver, so far ahead of everyone in those days," Gilmour remembers, "but he was a very bad putter when he was young. The game seemed to come easy to him, but he had to work on his putting."

"I had to play a little bit of a catch-up game," Norman concedes.

On the lightning greens of the U.S. Open, Norman showed how well he had succeeded. "I've never seen a guy play so well," Nicklaus said admiringly after a practice round. "If Greg doesn't win this tournament, then there's something wrong."

Shinnecock Hills, flanked by the Atlantic and the sparkling waters of Peconic Bay, is the nearest America comes to a traditional links course. Created in stages, first by Willie Davis, then Willie Dunn, then polished, extended, and transformed into a masterpiece by Bill Flynn, its gray-green fairways wind through scrubland, mounds, and clumps of blackberry bushes, toughened by gusting sea winds.

Those sea winds, whipping cold and salty through the tournament at twenty or thirty miles per hour, combined with rain and temperatures in the forties to turn Shinnecock into a brute on the first day of play. Of the 156 players who started, only 47 shot 75 or better, while 45 scored 80 or worse. Bob Tway, a tall, athletic player who had won the previous week at Westchester, led by one over Norman with a 70, an exceptional score in the conditions. He hit eight greens all day. Norman hit just seven. No player broke par.

"This is the most difficult day I have ever seen in American championship golf," Nicklaus said after his 77.

In the second round the wind eased and blue sky showed through thin clouds, and the scores improved accordingly. Norman went out in 31, stumbled a little coming home, but managed a 68 to lead the tournament by three strokes at 139, followed by Trevino and Dennis Watson at 142, with Tway, Watson, and Floyd at 143. Norman was brimming with confidence. After twelve holes of the third round, he was still three shots in front, playing with Trevino, and he was certain his time had come.

On the thirteenth hole, an imaginative par-four where the angle of the drive has the effect of narrowing an already narrow fairway, Norman pushed his tee shot into thick rough. Trevino almost holed his approach, but Norman sent his second sailing over the green and into the junglelike undergrowth that bordered a parking lot. His backswing restricted, he then attempted to punch a shot up the bank. It took off over the bank, across the green, and into the rough on the other side. He chalked up a six for his trouble. When Trevino holed from two feet for a three, they were tied.

By the time they reached the fourteenth, play had backed up and Norman, arms folded across his chest, stood steaming on the fairway with Trevino and waited for Floyd and Watson to putt out. The gallery had been noisy and excitable all day, rushing across the fairways and moving off while the partners of players they were supporting were still trying to line up putts.

Now one raised his voice above the mutterings and murmurs and called out, "Norman, you're choking."

Norman stiffened. His lip curled in an expression of amused contempt and he looked over at the heckler. Then he stared stonily ahead until the green cleared and played an iron shot to the heart of the green. Trevino was starting to walk up the fairway when, without warning, Norman marched over to the gallery, poked a finger at the man, and snarled, "If you want to say something to me, say it to me after this round when I can do something about it."

NORMAN . . . POKED A FINGER AT THE MAN, AND SNARLED, "IF YOU WANT TO SAY SOMETHING TO ME, SAY IT TO ME AFTER THIS ROUND WHEN I CAN DO SOME-THING ABOUT IT."

The heckler and his accomplices blustered and stammered, but they never took the Shark up on his offer. Norman, on the other hand, felt much better for the outburst. It appeared to release his pent-up anger, and he settled down and played flawless golf for a 71. At the end of the round, he held a narrow lead at 210. Trevino and Hal Sutton were at 211. Tway was at 212, with Floyd and four others tied at 213.

For the third time in his life, Norman was in control of a major, but he didn't seem to feel he was. Most mornings he could tell on the practice range whether he would be sharp or flat that day and on Sunday at Shinnecock he tended toward the latter. It was a clear, bright morning with a fresh, swirling wind, and even standing on the first tee with Sutton, he seemed tentative and unsure of himself. Trevino had just birdied the first and Sutton followed. Norman parred and they were tied for the lead.

Very quickly, a pattern emerged. So testing were the conditions that every player within shouting distance of the lead took one step forward and two steps back. Ben Crenshaw, Wadkins, Chip Beck, and Payne Stewart all came and went. Unnoticed, Floyd began to climb the leaderboard. The week before he had entered the last round of the Westchester Classic tied with Tway and collapsed to a 77. Distraught, he spent three hours riding around in a car with his wife, Maria, trying to work out what had gone wrong. Now he put the results of that analysis to work, firing perfect shots at the flag with his flat, ugly swing.

Norman was on his way to a 75. After a birdie at the seventh, he had bogeyed five of the next eight holes to virtually eliminate himself from contention. While Floyd played precision golf for a 66, becoming, at forty-three, the oldest man to win the U.S. Open, Norman was limping quietly to a share of twelfth place.

The hecklers had achieved their aim. Bender felt that the incident with the crowd had upset Norman and cost him his momentum, and "when you've lost momentum in this game, you've lost everything."

Norman always says that when he loses a tournament, he holds a private conference with himself about his performance, holding up a microscope to the errors in his round and trying to decide whether they were mistakes of judgment or execution. These postmortems marry uneasily with his assertion that he puts defeat out of his mind the second he leaves the course, but Laura insists that that's the case. "After the U.S. Open, riding back into New York City, everything was fine," she said.

NORMAN ALWAYS SAYS THAT WHEN HE LOSES A TOURNAMENT, HE HOLDS A PRIVATE CONFERENCE WITH HIMSELF ABOUT HIS PERFORMANCE, HOLDING UP A MICROSCOPE TO THE ERRORS IN HIS ROUND.

Tom Crow, vice chairman of Cobra and a longtime friend of Norman's, concurs. "In my opinion, Greg has always had a great ability to switch off and relax," he says. "He's very driven, very focused, and a perfectionist on the course. Off the course he's still focused, but he's got a sense of fun. He doesn't think about golf."

"Losing doesn't eat at him," Earp said to *Time*. "No sir. It makes him more determined. He says it's only a game. What are you going to do about it? Play again tomorrow. He says you bloody beat me this time, but you won't beat me next time. He isn't going to go home and lose sleep over it."

"We don't talk a whole lot about golf at home," Laura told the *Daily Mail*. "But when those horrible situations happen, like the Masters, it's nice to know that you can come back home to someone who is still going to love you, still think you're wonderful, and not be disappointed in you. Greg knows better than anybody what he's done wrong and why he's done it. He doesn't need to hear it from me. He doesn't need me to start on him because he feels bad enough."

Away from home the pressure mounted daily. Norman's close shaves had upped the ante. "I wasn't the only one who wondered where he would end if he continued on the trend he was on," Thomson says. "He was clearly standing still and people were going past him, and I didn't want to see that happen. Nobody here in Australia would wish that on him."

The Milky Bar Kid: Greg, aged ten, grins for the camera. (Merv Norman)

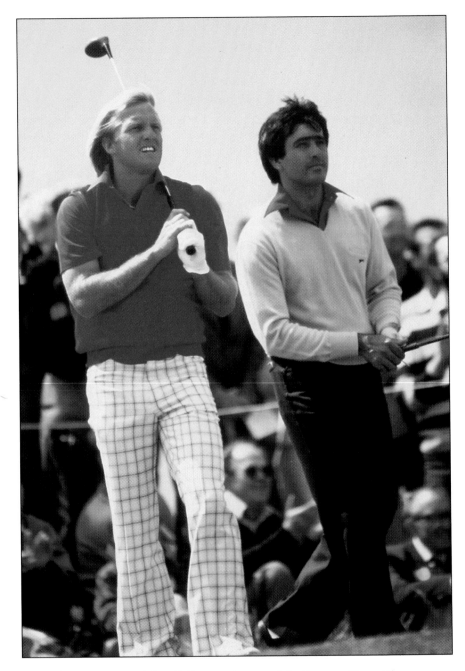

Young lions: Norman and Seve Ballesteros, the stars of the European Tour at the time, battle it out at Royal St. Georges in 1981. (© Phil Sheldon)

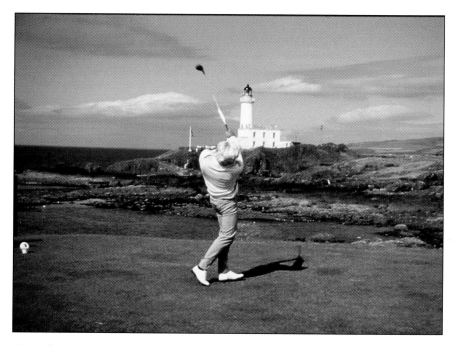

Favored son: Norman drives past Turnberry's famous lighthouse on his way to victory in the 1986 British Open. (Allsport)

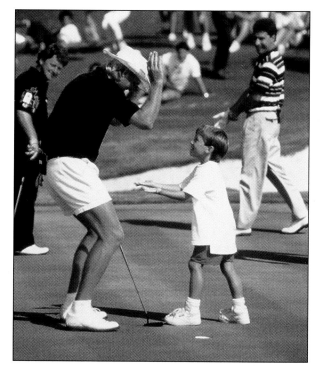

Watched by Jose Maria Olazabal and Ian Woosnam, Norman high-fives his son Gregory. (© Phil Sheldon)

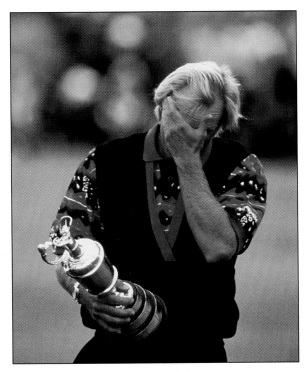

After the agony, the ecstasy. Tears of joy stream down Norman's face as he celebrates his second British Open Championship at Royal St. Georges, in 1993. (Allsport)

Norman follows through on a fairway shot at the 1995 Dubai Desert Classic. (©Phil Sheldon)

A prayer before dying: Norman collapses near the fifteenth green at the 1996 Masters after the chip he had pinned his hopes on skirts the hole in the final round.
(Allsport)

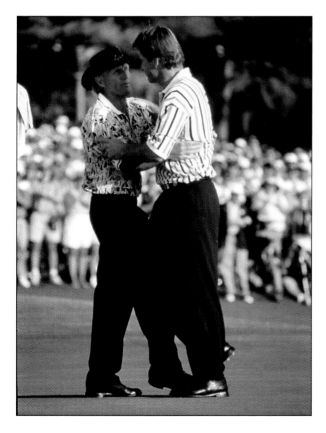

After a day in hell, Norman surrenders emotionally to Nick Faldo's embrace at the 1996 Masters. "It wasn't so much what he said," he told one writer, "it was the hug. I've never been hugged like that by a man."
(© Phil Sheldon)

Birds of a feather: President Clinton shows Norman how to play the game at New South Wales Golf Club in Sydney, Australia. (Associated Press)

The steps President Clinton made infamous lead the way to the Hobe Sound, Florida, mansion the Normans call home. (Associated Press)

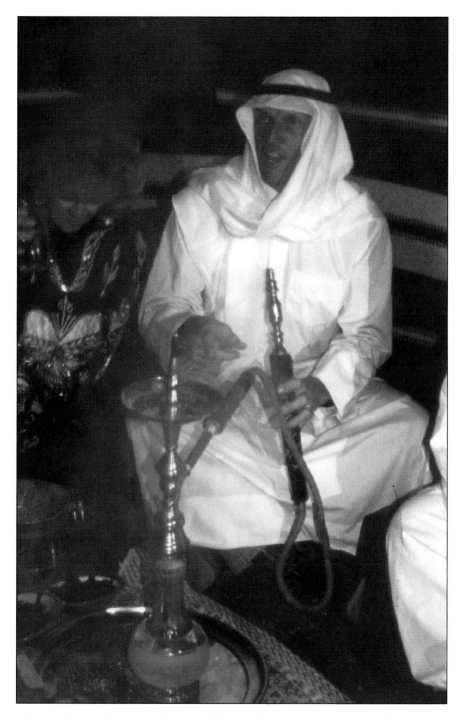

Greg and Laura Norman smoking "apple" in the Hookah, during the week of the 1997 Dubai Desert Classic. (© Phil Sheldon)

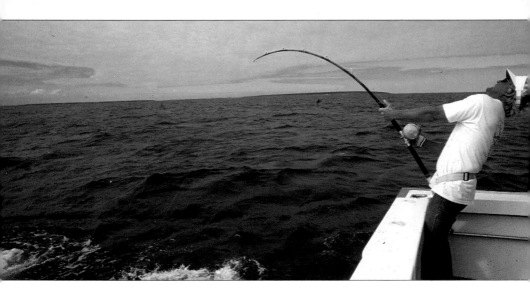

The Shark tries to extract another Great White from the deep. (Yours In Sport/Lawrence N. Lev

Top Gun: Norman and his alter ego—the boy who dreamed of being a fighter pilot. (Colorific/Robert

OPEN SEASON

"I'd like to win the British Open first. It is *the* tournament in the world. It has the tradition. One day I believe I'll be the Open champion."

Greg Norman, March 1983

It was midnight when Norman, drunk on happiness as much as champagne, walked down to the eighteenth green at Turnberry, accompanied by Laura, Norton, photographer Lawrence Levy, and Howie Baws, a friend of Levy's. Levy was wearing Laura's underwear, not having managed to find a clean pair of his own. They sat on the velvety surface where, hours before, a par had been sufficient for Norman to win the 115th British Open Championship by five strokes. Norman gazed up at the little black star that highlighted his name on the great yellow leaderboard. "Wouldn't it be great if I had that star to take home," he said wistfully.

Baws jumped up. "I'll get it for you," he said and departed to climb the grandstand. Hearing their laughter, eight policemen arrived with dogs, but not even they could bring themselves to detract from the most magical moment of Norman's career. They turned a blind eye to the champagne bottle upended in the cup and hid their smiles as Baws clambered back down the stands, triumphantly bearing the yellow placard emblazoned with Norman's name and the black star denoting him Open champion.

Just over a week earlier Norman had been staring unseeingly out of the window of a Concorde. He was on his way to the Ayrshire coast of Scotland for the British Open, and he was thinking about golf's cruelty versus its rewards, about how badly he wanted to bring home the claret jug and about destiny. "He felt it inside," Laura said. "He told me on the plane coming over, 'I'd like to lead for four rounds and win it going away.'"

Days later, standing waist-deep in the worst rough since Doug Sanders refused to leave the clubhouse at the 1966 Open on the grounds that "there might be Apaches out there," Norman was primarily concerned with a broken wrist. Grimacing, he wriggled down into the wet grass at the par-three sixth, his face red with cold and his trousers flapping like crazy in the gale, and prepared to hack his way out. The ball careened across the fairway and plopped into the hay on the other side. Turnberry's landmarks, the proud white lighthouse and the eerie volcanic outcrop of Ailsa Craig, rose out of the gloom like the twin points of a smuggler's run. When he eventually managed to hit the green, Norman three-putted for a six.

"The Survival Open," Nicklaus called it. Nine years after his epic duel in the sun with Watson, over a links so benign that questions were raised about its place on the Open rota, Turnberry had turned spiteful. On the eve of the championship, dark clouds moved in and icy winds gusted. "Everybody is going to drive into the rough and make bogeys," Norman said reasonably. "The secret is to take nothing more than a bogey. Level par will win because it will be hard to make more birdies than bogeys."

It was only when the gun went off that the full fury of the storm was unleashed. Spectators cowered beneath bucking umbrellas, and players and caddies leaned like suicidal lemmings into the rain. Norman opened with two birdies in the first three holes, before reality returned with a triple bogey at the 222-yard sixth. Despite problems at the eleventh and a three-putt at the twelfth, however, he returned an eminently respectable 74. Of the 153 players who started the round, forty-nine failed to break 80, and the scoring average was 78.19. Collectively, the field was 1,251 shots over par. A pint-sized Welshman named Ian Woosnam scored 70, and Faldo, Gordon J. Brand,

Robert Lee, and Anders Forsbrand were a stroke behind. Nicklaus and Floyd shot 78, and Gary Koch was the best among the Americans with a 73.

In the worst of the weather, the fourteenth, a 440-yard trip through a wind tunnel, was just one of eighteen nightmares. Only thirty-three players made par there, and only Woosnam—hitting the best one-iron of his life—reached it in two. "In the situation," said Floyd, who lost a ball there, "these are the hardest conditions I have ever played in." Faldo called it "the toughest course I have known." Norman was less complimentary. "That was the toughest ever, no question," he said. "You can throw in all your U.S. Opens. That was as tough as golf could be."

HE AND FLOYD HAD DISCUSSED WHETHER A PLAYER COULD SUE THE R&A FOR DAMAGES IF HE STRAINED OR BROKE A WRIST TRYING TO EXTRICATE HIMSELF.

There were times during the day when he had felt humiliated by the elements, reduced to a nonentity, "hacking along, trying to make no more than a five at a par-four." The rough was so savage that injury was a real possibility, and he and Floyd had discussed whether a player could sue the R&A for damages if he strained or broke a wrist trying to extricate himself. The fairways were ludicrously narrow. Watson paced them off and found that not one was more than twenty-three yards across.

In 1977 when Watson overcame the Bear, they shattered the British Open aggregate record so spectacularly that Hubert Green, who finished eleven strokes behind Watson, said, "I won the Open—those two were playing some other tournament." That was the year when the little-known Mark Hayes clocked up a second-round 63. Subsequently, Turnberry had acquired a reputation as a low-scoring venue, a reputation that the first round in '86 only briefly dispelled. By the second day the wind had ceased considerably, and there was a dramatic drop in the scores.

Norman had arrived at Turnberry fresh from a two-week vacation, and he had been assured by Bruce Devlin that his game was in perfect working order. He was full of confidence in his pretournament press conferences. In practice rounds Bender had worked overtime getting him to relax, joking and teasing and tossing balls into bunkers and betting him a Coke he couldn't get up and down.

On his way to the first tee in the second round, Norman repeated to himself like a mantra "blue skies and 65s," the phrase he liked to use to get himself going. It worked like a charm, and he made three successive birdies, starting at the second hole. At the fifth he came up short of the green and three-putted from thirty-five feet, but he bounced back almost immediately with an eagle at the seventh, hitting driver, one-iron to twenty feet, and then rattling in the putt. His mouth, white with chap-stick, was stretched into an uninhibited grin; his hair was as platinum as Barbie's. He was a lot happier than he had been the previous afternoon, when a local paper had photographed him sitting with his head in his hands and captioned it "Don't cry, Greg." Afterward, he said, "Everything seemed to flow. The ball was coming off the middle of the club, and I felt really confident and comfortable with my swing. I liked the speed of the greens. That suited me. There were no distractions. I was totally involved in each shot. Everything seemed just right."

He went out in 32 and then hit a six-iron to five feet at ten and a nine-iron stone dead at eleven for two more birdies, causing the gallery to erupt. "The crowd got me going," he said. "They really pumped me up. For the last four or five holes, there must have been fifteen thousand of them willing me on. It was difficult to keep my emotions in check." At the fourteenth, the monster of the first round, Norman hit a three-iron to three feet, then sank a six-footer at sixteen to get to seven under for the day. An eagle putt slipped past the hole at seventeen, and he needed a par at the last for a record 62, or a birdie for 61. With the sound of the crowd ringing in his ears, Norman hit a seven-iron to thirty-five feet on eighteen.

Bender tended the flag for him. "Pete, I want this one," Norman said urgently. "I want a 61." But he misread the speed of the green, rushing his first putt by and then pulling the return for a 63. "With four holes to go, I honestly felt I might break 60," Norman said later. "I mean, 59 looked like a real possibility."

"It would be tough to say he was disappointed with his round, but there's no doubt the last hole left a bitter taste in his mouth," Bender said.

Watson was awestruck, describing Norman's 63 as "the greatest round ever played in a tournament in which I was a competitor." It gave the Australian a two-stroke lead at 137. Brand was next at 139, with Tommy Nakajima and Faldo another two back at 141.

"In the Masters I was beaten by the brilliance of Jack Nicklaus," said Norman, who had nine one-putt greens and used his driver nine times to equal both the course record and the major scoring record. "In the U.S. Open, I beat myself. But I have learned enough from those experiences to believe that this time I won't let it slip."

Dan Jenkins, author of such classics as *The Dogged Victims of Inexorable Fate*, saw Norman's 63 as proof that Turnberry was a pushover. "All of this by a player who is still trying to learn how to golf his ball, as they say," he wrote. "Norman's feet move on almost every swing; he addresses his putts on the toe of the clubhead; he sprays his shots woefully to the right or left when he does bad; and he is always making you wonder about his judgment. Despite these things, his power can be awesome and his touch at times can be likened to a brain surgeon's. If he learns to keep it all together for a spell, everybody else can forget golf and go play polo with Prince Charles."

In 1973 a virtual tempest had flattened Turnberry, blasting through the John Player Classic and turning tents and tee boxes into kindling. The 1986 Open saw nothing to equal that, but the third round rivaled any event on the globe for sheer nastiness. Norman, trussed like a supermarket fowl in a blue rainsuit, struggled manfully through the wind and rain, his hands slipping on the club. He extended his lead to five after eight, and then proceeded to make six bogeys coming home for an inward 40. He needed two drivers at the twelfth, was in the rough again at fourteen and in the bunker at sixteen. "Four hundred and nine yards of terror," said Alliss.

"The difficulty of the rain was that you could not see," said Norman, whose demeanor was for the most part remarkably cheerful. "It was coming down horizontally and every time I looked up to see where I was going, it hit me in the face and stung. At the ninth and tenth I pulled the trigger too soon."

He used his driver from the rough at the last and smiled ruefully as he landed short of the green in the soaking grass. This time there was no applause as he finished a stroke ahead of Nakajima at 211; the gallery had long since abandoned him to sit by their firesides at home. Woosnam and Brand shared third place at 214, and Koch was the lone representative of a defeated American contingent. It was the worst Open for U.S. players since Royal Lytham in 1969.

Devlin rang Norman as he was getting into bed. "You can do it this time," he told him. Zoeller, John Mahaffey, and Green all lent their support, and when he phoned home to talk to Morgan-Leigh, she said to him, "Good luck, Shark." But it was the words of his boyhood idol Norman cherished most. Earlier that evening he had been eating dinner in the restaurant at the Turnberry Hotel when he was hit by the realization that everything he dreamed of was once more within his reach. "Though chatting pleasantly, Norman had the aura of a man who was to be hanged in the morning," Rick Reilly said in *Sports Illustrated*. Through the mist that was threatening to descend on him, Norman heard Nicklaus asking if he could pull up a chair.

"Jack said there was nobody in the world he wanted more to win the tournament than me," Norman recalled. "I got a little choked up."

"You deserve to win," Nicklaus said sincerely, advising him to "just concentrate on the pressure of your grip. That will orchestrate your tempo."

Back in his room Norman spent a fitful night clock-watching and fretting. He couldn't stomach much breakfast. When he made his way down to the range, it helped that the sun was shining and there was no breeze to speak of, but he was "nervous as hell. . . . I kept saying to myself, 'All right, let's not do another Shinnecock here.' " Finally, he decided that it was better to be nervous than overconfident.

"We're just going to win a golf tournament today," Bender said soothingly. "We've won plenty of tournaments. What's the difference between those tournaments and this one? They're all just tournaments."

Norman took out a one-iron on the first tee. Nakajima, the bespectacled Japanese best known for the thirteen he took at Augusta's thirteenth and the nine he took on the Road Hole at St. Andrews, was his main threat. He had won ten events in Asia in the past eighteen months. But Nakajima was feeling a little jittery himself. He missed the green and three-putted from five feet to hand Norman a three-shot lead after one hole.

At the third hole it occurred to Bender that Norman was not capable of regarding the British Open as just another tournament. His heart sank as he watched the Australian wrench his second shot into a big bunker, some seventy feet from the pin. But Norman's club flashed and the ball rose steadily into the wind, took one bounce, and vanished into the hole to give him a four-stroke lead. Excitedly, Bender took his club, confident Norman would now settle down. Instead, he bogeyed the fifth with a poor approach and hit a low snap-hook off the seventh tee.

"Right then, I knew something was wrong," Bender recalled in *How We Won the Open*. "With having all those years' experience, I know when a player is nervous or choking or whatever people want to call it. His ball had gone into deep rough and I noticed he was walking toward it much faster than usual and he was talking to me faster. I said to myself, 'Oh, boy, it's getting to him. He's feeling the pressure.' "

"PETE, I'M SO DAMNED NERVOUS I CAN'T SEE THE HOLE. YOU'D BETTER TELL ME WHERE TO HIT IT AND HOW HARD."

Norman, wearing a patterned yellow sweater and a curiously ill-fitting pair of gray trousers, was in the rough with grass up to his knees, but he had a good enough lie to hack out onto the fairway, put his third on the green, and save par. Walking to the next hole, Bender said gently, "Greg, do me a favor. You're playing too fast right now. You're real nervous and you need to slow down a little. You're the best player here and you'll win this golf tournament, but you've got to take your time and enjoy it."

The words glanced off Norman's tense frame and dissipated into the sunshine. He strode away as if Bender had not uttered a syllable. Bender grabbed his sweater from behind. "Whoa!" he cried. "Slow down and walk my pace. Let's talk and have fun." He cracked a joke, and Norman laughed and appeared to relax. "Pete, you're absolutely right," his told his caddie. "I've got this won. Why try and pressurize myself into losing it?" At the eighth he hit a four-iron to eight feet for birdie.

From that point on Norman enjoyed himself. He was still edgy but he began to believe that he might win. At the fourteenth he played the shot that effectively won the Open—a seven-iron from the rough that hit the flagstick and dropped beside the cup to give him a five-shot lead. Nakajima had fallen to pieces and Langer, the only player to present any real danger, putted himself out of contention when he missed a five-foot birdie at fourteen and then yipped the two-foot return.

Otherwise, Norman's only real threat was himself. He was so shaky when he hit his third shot to three feet at the seventeenth that he said to Bender, "Pete, I'm so damned nervous I can't see the hole. You'd better tell me where to hit it and how hard." On the green, Bender lined up the putt for him and said, "Inside right lip and soft, on the toe." Norman, who could hardly hold the putter, knocked it three feet by and somehow made the return. Bender breathed a sigh of relief.

At the eighteenth Norman wanted to take his driver, but Bender talked him into hitting a one-iron short of the bunker and a four-iron to the green. Hardly had the ball left the clubhead than the gallery broke through the barriers and swarmed across the fairway, engulfing Norman and bowling over Bender. Breaking free, Norman, hair ruffled, hands raised to acknowledge the crowd's ovation, was choking back the tears. "I was so close to crying, it was ridiculous," he said afterward. He putted out shakily for a 69 to win by five shots over Brand with a 280 total. He had become the first Australian to win the Open since Thomson in 1965.

"Apart from my wife and my caddie, Jack was the first person to congratulate me at the eighteenth," says Norman, who was sprayed with champagne as he hugged Laura. "He was under the bleachers waiting for me. Which I thought was very special."

Norman sent two crates of champagne into the press tent and followed them in with the claret jug wrapped in his arms, his face radiant with happiness. "Everybody knows how much I wanted to win a major," he said emotionally. "The media is always writing, 'Why can't he win here? Why not there?' and everybody's always saying, 'Come on, Greggy, you can do it,' and even if you know you can, it starts to get you down. You get a monkey on your back."

"With a major, it will all be easier for him now," Langer said.

Afterward, Norman, bubbling with joy, kidded around with the bagpipers, and McCormack hosted a celebration dinner for him at the Turnberry Hotel. "I've never seen anyone enjoy a victory as much as he did," remembers Bev Norwood, an IMG vice president. Norman stayed up until 3:00 A.M. with Laura, Norton, Levy, and Baws. Later, he would describe their party on the eighteenth green as a "magic little interlude."

He gave a press conference in the morning nursing a giant hangover and was planning to while away the flight home working out how much his victory was worth. "I couldn't tell you how much I earned off the course in

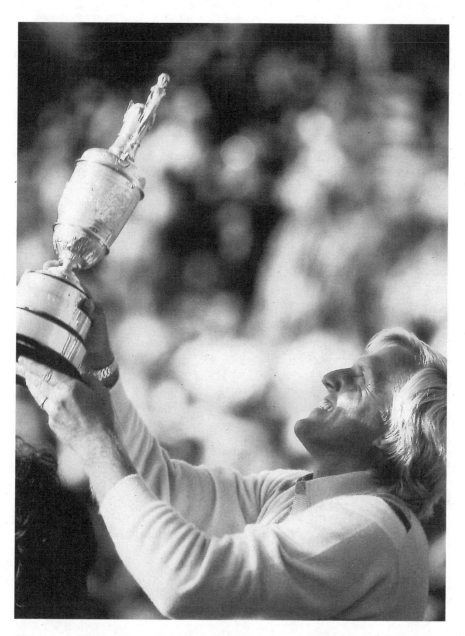

Heaven sent: Norman savors sweet success after winning the 1986 British Open at Turnberry.
(© Phil Sheldon)

a year, but if you multiply my golf winnings by four, you'd get pretty close," he smiled, adding, "Winning the Open was the greatest moment of my life, but I promise you this—it won't change me."

His next target was the U.S. money list. Along with his £70,000 first prize, he had already won $547,779 in America. "I appreciate everything golf has given me and I like to show it," said Norman, who was planning to buy an Aston Martin. "I like to spend money, and I'm lucky enough to have it to spend."

The celebrations continued back in Orlando and then in L.A. the following weekend, where a friend of Norman's was getting married. At the reception Levy pointed out to Norman that it was exactly one week and one hour since he had won the Open. Norman laughed. "And we've been partying ever since," he said.

"He's such a nice guy," said Bender, who had helped Norman to ten top tens in eighteen events. "Would you believe he took the Open trophy to a New York jeweler and had an exact copy made up for me? It's the proudest possession in my house."

Toini and Merv were overjoyed. So many people told Norman that his mother won the ladies' club championship at Royal Queensland within hours of his Open victory that when he phoned her, he said teasingly, "Hey, you're stealing my thunder."

It didn't suddenly become easier for Norman, as Langer had predicted, after he won his first major. Rather than diminishing, the burden of expectation increased. It was as though the Shark, having shaken his major hex, would now be unstoppable. He felt that way, too. In the weeks that followed his Open victory, he was carried along on a flood tide of pleasure and relief. When he teed up in the PGA Championship at Inverness in Toledo, Ohio, it seemed perfectly natural that he should shoot a course-record 65 to lead by two strokes over Craig Stadler and Phil Blackmar, and perfectly right and proper that he should follow it with a 68 to move four strokes ahead of Payne Stewart and Mike Thorpe on Friday. And what could be more appropriate than for Norman, so long denied, to put together a 69 in the third round, including a sixty-foot, par-saving chip to maintain a four-shot lead over Bob Tway, a fresh-faced Oklahoman, at 202? "Is this a soap opera or what?" Norman joked as he posed for his zillionth photograph.

Then the first black cloud came scudding over the horizon. Sunday's play was washed out and the final round was delayed until the following day. But Norman didn't anticipate any problems. "I am in a good frame of mind and it won't go away overnight," Norman said, declaring himself comfortable and ready to attack. "There's not a psychological problem. It's not like a sudden-death play-off. Everybody will come back and hit range balls, there'll be a gallery—it's all the same."

For ten holes of the final round, it was the same. Norman was four shots ahead of the field and in control standing on the eleventh tee. Now, looking back at the calamity that followed, he says defensively, "I didn't have two good holes, that's what it was. It was eleven and eighteen. That was it. The tide turned for me when I hit a perfect one-iron off the eleventh tee and I drove it into a half-filled divot, and I couldn't get the back of the ball. I hit it real fat, and I buried it in the front bunker about forty yards short of the green. And that was it. My tide turned there.

"There wasn't anything much I could do after that. It was just one of those things, when you look back on it and you pinpoint the exact moment when it all started. Hit the perfect tee shot and I'm walking up there thinking I had a pitching wedge to the green. And that was it. . . . I bogeyed eighteen because I was trying to make a chip shot. Eight out of ten times I'd get it up and down from that chip, because it was an easy chip. . . . Why does that stuff happen? Are you a fatalist? Do you believe in destiny?"

Norman did. At the fifteenth Tway conjured up a par after driving into the rough and hitting his second into the gallery. At the seventeenth, where he should by all rights have dropped a shot, he played an unbelievable pitch out of deep rough to within three feet to save par. Norman had bogeyed fourteen and they came to the last neck and neck.

At the eighteenth Tway drove into the rough and then put his recovery into a bunker on the right of the green. Norman had played a fine approach and watched in annoyance as it spun back into the thick fringe, twenty-five feet away. He wasn't unduly concerned. Tway was in the front bunker, anchoring his feet in the sand. He was looking back and forth from the ball to the flag. Norman watched him with one eye as he considered his own shot.

125

He saw Tway's club go back and the ball emerge in a pale flurry of sand, and then he saw Tway burst from the bunker like a jack-in-the-box, shouting with pure, unadulterated joy as the ball vanished into the hole.

"Oh, shit!" Norman said. He ran his own chip ten feet past the flag.

Later he recalled, "Even when he chipped it in, I still thought I was going to chip it in, 'cause I'll be damned if I was going to lose that championship."

Tway could hardly contain himself. "For something like that to happen on the eighteenth hole, it's just indescribable," he said tearfully. "I may never hit a shot like that again in my whole life. It was unbelievable. I just remember jumping up and down."

"You can't get much unluckier than that," Murray said of Norman's misfortune. "That's like getting run over by your own car."

"A lot of people have said to me my last-round 76 was a bad day," Norman says defensively. "But I say, 'I hit the ball as good as I hit it the first day. It's just that nothing happened.' Like at eleven . . . an inch either way, I win the golf tournament, simple as that." At the time he conceded graciously, "I did the wrong things at the wrong time, and Bob did the right things at the right time. Today he was the better guy."

Tway's victory left Norman with the unfortunate distinction of being the first man since Hogan to have led all four majors going into the final round, but unlike Hogan who won the Grand Slam, Norman actually won only one. "The Saturday Slam," it was labeled, or, as Jenkins cynically put it, "the Choker's Slam."

Only Ballesteros, who had lost the Masters in harrowing circumstances, thought that there was nothing surprising about squandering three third-round leads. "To win one out of four in those circumstances is not bad, it's about normal," he said.

"Bob Tway should never have been in the situation of holing a bunker shot to win," says Rodger Davis. "Everybody talks about how unlucky [Norman] was against Tway. Well, I looked at the scorecard and I saw him back in 40. Now that's not a good finish. It's just like match play. If someone keeps presenting you with things, then you start feeling really good and peppering the flag, and it's amazing how many times you can chip in or stiff an eight-iron because the other guy is giving you that opportunity."

"The PGA was kinda tough because he played so well," Norton recalls. "But in '86, particularly at Inverness, he was spinning the ball enormous

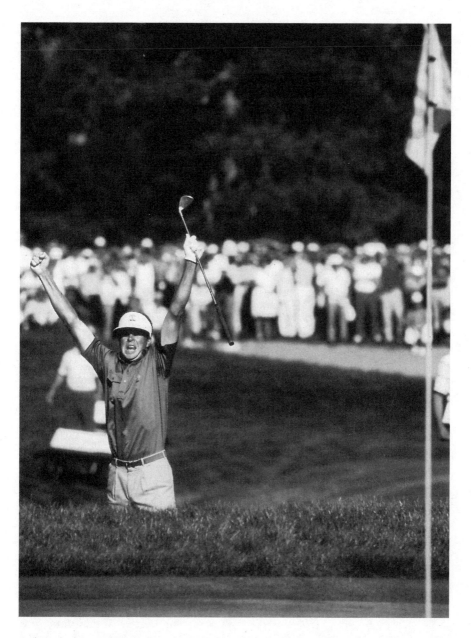

Jack in the box: Bob Tway bursts joyously from the bunker after holing out to beat Norman at the 1986 PGA Championship at Inverness. (© Phil Sheldon)

distances backward, and it certainly cost him. It was sad to see what he did on the back nine there."

Steve Williams, the New Zealander who caddied for Norman in some Australasian and Japanese events until '88, also believed that the Shark's ball held him back. "He was playing a Tour Edition golf ball that spun more than any other ball."

"Norman's problem is technique," Mike Clayton says. "People say he's a choker because he hits a four-iron eighty yards right of the last green at Augusta. That's not because you're choking, that's because your club is coming from the wrong place. His technique's killed him a lot of times. It's a measure of his talent that he's been able to play great golf with so many different methods, and he's never really stumbled."

When asked in his post-Inverness press conference if he felt that the monkey—the burden of not having the right ratio of majors to talent—was back, Norman snapped angrily: "What do you guys want? You guys are never satisfied. Face it. You know I did a hell of a job today. I don't understand you guys. Don't go saying the monkey's back on my back. I'll probably win next week and the week following that."

He strode from the interview room, jaw set, studiously avoiding looking at Tway who was still regaling reporters with details of his miracle shot.

Norman didn't win the next week or the week following that, but when he did start winning in September, it was to embark on a Byron Nelson-type streak. At the European Open at Sunningdale, he scooped the biggest first prize in the history of British golf. "I haven't felt as excited as this on a golf course since the Masters at Augusta," Norman enthused afterwards, a strange statement given that he had won the British Open, a supposed lifetime ambition, in between. "I was ready to play and I wanted to win. I felt I was ahead all the time."

At the end of October, *Time* magazine did a feature on the Norman phenomenon. Merv and Toini had been up until 3:00 A.M. two days in a row watching their son in the World Match Play. Before overcoming Lyle in the final, Norman had gone head to head with Nicklaus in the semifinals. They were tied after thirty-four holes, when Norman drained a sixty-footer for eagle and the eventual victory. "Well, you know it was tough playing Jack," Norman said. "I love the man as a person and for what he'd done, and I made that putt. I know he wanted to win, he wanted to prove that the older person is still as good as anybody—and he is still as good as anybody

The Shark and the Bear: Norman and his mentor, Jack Nicklaus, clown around during the semifinals of the 1986 World Match Play. (© Phil Sheldon)

in the world. And I just wanted us to finish even: Play all night and finish square and say, 'Guys, flip the coin. Heads he wins, tails he loses.' I really didn't want to see a result, and when that putt went in he just gave me one of those Jack smiles and a wink."

He was slightly less genial when he beat Lyle 2 & 1 in the final at Wentworth, marching off the course and declaring that he would never play in the World Match Play again. He accused the crowd of extreme partisanship, claiming that they had deliberately tried to put him off by making loud noises on his backswing and cheering when he missed crucial putts. "It didn't work," he said. "It made me concentrate even harder and be more determined to win. But if that's the way they want it, I'll stay away in the future. I hope my feelings change before next year, but at the moment I am very annoyed. Of the thousands who were following us, I reckon only 10 percent were good. The other 90 percent were bad."

Back home in Aspley, Brisbane, his parents found it hard to explain their emotions when they watched their son win another title. "One didn't ever think that he would ever be number one in the world," Toini said. "I sort of expected him to win a few tournaments, but not the number that he's won."

"Happy," Merv said, "proud. You sort of stand back and think, 'Well, there he is, walking the world stage.' "

GREEN JACKET BLUES

"I am going to win the Masters one day, there is no question about it."

Greg Norman, March 1988

For Norman, 1986 was, arguably, the best season any player had had since Arnold Palmer hitched up his trousers and kicked professional golf into the modern era. Between the European Open in September, where he beat Brown on the first extra hole of a play-off, and the Australian PGA, he won seven times, including the Dunhill Cup at St. Andrews (Australia beat Japan 3-0), the World Match Play, the Queensland Open (won by six shots), the New South Wales Open (by five), the South Australian Open (by three), and the Western Australian Open (by one)—perhaps the greatest run of form any golfer had enjoyed since Byron Nelson embarked on his eleven–victory streak in 1945. He won the U.S. and Australasian money lists, became the first player to earn more than a million dollars worldwide in a season, and was ranked No. 1 in the world. "It's incredible," Laura told reporters from Down Under. "We've almost forgotten how to lose."

"I'm just over the moon about it all really," Norman beamed.

To Jenkins and others, "The year became a haze . . . of Norman winning eight or ten dozen tournaments in various corners of the world, and almost winning eight or ten dozen others, or so it seemed. It got so bad that when Greg did not win a tournament, fans felt cheated. And if a newspaper didn't have at least three headlines a week that said, 'Norman Conquest,' you figured there was no tournament that week."

It wasn't until 1995 that Norman revealed that throughout the year he had been driven by something far greater than the fear of never winning a major. "You've got to be so careful because somebody can get into your business and destroy you so quickly and take everything," he told *Men's Journal*. "It happened to me in the eighties. In 1986 when I won the British Open, I didn't have a penny to my name."

He refused to divulge any details but went on to say that his recovery strategy had been to play the best golf he could. "One of Nicklaus's best years was when he won the Masters at forty-six. Why? It's not private information: He was having trouble financially. When a strong-minded person has his back to the wall, he comes out fighting. Nobody's going to stop the Bear when he's in a mood to get aggressive. Same [thing] with me. I was backed into a corner, and the only way I could get out was to play hard, be dedicated, focus. I had to pick myself back up from scratch."

Hughes Norton, who was not only Norman's agent during this period but one of his dearest friends, was rendered almost speechless by this claim. "Absolutely ludicrous!" he snapped, his voice shaking slightly. "It's just the weirdest thing I've ever heard. Now, several years before that he had to make a settlement with Marshall, which was costly, but by the end of '83 that was certainly over. In 1986 his income stream was fabulous. He's re-creating history. Why, I don't know. I'm amazed. I guess I shouldn't be, but I am."

"It was a very temporary thing," Frank Williams, who later took over from Norton, says hastily. "I think the severance with Marshall was very harsh and tough, and he was forced to pay out a lot of money, and I think there was a period of time when he *was* in financial trouble. But it was only very briefly, and it probably wasn't as bad as Greg thought it was."

Questioned about his *Men's Journal* comments two years later, Norman is adamant that the situation was very bad indeed. "In 1986 I probably couldn't have written you a check for a thousand dollars," he insists. "People warn you but you don't think it will happen to you. And yet it happens to everybody. You can go down the list—Nicklaus, Palmer, Muhammad Ali, Sugar Ray Leonard—in every area of sport. That's why, when my contract expired with IMG, I went looking for other things, to protect myself."

"That's pretty amazing," says Norton, who maintains that Norman was "thriving" and buying houses and cars all over the place. Indeed, a cursory glance over the Australian's purchases between 1983 when he left Marshall and the end of the 1986 season turns up Ferraris, Jeeps, twenty-year-old

Aston Martins, Jaguar sports convertibles, Rolls Royces, countless journeys on the Concorde, and a dream house in one of the most exclusive areas of Orlando. "I had just negotiated the Spalding contract at Turnberry," Norton continues, "which was the largest deal ever signed by a golfer. We were setting records for appearance money. That Spalding deal alone was so far from penniless on the spectrum I can't tell you. If he was penniless and he had just won the British Open, he would have fired IMG on the spot. He should have fired IMG if it was true."

But Norman didn't fire IMG—not that year at any rate. Why would he have? If the claims of his agents and the calculations of the press bore any relation to reality, he made ten million pounds in endorsements in the year following his victory at Turnberry, including a one-million-pound deal over three years to be a roving ambassador for Swan and Castlemaine XXXX Australian lagers; a two-million-pound deal with a Japanese hotel and leisure company; and up to seven million pounds over three years to promote Hertz rental cars, wear Reebok clothes and Niblick shoes, fly Qantas, conduct golf clinics at a club in Florida, and sport a calorie-injected McDonalds *M* on his sleeve.

But as the wealthy always say, there's more to life than money. Norman drew on the golden residue of the previous season and took what he could into 1987. He won the Australian Masters by nine strokes and immediately flew to Brisbane for a lesson with Earp, telling reporters there was room for 20 percent improvement. Then he tied for fourth place at The Players Championship in March. But his main, if not his only, focus was Augusta. "From the last day of the 1986 tournament, when I hit that second shot and missed the putt for par, from that very moment, and for the next year, twenty-four hours a day, I thought about the Masters," he admitted. "Every day it was in my mind. More than anything else in my life I wanted to win that one."

That obsession, a complex alloy of passion and desperation, was what forced Norman through two lackluster opening rounds to a third-day 66 on the flawless fairways of Augusta. It's what kept him clinging on when he went out in 37 on Sunday, bogeyed the tenth, and double-bogeyed the eleventh to lie one over par. It's what helped him claw his way back and sink a thirty-five-foot putt on the penultimate hole to recover a dropped shot at the water-rimmed sixteenth.

That morning, hours before he teed off, a group of writers, one of whom was Tom Callahan, golf's most eloquent chronicler, had encountered Norman in the locker room. "He was in there reading the papers," Callahan remembers. "Bob Verdi of the *Chicago Tribune* told him we'd all been in Australia for the Australias Cup. Instead of saying, 'Did you like it?' he just went, 'Hmm.' Then Dave Anderson said, 'We played Royal Melbourne,' and instead of going, 'What did you think?' he just went, 'Mmm.' Then, foolishly, I dropped the third shoe. I said, 'Yeah, we all bought one of those Akubra hats.' Well, he looked at me and said, 'Good, that's money in my pocket.' And somebody there—it wasn't me—put a curse on that hat and said, as long as he wears it, he's not going to [win another major]. Well, he gets chipped in there, and then he wins the '93 British Open [without a hat]. So among us, we kid that what he doesn't know is if he just took that hat off, he'd be all right."

With his hat firmly on his head, Norman arrived at the final hole, needing a birdie for outright victory. Ballesteros and Larry Mize watched his progress on television. They had tied at 285 after Mize, a gentle, mousy-haired local who had spent much of his childhood standing dreamily outside Augusta's exclusive gates, hoping and praying for a chance to compete there, holed a six-footer for birdie at the eighteenth.

Out on the course Norman watched a twenty-two-footer that would have given him the Masters slide past the hole. "I don't know how it stayed out," he said disbelievingly. "A foot and a half from the hole, I could just feel it going in."

"When Greg's putt just missed, Seve and I both looked at each other like, 'We just dodged a bullet,' " Mize remembers.

With the momentum in Norman's favor, the three men walked to the tenth for the play-off. The sun was sinking slowly below the pines, and the fairway, dropping away into the valley far below, was bottle green, crisscrossed with dark shadows. Between the Latin intensity of Ballesteros and Norman's presence and athleticism, Mize made a bizarre extra. At twenty-eight he was pale and slender with only one tour victory, four years earlier, to

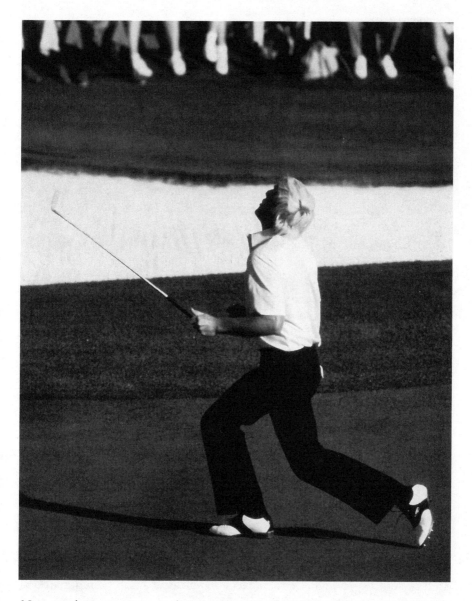

Norman reels in agony as a missed putt at Augusta's eighteenth drops him into a play-off eventually won by Larry Mize, who holed a miracle chip on the second play-off hole of the 1987 Masters. (© Phil Sheldon)

his name. Yet it was Mize who outdrove the stars on the first play-off hole. He was still bubbling over with the excitement of the birdie that had given him a tie at eighteen, so happy he could hardly contain himself. He hit a seven-iron to ten feet, Norman was twenty feet away, and Ballesteros putted up from the fringe.

"With Mize and Norman both having birdie chances, I gave it a little extra," Ballesteros remembered, running it three and a half feet past. The sun was directly in my eyes on the return. . . . I don't think I did anything wrong, but I must have aimed left."

With tears streaming down his face, Ballesteros began the long, lonely walk back to the clubhouse, as the other players made their pars. Even before he reached the top of the hill, history was being made on the eleventh. Mize had hit his five-iron second shot right, finishing some 140 feet away from the flagstick on a little rise near the twelfth tee. He went worriedly over to inspect it while Norman studied his long putt on the green.

" 'Pete, I think if we just cozy this little son down to within two feet of the hole, we'll have a two-footer to win the golf tournament,' " Norman remembers telling Bender. "That was my thinking, looking at the putt. It was a good fifty, fifty-five feet. I had hit it exactly where I wanted to hit it. Maybe it was six feet too far, because you'd rather have it hole-high than a downhill putt, but I was happy with it. Everything I did on that hole, I felt I executed right."

Norman looked over at Mize, who was preparing to chip. Thousands of miles away, in the pro shop at Royal Queensland, Earp "felt a cold shiver" pass through him as he watched the American set up over the ball on television. "My wife will tell you. I said, 'Mize is going to chip this in.' My hair went all funny."

The clubface flashed briefly and then the ball came bouncing gaily down the slope, took a quick skip across the green, and dived into the hole. For a split second nobody moved. The gallery stood aghast. Then Mize erupted, his purple-striped shirt flying upward. "It's just something that you dream about happening. I was so excited and thrilled, I'm running around screaming like an idiot. It was great."

Norman sank slowly to his haunches, the blood draining from his face. "I couldn't believe my eyes," he said afterward. "I just couldn't believe it was going in."

His own putt drifted away from the hole. "It was almost like somebody ripped that [green] jacket right off his back," Laura remembers.

"I felt for Greg a little bit at the end," Mize says. "You're kind of not human if you don't."

Back in the press center, Norman described that day as the most demoralizing of his career. "I'm just glad I'm playing for the next four weeks because if I went home right now, I might be throwing things against the wall for the next five days," he said with a laugh. But he was as sporting as ever. He cracked jokes, toasted Mize with a beer, and said smilingly, "I didn't think Larry would get down in two from there, and I was right. He got down in one."

FOR A SPLIT SECOND NOBODY MOVED. THE GALLERY STOOD AGHAST. THEN MIZE ERUPTED, HIS PURPLE-STRIPED SHIRT FLYING UPWARD.

As he walked out, his four-year-old daughter put her hand in his. "Daddy," she said, "I know you didn't win today, but can we still have a party?"

In the hours and even months that followed Mize's chip-in, there was no outward sign that this defeat was different from the rest, that it was, as Tom Weiskopf called it, a "stake in the heart"—the kind of blow that Watson inflicted on Nicklaus at Pebble Beach, or Trevino delivered when he chipped in to finish Tony Jacklin's career on the seventy-first hole of the 1972 British Open at Muirfield. That evening Norman flew back to Orlando with some friends on a chartered plane. They drank champagne and laughed so hard that when Laura looked at photos of the trip later, she said, "Is this after we lost?"

Back in Britain, Ballesteros told *Golf World* (of Europe) that Norman made a mistake by going for the center of the green rather than the pin on eleven, because it allowed Mize to believe he still had a chance. This ticked Norman off royally. "Seve is so detrimental to his name right now," he said. "He can't shut his mouth up, because he keeps chastising other players for what they've done. I don't understand the guy, I really don't. I thought I got to know him the years I played in Europe, but now I'm totally lost with him. If he's going to throw stones at a glass house, he [should] never have three-putted the tenth. If he was in exactly the same position I was, I promise you, Seve Ballesteros would've hit it to the middle-right of the green."

The media expressed Norman's own incredulity that he could be beaten twice in successive majors by a miracle shot. "Ever seen a Great White Shark eaten by an anchovy? Twice?" *Sports Illustrated*'s Rick Reilly asked, adding, "Another catastrophe and you can look for Norman on the cover of *Psychology Today*."

"Greg Norman will lose the next U.S. Open when Joe Bob Zilch holes out a wedge from the top of a eucalyptus tree on the third extra hole in San Francisco," Jenkins intoned. "Norman will lose the British Open when Sam Sausage holes out a wedge from ten fathoms beneath the Firth of Forth on the fifth extra hole at Muirfield. Norman will lose the PGA Championship in Palm Beach when Rex Shank holes out a wedge from inside a jewelry store on the seventh extra hole. Norman will then retire and autograph straitjackets for a living."

THEY DRANK CHAMPAGNE AND LAUGHED SO HARD THAT WHEN LAURA LOOKED AT PHOTOS OF THE TRIP LATER, SHE SAID, "IS THIS AFTER WE LOST?"

Outwardly, Norman was philosophical, admitting that it hurt but not saying how much. Earp thought that nothing in his life had hit him harder. "But he would not admit that. Greg says, 'Just forget it.' "

"Inside," Laura says, "he was dying."

It was not until 1991 that Norman admitted that it had taken him four years, not the four months he claimed at the time, to get over it. He hadn't wanted to tell people that after Mize chipped in, he sat on the beach at three o'clock in the morning and cried. "I was kind of, 'Ohhhhh, what have I done wrong?' I sat down in front of my house and just listened to the surf come in."

"I think the Larry Mize one was the most devastating loss for Greg," Laura says. "He tried to brush it under the carpet. He tried to pretend that it didn't hurt him and that he was just going to go on. But he had to deal with it eventually. It took a long time, and it kind of got deeper inside of him the longer he let it go."

A decade later, Norman is still trying to come to terms with the fact that the Mize defeat, still the most painful of his career, came so soon after Tway. "In all honesty, I didn't do anything wrong in either of those majors," he says.

Reminded that he came home in 40 at Inverness, he says, "Uhhh, yeah," before moving smoothly on. "So people had to do something dramatic. Anyway, Larry Mize was the hardest one of the lot. I can deal with it when I screw up myself, but it's pretty hard when it happens back to back. People say, 'Well, it's never been done before,' and you start analyzing it and you think, 'Shit, it's true. I did lose back-to-back majors with somebody holing miracle shots. I could have been on my way to a Grand Slam, but no. And then you sit back and look at all the people who holed shots against me—you can go down the list. My life, my career, has been so much better than theirs. I kept on winning. Larry Mize hasn't won.''

"If you actually look at Greg's failures, if you want to call them that, if you actually analyze them, it isn't just that he's been unlucky and lost," Marshall says. "To me, that's the easy way out. People have been able to parlay that around and say, 'Poor guy! Larry Mize chipped in or Bob Tway came out of a bunker.' But people forget that he dropped four or five shots, so he didn't lose to Bob Tway, he let him in. So I think he's been cushioned by that over the years."

"They were all his fault, except the Larry Mize one," says Clayton. "I mean, that was outrageous. But he shot 40 on the back nine at Inverness. He made a double bogey at eleven with a pitching wedge. He was in a divot, sure, but he made a double bogey. He played so well for three and a half days and then he shot 40. Bob Tway was never in it. Sure, the guy made a bunker shot, but when was the last time you saw someone shoot 40 on the back nine of a major and win?"

One of the guiding principles of Norman's life has always been that of rewarding himself for his hard work. Since he had worked hard for seventy-four holes of the Masters, he rewarded himself with a $118,000 Ferrari Testarossa, a trip to the Indy 500 to hang out with Roger Penske in the pit, and spent three million dollars on a new oceanfront house in Lost Tree Village, North Palm Beach, close to Jack and Barbara Nicklaus. The Normans had not been happy with the standard of education in Orlando, and the Nicklauses had convinced them of the advantages of sending their children to the exclusive Benjamin schools in Palm Beach, which all the Nicklaus children had attended.

To Coleman this typified Norman's penchant for befriending the rich and famous. "He's a showbiz man," he says. "He moved to Bay Hill and was playing with Arnold Palmer when Arnold Palmer was still a bit of a name, then he went to North Palm Beach where Jack Nicklaus lived and was always flying and playing golf with Jack Nicklaus. He's promoted himself very well by being seen with the right people all the time . . . and when you're doing that, people talk about you in the same breath. They say, 'Jack or Greg or Arnold.' And if he'd come and play a practice round, it was mostly with Jack or Arnold or Nick Price. It was always a name. He's completely different from somebody like Bernhard who'll roll up and go out and play with Joe Bloggs or Jack Smith or anybody who wants to play. But I think Greg was a guy who wanted to promote himself."

"Greg makes a lot of money; he flaunts it and that pisses people off," said former Masters champion Cary Middlecoff, who was living at Lost Tree at the time. "He is very popular, but that's the reason he is not more popular."

But according to Williams, the opposite was true, and in fact the Normans had moved away to Jupiter Island in Hobe Sound, Florida, within three years. "They hated it," he says. "It was too snobby for them, for want of a better word."

When Laura first saw the North Palm Beach property, she called Norman in Australia. "Should I spend a million dollars without you seeing it?" she asked.

"Do you like it?" Greg asked.

"I love it," Laura said.

"Well, go ahead and get it," he told her.

The existing house was then leveled and replaced with a six-bedroom French villa with a fountain and lots of arches. The dining room could seat one hundred or more, and the trophy room housed the billiard table used in the 1932 world championships.

"I feel that my place is to do anything and everything to help Greg's success," Laura told April Tod of the *Mail*, "and that means keeping a low profile and helping with all the trivial background stuff. . . . There are times when we are forced apart because of all of Greg's golfing commitments, and I know there are women out there who love to follow him because of who he is. But I don't think I've ever been jealous of those attractive girls who follow golfers. Greg is smart enough never to risk anything."

The anxiety of watching Norman play often caused her to shed pounds in weight, and she felt physically ill after his Mize defeat. Asked whether she was concerned that Norman would be felled by another miracle shot at the forthcoming U.S. Open, she cried, "No, no, no! It just couldn't happen again. In fact, I really feel more of a relief now. It's all over. And you know what? I have a feeling that this time Greg is going to pull one of those miracles on somebody else."

"BUT I DON'T THINK I'VE EVER BEEN JEALOUS OF THOSE ATTRACTIVE GIRLS WHO FOLLOW GOLFERS. GREG IS SMART ENOUGH NEVER TO RISK ANYTHING."

But there were to be no spectacular feats from Norman in the majors that year. Quite the reverse. He tied for fifty-first at the U.S. Open and was thirty-fifth at Muirfield the year Faldo won the British Open in horrific conditions with eighteen straight pars. Afterward, Norman stood in the cold in a garden illuminated by car headlights, giving a lesson to Andrew Mitchell, the head chef of the Greywalls Hotel. Having shouted at Mitchell at the start of the week for underfeeding him with half a lobster, an entire Dover sole, vegetables, and dessert, Norman was so pleased when the chef responded with giant portions of roast pork, duck, lamb, apple strudel, and raspberries that he offered to give him a thirty-minute lesson rather than the five-minute lesson he had cheekily asked for.

Only the hotel manager was not amused. "I shudder to think what would have happened had the club secretary caught my chef and Norman on the course," she said.

Norman's own game had gone into decline. After the Masters he had tinkered with his basic fundamentals in an effort to eliminate the blocked shot he sometimes hit from his game. As a consequence he had begun hooking the ball. "At the British Open, I hit a couple of iron shots that I really didn't like, so I said, 'Screw that, forget it.' I've gone back to my old left-to-right method, and I've stuck with it."

At the PGA, where Norman trailed in seventieth, a row brewed when the *Orlando Sentinel* published remarks Paul Azinger had made during a friendly round of golf, to the effect that a lot of the people Norman had beaten in his time had only been mediocre players. He was responding to comments Norman had made about the foreign players being more dominant than the Americans at that time—comments not dissimilar to those of McCormack, who called the U.S. pros a bunch of pampered prima donnas. "They can't face up to the fact that they aren't the best in the world anymore," McCormack said scornfully.

"He confronted me with [the article]," Azinger remembers, "and said, 'What is this? Why have I whipped you into a frenzy?' I said, 'That's trash, man, you never whipped me into a frenzy.' I mean, I'm sorry, it was nothing. The press made such an issue of it, like Greg and I had this big falling out. It was nothing like that."

"We had a discussion," was the way Norman phrased it to *Golf Digest*. "One thing I've always believed in is that you never mention another player's name in a derogatory fashion . . . because it will always backfire on you. Always."

He conveniently forgot about the forty or so character assassinations he had performed in his autobiography or his criticisms of Ballesteros and even Mize the previous November, when poor Mize was chosen by his fellow pros, in an informal magazine poll, as the player with the least intestinal fortitude. "I almost hate to say it, but Larry just doesn't show that special look at any time," Norman told *SI*. "He never seems to say, 'Hey, I've got a chance to make a birdie here.' I've played with him a couple of times and I've never seen that. He pulls that shoot-to-the-center-of-the-green routine way too often."

The day before Thanksgiving, Norman sacked Bender from his car phone in Australia. "He just said, 'It's time to change,' " Bender recalled. "I said, 'Give me one reason why you're firing me. What's your excuse?' He said, 'I don't have an excuse.' "

Bender told *Golf* magazine that Norman fired him for no reason, but the feeling among some of the caddies was that he had grown too cocky and boastful. He was nicknamed "the Million Dollar Caddie." However, Bender's friend Andy Martinez, Tom Lehman's highly regarded caddie, says that no caddie worked harder. "I think it had to do with some of the flaws Greg has, like maybe finding a scapegoat. I don't know. With Greg, it seems like he's tried a lot of different realities."

To Martinez, in the three-year period Bender had caddied for Norman, Bender had changed from being fun, one of the boys and "loose," to being "wound so tight all the time." Martinez, who carried Norman's bag for a day at the 1987 International when Bender was sick, actually experienced the effects of this change firsthand. "I tell you, in that one round, I saw the whole gamut of emotions. I even had to give him a pep talk. He was having one of those days and he was forcing shots and putts were lipping out. I said, 'After the year you had last year, this should be a piece of cake. What you did last year, it's in the history books. You've got nothing to prove.' But it seems like he always feels like he's got something to prove, every week."

"Greg intimidates caddies, too," Bender said. "You're afraid to say stuff to him, even if you're right, because you don't want to be fired for it."

It was almost the last controversy of the year, but not quite. On November 29, the fourth round of the Australian Open had to be abandoned when Norman and Sandy Lyle led a walk-off in protest at the third green at Royal Melbourne. Players and reporters crowded into the locker room after officials refused to do anything about the farcical position of the cup, cut into a slope on a triple-cut, quicksilver green in a howling gale. Rodger Davis, who was in the first group out, thought that the decision to quit was entirely reasonable. "Guys were eight-putting and penalizing themselves for all sorts of stuff. It was on a hill. You putted up, it rolled back fifteen feet. Sandy Lyle was the one who refused to putt. Greg found out and walked off. Fair enough. I mean, it was absolutely stupid. You can't have a shot at him for doing that. And then they blame some fifty-year-old greenkeeper, when at the end of the day the AGU didn't go around and check all the pins."

When the tournament resumed the next day, Norman won by ten shots.

The story of Jamie Hutton and the Heritage Classic is an integral part of the 1988 season. Shortly before the tournament, Norman had been contacted by a charity called Thursday's Child, which helped to fulfill the wishes of children suffering from extended or terminal illnesses. Hutton, a small, slightly built seventeen-year-old from Wisconsin, had suffered from Crohn's disease since he was seven, and in February he had discovered he also had leukemia. He idolized Norman. Like the Shark, he was a Boston Celtics fan, and his dream was to watch Norman play a tournament and win.

Norman willingly agreed to meet the boy and promised to do what he could about winning. Hutton was so excited about meeting his hero that, when he reached Hilton Head on Thursday night, he phoned Norman at 11:00 and woke him up. They arranged to have breakfast together. "I couldn't believe he eats cornflakes," Hutton said. "He was like a normal person." Norman, in his own way, was equally overwhelmed. After breakfast he had taken Hutton down to the Atlantic. The boy stopped and stared. "My God, it's so big," he told Norman, who realized with a shock that Hutton had never seen the ocean before.

That afternoon, Norman, who had opened with a 65 to share the lead with Azinger, introduced Hutton to some of the stars. By coincidence, Curtis Strange was also looking after a young boy with leukemia. After Saturday's round Norman was four strokes off the lead. Out on the course he was conscious that Hutton was willing him to win. When he found out that Hutton would have to leave before the final round on Sunday, he and Lawrence Levy chartered a plane to take Jamie and his mother to Madison for bone marrow transplant tests on Monday.

"He's very generous," Laura says. "He has no problem giving or doing things for other people. He does a lot for sick kids and kids who don't have anything."

Norman had arrived at Hilton Head filled with more confidence than he had had in months. A tip from neighbor Nicklaus, to quicken his hands and be more aggressive through the ball, had helped him win a succession of early-season events in Australia, including the ESP Open at Royal Canberra, where he opened with a course-record 62 and left the field behind by seven shots. When he read in a Sunday paper that the other Australians felt they were playing for second place at the Australian TPC, he took them at their word. "I had those guys beaten even before I walked onto the first tee," he said with typical modesty. "No guts, no glory."

In America he had battled to a final-round 64 for a share of fifth place at Augusta the previous week. Had it not been for opening scores of 77 and 73, the outcome might have been very different. "The old saying is that you don't go out to shoot 64s, they just happen," Ken Venturi, who had allowed three Masters titles to get away, told *Golf Digest*. "Norman has to let it happen. He's tried to make it happen. His first rounds have been horrendous because he puts so much pressure on himself to live up to expectations."

HE AND LAWRENCE LEVY CHARTERED A PLANE TO TAKE JAMIE AND HIS MOTHER TO MADISON FOR BONE MARROW TRANSPLANT TESTS ON MONDAY.

On the final day of the Heritage Classic, Norman struggled to concentrate, distracted by the "freedom of expression" with which Hutton talked about the illness which made him measure his life in months. When he stood over a six-footer at the eighteenth with a chance to win, he said to himself, "This one is for Jamie." He holed it for a 66 and victory. "That was probably more pressure than I have ever put on myself—because I knew I would break the boy's heart if I missed it," he recalled later.

It could have ended there, but it didn't. Norman, who presented the boy with his trophy and sent him clubs inscribed "To Jamie from Greg," keeps in touch with Hutton to this day. Honored for what he had done for Hutton at a New York golf writers dinner in June, the same month Hutton underwent his bone marrow transplant, Norman stepped up to the microphone and broke down. Tears poured down his face. "Pardon me," he said. "I've never done this before. Please excuse me." When he could finally speak, he spoke unevenly: "I don't think that many people know what goes on with a sick child. Heck, they haven't reached one-quarter of their life. They don't have a chance."

He received a standing ovation.

145

If the Hutton story represented one side of Norman's character—warm, compassionate, and infinitely generous, the Italian Open in Milan represented the profligate, flamboyant, and overbearing aspect. He arrived there with Laura from the Monaco Grand Prix in May, followed by a taxi transporting the luggage that hadn't fit into the trunk of their car. "It cost around eleven hundred dollars—the guy ripped us off," Norman said with a laugh. "He just took advantage of a couple of foreigners."

By the end of the week, he had paid for it with a £60,000 appearance fee and the £35,000 winner's check. In between, he found time to criticize the world-ranking system and Ballesteros and Woosnam's decision to change their clubs, which he said was "like cutting off the hand that feeds you." He also ordered a £200,000 Ferrari F40.

Norman was addicted to high-octane activities. People unlucky enough to find themselves in a vehicle with him experienced near heart failure and sudden aging after hand-brake turns at eighty miles per hour, although Norman claimed that he had received just four speeding tickets since he first moved to Florida in 1982.

"It used to bother me," Laura once said. "Anything dangerous he likes."

"He's just that way," Laura told *Golf Digest*. "People used to tell me he'd change. But he never will. I've learned to live with it." She admits, "When he dives, I'll still watch the bubbles and I'm always thinking about what could happen. But I'm not afraid, I'm just overcautious. He's always fine."

Norman's passion for speed led to his friendship with Nigel Mansell, the British Formula One driver. They had met the previous year in a pro-am and had formed a "brotherly" relationship based on a mutual love of golf and cars. "We have the same chemistry," Norman said. "He loves to be a winner; so do I. When you feel comfortable with a friend, you can get a lot off your chest. It makes you feel relaxed."

Norman had watched Mansell win the British Grand Prix at Silverstone in July 1987, and Mansell had visited him at the European Open at Walton Heath a few months later. "He was in his helicopter and I had a Jag," Norman told *Golf World*. "I was staying at a hotel near Gatwick, normally about thirty-five minutes' drive round the M25, so—I guess I was crazy doing this—I bet him dinner that I could beat him back. He had to give me ten minutes' start before he could even start the engines. Typically, because he didn't want to get beaten, he only waited five minutes. I had the car off the clock all the way and he landed at the same time as I pulled into the hotel. That's how we are—both very competitive."

"He'd probably scare some people who don't know about automobiles," Steve Williams says, "but he knows how to drive a car."

For Norman, the Italian Open turned out to be the high point of the season. In June he lost a play-off to Ballesteros at the Westchester Classic, and he then damaged ligaments in his left wrist when his club hit a rock on the ninth hole at the U.S. Open. Golf writer Melanie Hauser remembers Norman's flying into the locker room "half-hysterical. He was on the phone to his doctor and just going crazy. You could tell he was scared to death that he had ripped up everything in his wrist. He said something to the effect of, 'This is my career and I need to be seen now!' "

Norman was out for eight weeks. By the time he realized he might be fit enough to play the British Open, it was too late to re-enter, and he was desperately disappointed to find he would miss that, too. A top ten in the PGA Championship provided little consolation.

By then he was embroiled in two new controversies. Not only had the PGA of Australia decided to pick Peter Senior and Roger Mackay, leaders of their 1987 Order of Merit, over Norman and Ian Baker-Finch, the highest-ranked Australians on the Sony World Rankings, to represent them in the World Cup, but Norman's inability to play the obligatory fifteen tournaments required to maintain membership on the U.S. Tour had provoked a storm of protest. There was still plenty of time for him to play all fifteen events, but he was committed to events in Australia and the Far East.

"I can't believe that Greg would challenge the rules," said Strange, the U.S. Open champion and, until that point, a close friend of Norman's.

"Why should Greg be different?" Doug Tewell demanded. "The rules are the same for everybody."

Ballesteros was angrier still. Two years earlier he had fallen out with PGA Tour commissioner Deane Beman when Beman had stripped Ballesteros of his membership after his father died and he did not complete the requisite number of events. "If Norman breaks the rules, he should be suspended just as I was," Ballesteros said.

But Beman was in fact completely sympathetic to Norman's cause. "Deane told me there was no problem," Norman said defiantly. "I don't want to get into a slanging match with other players. I've supported and stuck up for this tour."

10

LONE SHARK

"With the glory goes the pressure."

Jack Nicklaus on Greg Norman, 1989

The season rolled out from under the new year, heavy as lead. "Is Greg Norman overrated?" That seemed to be the burning question. Or as one magazine put it, "Is Norman overanxious? Overwrought? Overdue? Overrated?"

There was no escaping the endless analyses and speculation. Norman had won fifty-two titles around the world, but everywhere he turned he was competing with ghosts—his own and the paragons of history. Nicklaus said that the Australian worked harder than he himself had ever done on his game—"He's on the practice tee at eight in the morning"—and let it be known he thought Norman and Ballesteros were head and shoulders above anybody else in golf. "I think Greg is a better shotmaker than Seve," he said. "It's just that Seve has greater imagination and a short game that is out of sight." But it was not enough, not for the media and not for Norman. Norman might have been number one in the World Rankings for the best part of three years, he might have an estimated income of ten million pounds, and he might, as *Golf Digest's* Nick Seitz said, be a "tall, powerful Australian with the meat-cleaver features and the regal bearing of a Degas stallion," but at thirty-four he had just one major and five U.S. Tour wins to his name. At the same age Nicklaus had won twelve professional majors. Even Ballesteros had won five.

"He has the ability to be the finest player in the sport, but his record in the States has not been that outstanding," Johnny Miller told *Golf Digest.*

"There's a very close correlation between Greg Norman and Tom Weiskopf. Tom should have been the best golfer in the world but he never was."

"I don't think Greg will ever win a lot of tournaments because he's big business," Strange said disparagingly. "He could quit today and spend a lot of money."

For the first time ever Norman admitted that burnout, the extinguishing of desire by off-course pressures, was a distinct possibility if he continued at his current pace. Reebok, McDonalds, Akubra (he was reportedly paid forty to sixty thousand pounds a year to wear his trademark hat) and other sponsors all demanded their pound of flesh; and his obligations to two tours—the Australian PGA was rumored to be forking out five hundred thousand pounds over five years in appearance money—meant that he flew back and forth to Australia as frequently as most Wall Street bankers commuted to their day jobs.

"I have been overloading my schedule," conceded Norman, blaming himself rather than IMG for his reluctance to turn down appearance fees averaging seventy-five thousand pounds. He planned to take things easier. "The bottom line is that I've tried to please other people ahead of myself and my family. I thought I could go charging around, playing all over the world, and I've enjoyed doing it, but it's been affecting the way I am as an individual and it's been affecting my game," Norman said. "I'm mature enough to say no. From now on the majors will be more important than making money."

But in reality slowing down was not an option. Driven by his fear of failure, poverty, or anonymity—sometimes it was hard to know which—Norman confronted his demons at Augusta in the spring of '89. A sense of urgency inhabited his game. A naturally quick player, he seemed to fidget and deliberate more over shots, executing a series of careful waggles and then launching himself at the ball. Lackluster rounds of 74 and 75 left him eight strokes behind Faldo and Trevino at the halfway stage.

As seemed so often to happen, Norman was at his best when coming from behind. He shot 68 in the third round and, on the back nine on Sunday, caught fire. He made birdies at the tenth, thirteenth, fifteenth, sixteenth, and seventeenth holes, before a five-iron shot to the final green fell like a pricked balloon short of the green and cost Norman a bogey. His 67 left him a shot out of the Faldo–Scott Hoch play-off.

As twilight cloaked the pines of Augusta, Norman pasted a smile on his face and joined Mark O'Meara and Stewart in the clubhouse for a beer. "I may not show it," said Norman, who had declined to be interviewed, "but I'm incredibly disappointed, incredibly down."

"You will win the Masters sooner or later," a bystander promised.

"Sooner or later?" Norman replied, smiling as if his life depended on it. "How much later is it going to be?"

For all of Norman's macho image, Weiskopf, among others, wondered whether he was too soft to win as many majors as he should, whether he lacked a killer instinct. "He wants to be the best, no doubt about it, and I wish it to him," the former British Open champion told Bob Verdi. "But to be the best, you have to be a motivated, selfish, egotistical, demanding perfectionist. But I give him lower marks on selfishness and ego, as far as golf is concerned. In life, Greg's a great guy, a man's man, who cares about friends and spends a lot of quality time with them and his family. He might not be mean enough to be the best in a cutthroat business, which is okay as far as I'm concerned. That was never a priority of mine, to be the best golfer in the world at all costs. I don't know about Greg. He's not a phony. He's a whole person who enjoys having a beer with friends and fishing with his kids. Is that bad? You tell me."

"Well," Norman said, "I do want to be the best golfer in the world, very much so. But I am a nice guy, and I also want to be that. You know, when I don't win, I feel worse for the people who root for me than for myself. I feel as though I've let them down. But I don't want people to feel sorry for me. I came from very little and I've done remarkably well, surrounded by great people, starting with Laura . . . I'm not comfortable though. I'm driven to win."

Norman told Verdi that he didn't think he could be meaner if he wanted to. "I give 110 percent on the course, but I also sleep at night. Where I was brought up, you give it your best, and if somebody beats you fair and square, you congratulate him for it and move on. Keep trying. Try harder. Too hard? Perhaps."

Nonetheless, the ticking of the clock wore on Norman's nerves like water torture. Privately, Nicklaus thought that Norman allowed himself to be discouraged by too many encounters with players with hot putters, but Norman felt there was more to it than that. He prayed there was more to it. "When I won the British Open, I wasn't ready to win a bunch of majors," he admitted. "I feel ready now, but first I've got to get the next one, and I'm very aware of wanting it too much. If I try too hard, I could lose. I also know that if I reach thirty-nine and haven't done it, it might be too late. I don't want to be remembered as the poor fellow who was there for those two chip-ins. I've got to believe there will be a day . . ."

Norman stood nervously on the first tee at Royal Troon in the British Open Championship play-off, with Bruce Edwards at his side. A veteran caddie, with the weathered, slightly hard aspect of a range rider in a spaghetti western, Edwards had spent sixteen years working for Tom Watson. When Watson cut back his schedule to watch his children grow up, Edwards took Norman up on his oft-repeated offer of employment. Their first tournament together had been the Westchester Classic in June.

"I thought he'd be fun to work for," Edwards recalls. "I thought, having worked for Tom and seen how he won, how he became a champion, maybe I could bring that to Greg. So the first two years I worked for him, we got along great."

Right at this moment Edwards was having all the fun he could have wished for. It was blazing hot, for starters. Frog-bellied Brits waded in the muddy-blue shallows of the sea, and Troon was dry and dusty and not a fraction as vicious as usual.

"People say the field is bunched because of the benign conditions," Watson had said. "But even if the wind doesn't blow, that'll probably change on Sunday because of the choke factor, the pressure factor. . . . You've got to have bottle."

Wayne Grady, the gentle Australian; Watson, looking like a Scottish shepherd; and the entertaining Stewart, were, respectively, at 204, 205, and

206 when Norman teed off on the final morning. He was seven shots off the lead, with only the remotest possible chance at winning the title, and yet he felt good about life. He rolled in a birdie putt on the first and his grin broadened. He rattled in another at the second and laughed. By the time he reached the third, he was in heaven. Six straight birdies brought him to within a stroke of Grady. At the sixteenth he narrowly missed an eagle. At the par-three seventeenth he holed his chip to save par. At the eighteenth he used his putter from the thin rough skirting the green and almost birdied again. His 64 was a new course record and set a clubhouse target of thirteen under. When Mark Calcavecchia hit an eight-iron to five feet at the last hole for a birdie soon afterward, and Grady bogeyed the fourteenth and seventeenth, they were tied with Norman.

Standing on the first tee of the play-off on that golden evening, Edwards felt confident that the tournament was theirs. There were lots of laughs. Calcavecchia, with his red- and white-banded shirt and mischievous face, looked like an irreverent high school footballer, and he kept asking the R&A officials if it really was a four-hole play-off. "You're sure now? After one hole, nothing changes, right?"

Norman and Grady were more tense, their smiles a little strained. Even when Norman birdied the first to gain an early advantage, he didn't seem to relax. At the second he hit his approach to about fifteen feet and birdied. The American followed him in from the back fringe to be a shot behind him. Grady trailed at even par.

At the seventeenth Norman hit a four-iron through the back of the green. He contemplated his lie in the pale grass. Grady was busy making bogey from a bunker, and Calcavecchia was waving his putter jauntily, laughing at some private joke. Norman took out a putter. "What I remember most vividly," Edwards says, "is that there was a long piece of grass, like kind of a straw, and as he took his putter back it was kind of catching it. But he still liked that play. The ball was just through the green on the fringe. I wanted him to putt it."

Edwards shouldered the bag and prepared to move back.

"Don't go away," Norman ordered, "I might chip it."

"I thought, 'Oh, man,'" Edwards remembers. "I've always felt, as a caddie, that you never say anything around the green. I mean, it becomes a touch shot. I really don't think a caddie should tell a guy, 'Don't putt it, chip it,' or, 'Don't chip it, putt it.' So I didn't. I don't know what he was thinking,

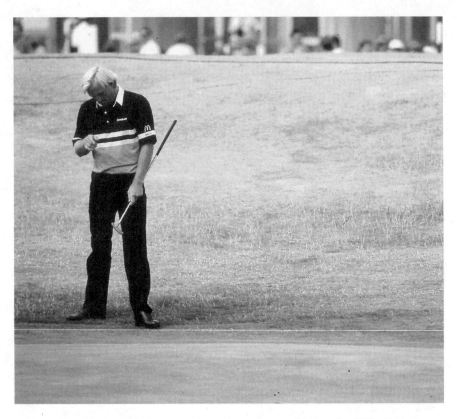

Despair shows on Norman's face as another major gets away, this time the 1989 British Open at Troon. (© Phil Sheldon)

but when he hit the chip I knew it was too hard. At that point we didn't need a birdie, all we needed was a three, and we would have had a one-shot lead going into the last hole. And it went about ten feet by and he missed the putt. I felt right then that we had thrown a shot away due to him being too aggressive. We didn't need a birdie, and I felt like he was trying to chip it in."

Grady thought it was bizarre. "He used about an eight-iron, which is probably not the right sort of club in that situation. I would have used a sand wedge."

"He could have putted it, hit it with a seven-iron, anything," Newton said. "Instead, he tries to hit a fancy, spinning chip. Seven years later he tried to hit the same fancy chip at the tenth hole in the final round at Augusta. He still wants to play the low-percentage shot he'd play in the first round, and that isn't the way to win majors."

Drake Oddy, Calcavecchia's caddie, said that the American had also been surprised. "There didn't seem that much between him and the green that would cause him trouble," he told Norman Dabell in *How We Won the Open*.

Norman's mouth tightened when he missed the putt. "It didn't go left," he told Edwards with a scowl as they walked to the eighteenth tee.

Whenever the 1989 play-off appears on the list of Norman's perceived failures, the chip on the penultimate hole is rarely mentioned. It is his tee shot at the last that is held up as symbolic of the overzealous approach that has cost him so dearly in the majors. Yet not one of the five who stood with him on the tee will condemn him for it.

Calcavecchia drove first, careening the ball off the metal railings way out to the right and rebounding into the rough. Norman considered his options. He had taken a driver off the eighteenth tee in all four rounds and, with Edwards in complete agreement, he was quite comfortable using it again. In the television commentary box, Nicklaus gave a little gasp of surprise. "I can't imagine what Greg is thinking taking out a driver here," he said. "The only thing he can do by hitting a driver is bring the bunker into play, which is the one place out there he wants to avoid."

Standing on the tee Norman and Edwards didn't see it that way at all. "I really didn't feel like that far bunker was in play for him," the caddie says, "and as well as he was hitting it, I didn't see it going anywhere but right down the middle. Which basically is where it started out. It hit a little mound and it kicked a little right and just fell into the bunker. Dead."

"People said I shouldn't have hit a driver," Norman said later. "But if I'd hit it three yards to the left, they would've said I hit the greatest drive ever."

Grady, whose own tee shot skated along the bone-dry fairway to within ten yards of that fatal bunker—"about twenty yards closer than I'd been all week"—thought that Norman's choice of club was entirely appropriate. "It was one of those shots where, as soon as he'd hit it, he bent straight down to pick up his tee, thinking it was perfect, and I thought it was perfect and bent down and teed my ball up," Grady says. "Then we heard the oohs and aahs as it went into the bunker." In his opinion Norman hit a flawless fade and was cruelly punished by a bad bounce. Grady refuses to accept that Norman picked the wrong club. "It might have been the adrenaline or something, but at no stage did any of us think that that ball was going to reach the bunker. Somehow it got there, and I don't think he deserves the criticism that he's received on that tee shot. It was just one of those things that happened."

Norman's position in the bunker was about as bad as it could be. He stood in the sand with his hands on his hips and his eyes empty. The sod-face of the pot bunker, just three feet high and about 120 yards from the green, was as insurmountable as any obstacle in golf in those circumstances. He looked over at the American. Calcavecchia, his freckled, roguish face aglow, was swinging at his ball with a five-iron. "It's a shot I'll never forget," Calcavecchia said later. "I watched it and I said, 'I don't care where it ends because that's the best shot I've ever hit.' "

The ball flew 205 yards to the heart of the green and ran to within six feet of the hole. Grady, who needed to hole his approach shot, put his best swing on it and got it to four feet.

"Is that close?" Norman asked Edwards, knowing the answer.

"Yeah, it's close," his caddie replied.

Norman frowned at his ball. "What do you think?" he asked Edwards.

In the commentary box Nicklaus tutted. "What he has to do now," he opined to the viewers, "is play a wedge of some kind safely onto the fairway and hope he can pitch the ball close enough from there to make par. If he goes for the green from that lie, the best he'll do is knock it in the bunker in front of the green. If he does that, he's in serious trouble."

Edwards, meanwhile, was telling Norman that if he thought he could get the ball over the lip and on to the green, he had to try. Norman agreed. He took an eight-iron and gave it everything he had. The ball caught the lip and dropped like a stone into the trap near the green. Behind him, the crowds broke across the fairways like surf, pouring through the barriers and rushing toward the green in an uneven wave.

Trying to escape the second trap, Norman caught the ball thin. It emerged from the sand as if it were rocket propelled, airmailed the green, and disappeared out of bounds. His score on that hole was X, just like an amateur hacker. "I just walked away, thinking, 'God, we should have won this thing,' " Edwards says. "And I felt for him. I really felt sorry for him. But that's the nature of the game. That stuff happens."

Norman was crushed. To shoot eight under par and then birdie the first two holes of the play-off and not win was hard to take. Yet when a roar of applause greeted Calcavecchia's final putt, Norman was the second person to congratulate him, smiling warmly and sincerely at the American. "He didn't moan and groan about it, which I liked," Edwards says of Norman's reaction, "but he was hurt. That hurt."

Grady was gutted. "Don't you feel sorry for Greg?" someone asked him. Grady stared at him in disbelief. "I thought, 'With all due respect, no.' I mean, I did, but I had the tournament there for two and a half days and I lost."

In the press center a wall of black-eyed lenses and cynical journalists waited to hear Norman's explanation for the latest black mark in his checkered career. "Destiny has a funny way of saying, 'Hey, this is the way it's got to be,' " Norman said, gazing steadily and courageously back at his interrogators. "But we all accept fate. It's what keeps us coming back hoping. You've got to keep thinking positively. I have to believe my time will come soon."

Asked if he felt destiny owed him a major, he gave a dry laugh. "Shit," he said, "it owes me four."

Later, when he read the papers and had time to think about what had transpired, Norman found Nicklaus's remarks almost as hard to deal with as defeat. Laura was upset on his behalf. "It's easy when you're sitting in a chair to make a guess, but what Jack Nicklaus would do or Johnny Miller would do is not what Greg would do, and that's all you can go by, what you feel at the time. I don't think Greg to this day would tell you he made a mistake there. It was a bad bounce, it went into the bunker. . . . When we got off the airplane in Washington, they never once said, 'You know, he made it so exciting in the last round.' There were guys leading and they never mentioned that those guys lost the tournament. They talk about Greg. Well, Greg came from seven shots behind to get there."

To Norman, held accountable once again for failing to live up to history, that was life. "Sometimes you play bad golf and win. Sometimes you play good golf and lose," he told *Esquire*. "Because of the way things ended up, people forgot what I had created that day. I had painted this beautiful picture, and I didn't win."

Typically, Norman used defeat as a springboard to victory. Nicklaus had described the United States as the Shark's last frontier. In the second half of 1989 he conquered it, winning the International at Castle Pines and the Greater Milwaukee Open and finishing fourth in the World Series. In Australia he won the Tournament Players Championship at the Riverside Oaks. "I hate failure," he growled at a reporter from the *Sunday Express Magazine*. "The idea of failure is, I think, my driving force."

"WHAT JACK NICKLAUS WOULD DO OR JOHNNY MILLER WOULD DO IS NOT WHAT GREG WOULD DO, AND THAT'S ALL YOU CAN GO BY, WHAT YOU FEEL AT THE TIME."

For Norman, still smarting from the disappointments of the previous season, 1990 could hardly have started better. Not only did it involve a spot of deep-sea fishing, but it carried the threat of danger, and as Steve Starling, who recorded both for *Modern Fishing*, observed, Norman is "an unabashed adrenaline junkie." A promoter had combined golfers and anglers in a worldwide fish tagging and fairway contest, involving, among others, Strange, Jumbo Ozaki, and Faldo; and the Shark was required to face a Great White through the bars of a steel cage.

On the appointed day Norman donned a heavy cold-water wet suit, mask, and oxygen tank in Spencer Gulf, Australia. The film crew was as slow and laborious as film crews always are, and the Shark quickly grew frustrated. "He bristled at each delay and openly resented the director's instructions," Starling reported. Finally, it was time to enter the water, and Norman splashed into the cage and then surfaced in a cloud of bubbles. He was handed a beer and was swigging it back and grinning and giving a thumbs-up to the crew when a deckhand shouted, "Here she comes! Get that bloody cage closed!" In an instant Norman snapped his mask on and retreated into the blue-green depths. A bucket of minced tuna was tossed in after him.

The silver outline of a shark came curving slowly out of the darkness and slammed against the steel bars. "Greg Norman had a ringside seat to the show of his life and all the adrenaline rush any mortal man could desire," Starling wrote. Afterward, the human Shark, who had hand-fed the Great White with a salmon and punched it playfully on the snout, was "wide-eyed and pumped up. . . . As his American minders surrounded him and slapped his back in congratulations, a steely glint entered Greg's expression. '*Man!*' he exclaimed. 'I gotta get one of those suckers! There's a twenty-five-foot feature wall in my house back in Palm Beach that's just waiting to have that mother hanging on it.' "

NORMAN RE-TURNED THE NEXT DAY WITH THE CAMERAS TO ATTEMPT TO CATCH A WORLD-RECORD SHARK, WHICH WOULD THEN BE TAGGED AND RELEASED.

Norman returned the next day with the cameras to attempt to catch a world-record shark, which would then be tagged and released. After maiming and losing one sixteen-hundred-pound shark in a four-and-a-half-hour struggle with a rod and line, Norman and his friends managed to land a one-thousand-pound Great White. Sadly, as he was reeling it in, it became tangled in the wire trace at the end of the line and died horribly.

Across Australia, environmentalists rose in outrage. "Sad Trophy Boosts Golfer's Ego" was one headline; "Great White Golfer Savaged over Shark" was another; and Norman was depicted beaming proudly beside the bloody carcass. Ian Gordon, Australia's top authority on sharks, said that there were probably fewer than fifty Great Whites in the country's southern waters and declared that the shark had been "sacrificed for the sake of publicity. . . . This creature died while the cameras rolled."

When "bloody [Jacques] Cousteau," as Norman referred to the man who had been his childhood hero, added his voice to the litany of complaints a month later, Norman said it was because he thought mistakenly that two sharks had been killed. "Things are said without the facts," Norman told *Esquire*, choosing to overlook the fact that the first shark probably died or suffered immeasurably after the injuries inflicted upon it. "[For example], people say I hit the wrong chip at the British Open. But I was the only one who could see the lie." His only regret was that the maimed shark had escaped. "We had that big sucker in the boat twice," he said in frustration. "Twice we had our hands on him. And he got away."

When it comes to hobbies, professional golfers are almost universally drawn to four things: televised sport, fast cars, gardening, and hunting. Angelic, sweet-natured men like Davis Love III and Tim Simpson shoot at all manner of creatures with bows and arrows, others just use guns, and one smiling, cuddly legend is reported to have slaughtered elephants with a machine-gun from a helicopter.

"I guess it's the challenge," Norman said lamely when asked what appealed to him about hunting, before resorting to the age-old hunter's defense. "Where I go hunting, it's culling. I don't go out and indiscriminately shoot. I've never done that. Where I go hunting in Australia, they ask you to go out because they have problems with the pigs. Where I go hunting in America, you have to buy a license and then you're only allowed one animal."

The trip to South Australia was one of the first major excursions Gary Stuve took with Norman in his capacity as the Shark's boat captain. Originally, he had been Nicklaus's boat captain, working with the Bear from 1967 to 1977 and from 1984 to 1989, and he had met Norman when Nicklaus and Norman went into partnership together to build a boat. "I thought he was kind of a fancy dresser," Stuve remembers, "and he had a fancy car. To my style, he was overdressed for the occasion."

Stuve was more down-to-earth, but he and the Australian hit it off quickly because they shared a love of sportfishing, and, since Nicklaus was using his boat less and less as his businesses expanded, they often went out together. The custom-made boat was a two-year project, but midway through Norman decided he could afford a similar boat of his own and he offered to either buy Nicklaus out or sell his share. The Bear kept the fifty-eight-foot boat, and Norman ordered a sixty-five-footer of his own.

"It seemed like one was always trying to get a bigger boat than the other," Stuve said. "It was a kind of one-upmanship, was how I saw it. Jack bought an eighty-foot boat, then Greg bought an eighty-seven-foot boat and that's where they stand now."

The problem was that Norman then went a step further and hired Stuve. Nicklaus hit the roof. "There was conflict because basically they each wanted me for themselves," Stuve explains. "There was resentment on Jack's part because even though they're friends, they're competitors on the golf course, and anytime you take an employee away . . . Jack was a little annoyed about it, and it wasn't an easy decision for me to make because Jack had done a lot for me. But I saw a better future with Greg."

To Edwards there was a pattern to Norman's recruitment strategy that started when Norman lured Coleman away from Ballesteros and Bender away from Nicklaus. "He hired Jack Nicklaus's boat captain away from Jack, he hired Jack Nicklaus's helicopter pilot away from Jack, and he hired me away from Tom Watson. He wants the best that he can afford. He wants to surround himself with top people."

Between 1989 and September 1996, Stuve went on hundreds of trips with Norman, spearfishing and scuba diving in places like Mexico, Belize, and the Bahamas, sometimes accompanied by Laura and the kids, sometimes with Price, and sometimes just with the Australian. "He was a really fun guy," Stuve said. "He was really regular, liked to hang out with the crew, and get drunk and party. Jack was a good person, but he was a little more reserved. He was always with his family. Greg would like to get away, to be one of the guys and hang out and drink beers."

Flash, the first mate on Norman's $4.8 million sportfishing yacht, *Aussi Rules*, told *Sports Illustrated*, "Here's a vacation with Greg: Get up early, wolf down breakfast, dive, come up, fish, then a quick lunch, bottom-fish, dive, troll for sailfish, then dinner, sleep, and start again the next day."

"He likes to be busy," Price laughs. "I can put my feet up and relax and watch the world go by for half a day. Greg can't relax for an eighth of that time."

Aussi Rules had been designed to Norman's own specs and included two staterooms finished in Australian silky oak for his children, both keen anglers. According to *Motor Boating and Sailing*, the list of TVs, videos, CD players, and other appliances ran to two pages. A cushion in the plush master bedroom read: "I love my wife but, oh, that boat." Norman felt he needed more space. "In a few years, we may look at a mothership and maybe take off for two or three years to really have a look at the world," he said.

But as the years passed, Norman spent less and less time on his boats, and, according to Stuve, they became more of a business than a pleasure. "I think he thinks that just because he puts his name on it, people are going to rush out and buy it. People in boating could care less about Greg Norman." Stuve added, "He knows a lot about boats, but he doesn't know as much as he thinks he does and that was probably the cause of the friction that we had. I'd make a recommendation that he shouldn't buy a boat, and he'd buy it anyway and lose money on it or not like it."

Stuve felt that they gradually grew apart. Norman was perpetually buying larger and larger boats, while simultaneously trying to downsize his crew, and Stuve, who was a sportfishing captain at heart, quit. "I think the sport he is in, boating, is a very expensive hobby. You don't get any return from it. They're not investments; you're just throwing money away. I think Greg was okay with that, but his wife wasn't into it—she gets seasick and she's not really into fishing—and she was always trying to get him to not spend so much money on it. He was torn between trying to keep her happy and keep the crew happy, and in the end you've got to stick with your family."

Norman was five thousand feet above the earth, fighting with the joystick of his helicopter. Black rain battered the doors and drowned out the engines, and a gale-force wind tossed the craft like a paper plane. His passengers said their prayers and reached for the sick bags. They were on their way back to West Palm Beach after the third round of the 1990 Doral Ryder Open, and it was beginning to look as if they might not make it. Miserably, one man raised his head to see how Norman was coping. Norman's steely eyes were on the controls, his hands gripping the joystick. He was laughing.

The next morning the Shark returned to Miami in the same helicopter. He teed up on Doral's notorious Blue Monster course seven shots off the lead. "This year will be different," he had said. "I'm young enough, I'm strong enough. This is the year I start turning those negatives into positives." He planned to try Nicklaus's approach to course management—visualizing holes in reverse, from green to tee. "In other words, where do I have to hit the ball on the tee shot to have it in the right spot for the approach shot to have it in the spot where I want to reach the green?"

At Doral, Norman chiseled steadily away at the leaderboard. At seven thousand yards, the Blue Monster is one of the most brutal layouts in America, and its tree-lined fairways and yawning water hazards have been the final resting place of a million golf balls. But Norman had a feeling it was going to be his week. He birdied the 514-yard first with a drive and a two-iron and hit eight-iron shots to four feet at the third and five at the seventh. At the eighth he holed a sand wedge.

"THIS YEAR WILL BE DIFFERENT," HE HAD SAID. "I'M YOUNG ENOUGH, I'M STRONG ENOUGH. THIS IS THE YEAR I START TURNING THOSE NEGATIVES INTO POSITIVES."

It was a mesmerizing performance. His bottom lip caught between his teeth, his hair shining snowy white, he lashed from the tees as if there were no tomorrow. He took twelve putts out and twelve putts back for eight birdies, an eagle, and a 62.

The most hair-raising moment came at the eighteenth, where Norman insisted on cutting a seven-iron into the water-lined green after Edwards tried in vain to persuade him to hit a relatively safe eight-iron. "I feel comfortable with it," he assured Edwards. The ball bounced off the hill and trickled dangerously near to the water.

"We get down there," Edwards recalls, "and I thought, 'Well, Tom would take out a sand wedge and lob it up there.' Greg takes a nine-iron and tries to bump it into the hill. It goes thirty feet past the hole and he makes the putt for par."

As fate would have it, Norman met Calcavecchia in the four-man play-off and redressed the past by holing an eagle chip for victory on the first hole to end one of the most impressive rounds of golf ever played in ordinary competition.

"We won, we won, we won!" cried Nigel Mansell, leaping up and down beside the green, his arms around his wife, Roseanne, and Laura, who was crying with joy.

In a practice round the following week, Edwards asked Norman whether, if he had the shot at eighteen again, he would hit an eight-iron instead of a seven. "No," Norman said stubbornly. "I'd hit the same shot again."

"I thought, 'Well, there you have it,' " Edwards says. " 'You just don't get it. You don't understand what we're trying to do here.' " Five years later Norman hit a six-iron into the water on the same hole at Doral to lose to Faldo.

Norman, meanwhile, credited his caddie with guiding him to one of his finest victories. "He tells me a lot of the things that Tom used to do, and so in getting Bruce as a caddie I'm also getting Watson's knowledge," he said. "Bruce is very positive. Just before I played the chip on the play-off hole, he told me to chip it in. He said I was due one. That helps. The reason I'm playing so well now is that I'm getting the ball in the right place and doing the right things. I'm not as brash as I used to be. That means I can be aggressive when I want to. As Bruce says, I'm painting beautiful pictures now."

Three weeks later Robert Gamez, a bright, fearless rookie from Las Vegas, holed a seven-iron from 176 yards for eagle on the seventy-second hole at Bay Hill to beat Norman by a stroke in the Nestle Invitational.

"GREG DOESN'T SHOW CREDENTIALS BECAUSE HE'S SUPPOSED TO BE SO RECOGNIZED," EDWARDS SAYS. "THE GUY WOULDN'T LET HIM IN, SO HE RAN OVER HIS FOOT IN THE CAR."

For a man who had already been tried to the limits of endurance by the wicked machinations of fate, it was a cruel blow. Norman's nerves were still frayed a month later when an incident took place at the USF&G Classic in New Orleans that could well have affected the outcome of the tournament. Walking off the ninth green after a bogey in the final round, Norman was infuriated when an ignorant spectator asked him for his autograph. "The guy was wrong to ask him for an autograph," Edwards says, "and Greg stormed by him. The guy said, 'Well, I hope you bogey the next hole, too,' and with that he stopped, wheeled, and went right back in this guy's face and confronted him. I just kept on walking. I thought, 'I'm not going to go back and separate this.' Greg ought to know better."

There was more. Edwards claims that, in a darkly comedic scene, Norman had accidentally ridden over a security guard's foot at the golf club entrance that morning. "Greg doesn't show credentials because he's supposed to be so recognized," Edwards says. "The guy wouldn't let him in, so he ran over his foot in the car."

The net result was that, through divine intervention or plain old bad luck, lightning struck Norman a second time. David Frost, a South African living in Dallas, holed a fifty-foot bunker shot on the seventy-second hole of the tournament to beat him by a stroke. Numb with despair, Norman hardly knew what to say. It was no great surprise when he missed the cut at the Masters, surrendering the Green Jacket to Faldo for the second successive season. As Norman said, "The law of averages says you win 50 percent of the time, not lose 100 percent of the time."

The previous Christmas, Norman had stood for an hour in Nicklaus's driveway, communing with the Bear. Absorbed in conversation, he had no idea it was raining until Barbara, Nicklaus's wife, came out fussing that they were getting wet. They were discussing the Tway incident and other factors that had prevented Norman from winning more. "Greg, you just have to understand that when you're a certain type of player, people want to beat you, whether it's holing a shot or playing a phenomenal round to catch you, whatever," Norman recalls Nicklaus telling him. "You're going to have to learn to accept that, because you are one of those players people want to beat. And you should take it as a compliment. I know, because that happened to me a lot."

"The things that have happened to him are extraordinary, to say the least," Price says. "What would you call it? Is it fate? Is it luck? If I was Greg, I'd feel a little picked on. But as Trevino said, 'God never gave golfers everything, he always held something back.' Jack didn't get a sand wedge and Greg didn't get any luck."

Norton, who was closer to Greg than anyone apart from Laura, despaired on Norman's behalf. "He's certainly carried on as well as anybody who's had the disappointments that he's had," he says now, "but we're all human. I think that those were wounds that hurt him—the multiplicity of them was something that was tough for him. I think he thought about that a lot more than he let on. It seemed to be a situation where, every time that he lost, not only in the majors but at Bay Hill or New Orleans, someone rose to the occasion. It was absolutely uncanny. The other side of that is that people say, 'Look at his back nines of those tournaments.' Okay, fine, but still there was always this conspiratorial situation, and you really felt for the guy because he's really a good guy. I think he gets in his own way sometimes and is maybe misunderstood, but he's a good person. And you hate to see that happen to any great player."

11

FLIRTING WITH DISASTER

"Golf to me is a battle within yourself, it's the struggle to understand yourself. There's no doubt about it, golf could drive you crazy."

Bob Tway, 1993 PGA Championship

Norman was flirting with disaster again. His favorite quotation—Teddy Roosevelt's assertion (as remembered by Norman) that it is better to "know the agony and the ecstasy of defeat and victory than live forever in the twilight of never having felt either one"—had become a one-line script in the play of his life. "Greg Norman reminds me of the movies," said Rick Reilly. "Every time you think he's going to get the girl and ride off into the sunset, his horse breaks a leg."

The ecstasy part had come early in the week at the British Open at St. Andrews in the summer of 1990. He had taken a ride in a 111 Squadron Phantom, flying, along with two other jets from the RAF base at Leuchars, at 550 knots and pulling three G's. "It was a great thrill and something you really can't describe," he said. "The nearest thing to the feeling is seeing your baby born or walking down the eighteenth at Turnberry."

His happiness was complete when he shot a 66 to share the lead in the opening round, and then he was tied with Faldo at 132 after the second. When they were drawn together on the third day, many saw it as a showdown between the two best players in the world. A kind of day of reckoning between the giants of the game.

To David Leadbetter, who had coached Faldo to three major victories by then, Norman's relish for the dramatic had cost him dearly in the race for golf's greatest titles. "The fact is, it's not always about being the most aggressive and hitting the most startling golf shots. It's about getting from A to B. And Nick's a master of that. Greg tends to try and take the course by the scruff of the neck and as a result it can be an all-or-nothing sort of experience. Nick is a very methodical, workmanlike player, and majors require that sort of game to a large extent."

Analyzing the rivalry between the two players in his *World of Professional Golf*, Mark McCormack calculated that, on the thirty-two occasions they had gone head to head in the previous three years, Norman had come out in front nineteen times to Faldo's eleven. Each had won three times when the other was in the field, but all Faldo's victories were majors.

When morning came Norman stood on the first tee in front of the Royal & Ancient clubhouse, gripped by the peculiar flatness that had dogged him in the Winged Foot play-off. The sun was blazing down, the historic gray town was etched against the skyline, and the sea was a cornflower blue, but Norman felt no rush of enthusiasm or adrenaline. When Faldo holed from outside of him for a birdie at the first hole, Norman was unable to respond. "You have to feel invincible to be invincible, especially with putting," he said later.

The agony began there and never let up. Norman three-putted three times in the first ten holes. "I lost my rhythm with my putter," he said sadly. "The putt I missed on the second was a very makable putt, but I just hit it too hard and hit it through the break. The next putt I missed, I hit too soft. So now I'm second-guessing myself on the line and speed, and as time goes by I'm getting worse and worse in a hole about my putting. Then I hit a good drive on twelve, which I thought was perfect, and it trickles into the bunker; and I hit a drive on thirteen, which I thought was perfect, and it rolls into the bunker." He felt that the twelfth, where Faldo made par from a gorse bush and Norman three-putted, was where he lost his momentum. "Nick was making everything he looked at, and he had a lot of confidence. And he kept the momentum going. So that's what happened: It was the ebb and flow of momentum."

At the end of the day, it added up to a 67 for Faldo, which helped him to a five-stroke victory the next day. Norman shot 76 and was shattered. Wiping sand out of his eyes after the bunker shot at the thirteenth, he looked on the verge of tears. But as hurt as he felt, he did not, as was wrongly reported, refuse to talk to the press.

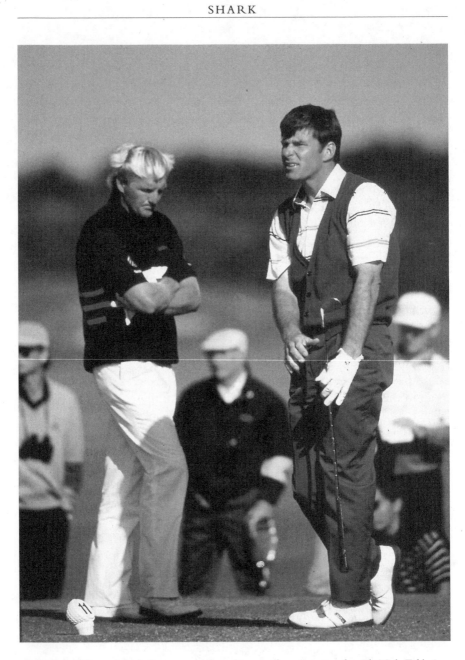

Arch rivals: Norman's body language speaks volumes as he crosses swords with Nick Faldo in the third round of the 1990 British Open at St. Andrews. (© Phil Sheldon)

"Greg feels the knocks, but he forgives and forgets even though he's seething inside," Earp said. "He keeps his pain inside."

"That third round killed me," Norman conceded reluctantly.

It's hard to pinpoint the exact moment Norman changed, or even why he changed, or to show when precisely he entered a slump so deep that at times it threatened to consume him. Was it, as everyone suspected, the humiliation of that third round at St. Andrews, following as it did on the heels of Tway, Mize, Calcavecchia, Gamez, and Frost? Was it the harsh treadmill of tournament golf? "You wake up every morning and go through the same routine, so it gets kind of monotonous and boring," Norman admits. "Sometimes you just want to say, 'I'd love to walk away from it for three months.' But you can't."

Or was it the bittersweet side effects of fame? "Success is wonderful, but it can also be very painful," muses Norman, back at St. Andrews for the Dunhill Cup in October. "I've been pretty good with it, but in the last twelve months it's been a lot harder to take. People have been a lot more critical."

It's ironic that, some eighteen months earlier, Norman had clashed with Jack Newton at the 1989 Australian Masters over the chief cause of that criticism: his propensity for opening his mouth and telling the truth as he saw it to anyone who would listen, regardless of the pain it might cause or the consequences to himself.

"You can't just open your mouth and blurt out the first thing that comes into your head," Newton warned him.

"All I'm doing is being honest," Norman protested.

"I said, 'Well, you can't do that,' " Newton recalls. "Now here we are seven or eight years later, where he hates the press, mistrusts the press, because he feels he's been hard done by."

In spite of their differences, Newton liked Norman and felt he had a lot of good qualities which were worth salvaging. Having taken him to task over his misplaced candor, he added more gently, "Look, Greg, you've lost your mates, you've lost your real roots. The guys here that you started out with, they all feel that you're unapproachable. Why won't you go and have a beer with them and sort of shoot the shit about what happened in the old days, just to get away from all the tension?"

Norman was stung but he had to concede that Newton was right. After some discussion, he went along quite enthusiastically with Newton's plan to round up his mates from the early days, men like Stewart, Ginn, Brian Jones, and Mike Ferguson, Payne Stewart's brother-in-law. They arranged to meet at a club on the outskirts of Sydney. "We drove there to have dinner with him and there's a guy from IMG," Newton remembers. "It just put a damper on the whole evening. So I guess you'd have to put some of the blame for that on Greg."

It was true that the speed of Norman's ascent in golf and the staggering demands on his time had left most Australians behind from the day he won the West Lakes Classic. Despite the fact that he went out of his way to help other Australians, often financially, many felt that Norman moved in more elite circles, and they admired him from a distance. "Wayne [Grady] and I respect Greg's privacy because he's always so busy," said Baker-Finch. "But he's one of the guys and he's very generous."

Norman's busyness was a constant refrain. "He doesn't have time to go to dinner," Clayton said. "The demands on his time are greater than on anyone else's."

Newton thought that friendship was a two-way street. "Some of the guys felt that he had got so big he was on another level, and from Greg's point of view, I think he probably expected them to call him. I can remember some of the guys who lived near him in Florida saying Greg had complained because they never called him about going fishing. But whenever they did, they always had to go on his boat, because it was bigger and faster and their boats weren't up to speed."

The relationship between Norman and Australia has always been a complex one. In many ways it was epitomized by the events of 1990 and 1991, when the media, variously labeling him "the Great White Carp," "the Great White Minnow," and "the Great White Fishfinger," savaged him for a "pathetic performance" in the Australian Open and found reasons to condemn him for disqualifying himself from the Palm Meadows Cup after officials acted on a rules violation he'd made in the first round, shortly before he teed off in the third. He had shot a record-breaking 63 in the second round.

He could do nothing right. When Bob Hawke, the prime minister, offered Norman the position as Australia's ambassador of tourism without telling Paul "Crocodile Dundee" Hogan, who had done the job for years and who had made Australianisms such as "Toss another shrimp on the Barbie" common currency, it caused a diplomatic incident. When Laura begged him to forgo the Australian Open just once to spend Thanksgiving with his children in 1991, newspapers reported that the AGU was considering legal action because he was playing in a Skins game at the same time. They were not and he was not. There were tabloid reports that he and his entourage were thrown out of a nightclub and that he came within an inch of hitting a man who had punched him in the shoulder and shouted abuse at him in a restaurant.

"I wanted to hit him back," Norman said, "but of course no one, let alone someone like myself, can go around doing things like that. We're just supposed to sit back and take it. But it's becoming pretty hard."

Norman himself was not blameless. He had expended a huge amount of effort trying to persuade the recalcitrant members of St. Michael's, a windswept course near Sydney, to allow him and his mate Kerry Packer, Australia's richest man, to turn the course into a $300 million resort aimed at Japanese tourists. When the members balked, Norman said patronizingly to the *Australian*: "I guess they didn't understand the document. You try to make them understand . . . you try to be rational with them. The crazy thing about it is that the golf course is in desperate need of attention. I mean, they can't even afford a mower out there."

His first course-design venture in Australia, on the Gold Coast, opened for just one day in July 1991 before the Japanese conglomerate behind it went bust. The Grand Golf Club became a dense, snake-filled jungle before a group of Australian businessmen bought it six years later and persuaded Norman to come back on board.

Then there was the ever-controversial issue of appearance money. James Erskine, head of IMG's Sydney office, said that anyone who ran a tournament in Australia or anywhere else without getting Norman to play in it needed to "go see a doctor" because Norman generated "an increased turnover in gate takings, world TV, sponsorship, and the like of $1.2 million." But when Norman, fed up with being attacked over it, announced he was forgoing appearance money for three years beginning in 1996, the sponsors rushed straight out and paid Tiger Woods record appearance fees.

"Appearance money is something that's always irked me, I've got to say," Newton remarks. "Not that he doesn't deserve it, but I've said to him lots of times, 'Greg, I couldn't care if you want to go to Italy and get five million dollars and five Ferraris to play, but when you come back to Australia there's something ethically wrong with holding your hand out for huge sums of money.' Now his answer to that would be, 'Other blokes are getting it, why shouldn't I?' Which is true, but, you know, you've got to remember that he is a guy who gets ridiculous sums of money all because of IMG, who created all this, and now it's become a real cancer in the game. In [the old] days in Australia, fair enough, the prize money wasn't that good. Now he's sort of playing for a million dollars and instead of the appearance money going down, it's gone up."

Peter Thomson agreed that appearance money lay at the heart of the anti-Norman feeling, but he felt that IMG should shoulder a lot of the blame. "It was said he exploited our tournament scene here almost unmercifully. However, I even defend him on that score because, at first, when IMG did all the deals, they were getting part of the money. Once he knew how much money they were making out of the tournaments, it made him very angry. And he reckoned if they were going to make money out of it, so was he. . . . That truth didn't come out. He got the rough end of the stick there, but perhaps he didn't handle it perfectly."

When all was said and done, it had much to do with the "tall poppy syndrome," the natural antipathy of Australians toward people who appear to be too rich, too famous, or too pleased with themselves. "The ambivalence is a result of uncertainty," the Australian magazine *Inside Sport* reported. "Ours. We're no longer sure if he's one of us, if he feels Australian any more. His staggering wealth . . . and seemingly insatiable thirst for more puts distance between us."

"In the U.S., they see a big car and they want to get a car like that," Norman said. "In Australia, they run a key down the side of it. I don't understand that mentality."

There were countless unpublicized examples of his generosity. He and Laura gave freely, raising millions for children's cancer research, other charities, and Australian golfers through the Greg Norman Foundation and the Greg Norman Junior Golf Foundation.

In 1990, Norman made a four-hour helicopter journey to the bedside of Sam Roberts, the desperately ill son of Australian television presenter Sandy

Roberts. He had visited and telephoned Sam, a hemophiliac who had contracted the AIDS virus, numerous times before. Later, when news of the boy's death reached Norman shortly before he teed off in the Australian Masters, he wore Sam's name on his hat and walked down the fairway with tears streaming down his face. "We both feel very fortunate, so we want to do what we can to help those who are not," Laura says. "It helps balance you. It makes you feel okay about what you have." In his pocket Norman carried a thank-you letter from the mother of a boy to whom he had spontaneously donated a putter. But none of it made up for what were perceived 'as "ostentatious displays of wealth" and "frequent ego trips."

HE WORE SAM'S NAME ON HIS HAT AND WALKED DOWN THE FAIRWAY WITH TEARS STREAMING DOWN HIS FACE.

"The Australian philosophy has always been to build people up and chop 'em off at the kneecaps when they get too big for their boots," Newton said. "I don't think that way about Greg, but I think that the average guy on the street likes to see his champions with a bit more humility. I don't really think that the average guy on the street gives a damn about how many Ferraris he's got."

Marshall agrees. "Australia is a funny society," he says. "They like their sportsmen to be down to earth, and I don't think there's any question that Greg has succeeded in rubbing a lot of the sports world up the wrong way in Australia. That's self-evident. If you look at Seve or Faldo, they don't spend their time letting people know that they've just bought a new car or a new house or they've just made another couple of million. I think it's a great pity that Greg is not . . . well, he's not a humble person."

But Thomson, who has, over the years, been one of Norman's harshest critics, felt that behind the facade Norman was "very likable. His public image doesn't match his private personality. I honestly think that under the guidance of a management structure, an image is created in order to make everybody wealthy, and that doesn't necessarily reflect the real person. Some people throw it off. Sam Torrance, for instance, would never be anybody other than who he is. Peter Senior is another. You couldn't possibly invent an image for either one of them. But in the case of Greg, I think he enjoyed the image making. So there it was."

All of these things—the on-course pressures and the off-course stresses—combined to shake Norman's hitherto unshakable confidence. That October of 1990 was only the second time in their long relationship that Norman had flown Earp to a tournament for an emergency session on his game. Even when he had won the Memorial, he felt that he was playing "horrible golf, probably the worst golf I've ever played." Now his old friend had come to help him find a cure. For two hours they worked in driving gray rain, cold enough to chill a polar bear, and at the end of it they felt they had found the problem: Norman wasn't swinging down the line.

Back in his room, Norman, golden and larger than life, downed a beer, read a fan letter, bantered on the phone with Mansell, and gave every impression of being a blissfully contented man. "Sometimes I wish I wasn't as committed," he remarked at a cocktail party, "but when things are going well I don't pay any attention."

On paper the 1990 season was one of the best of his career, earning him the Australian Masters and, in the United States, two prestigious titles, eleven top tens, $1,165,477, and first place on the money list. But every day Norman felt himself sliding closer to the abyss. "This IMG mob is milking the cow dry," Earp ranted to the *Australian* after Norman, who had not slowed down as he promised, finally reached overload on the Australian circuit. "I mean, Greg Norman is the greatest draw card on earth. People would scramble over broken glass to watch him hit golf balls, and IMG's demands on his time mean that golf is third-rate now to Greg. He's too bloody busy all the damn time. The person hasn't been born that can hit a ball like he can. And these people are roping him down and tying him up. But Greg can't see that. He says, 'It's okay, Charlie, it's okay,' but I can see it isn't. It damn well isn't."

Erskine was not pleased. "His words are childish and ill informed," he snapped. "Greg Norman decides exactly what he wants to do himself. Charlie's argument is that because Larry Mize or Bob Tway chip in to rob Greg of a major tournament win, or he gets the yardage wrong on the last hole of the Masters, or loses the British Open in a play-off, then somehow it's IMG's fault. That's absolute bloody nonsense."

Norman was forced to mediate. "[IMG] works for me, not the other way around," he insisted. "Golf is my number-one priority."

Earp was unconvinced. "What Greg doesn't see is that people are using him," Earp insisted. "Do you really think the PM [the prime minister, Bob Hawke] wanted Norman to leave the tournament in Melbourne, fly to Canberra for the night [to attend his sixtieth birthday party], then fly back to Melbourne again for the last round because Hawke considers him a bosom pal? I doubt it. But Greg is blind to all that. He just can't seem to say no."

It was years before Norman would admit that burnout had been a large factor in his slump. Laura wanted him to take six months off; he wanted three; his schedule barely allowed for one. "For five years I put my blood, sweat, and tears into it, because I had to," he said. "I wanted to, but I had to. And I was just plain tired."

He made one last attempt to put things right, consulting Mitchell Spearman, Leadbetter's assistant, at Royal Melbourne. Spearman had written an article describing Faldo's technique as an "iron swing," meaning that he hit down on the ball, and the Shark's as a "driver swing," meaning that he tended to hit the ball a little on the upswing. "His stance was too narrow and his left-hand grip was a little too much in the palm," Spearman says. "I remember him showing me how much he was wearing out his gloves. His swing was very upright at the time. He said he felt that he didn't have the control at the top of the swing. He was trying to get it a little flatter."

When Norman returned to the United States, they tried working together for a few months. "Very strong character," Spearman says. "Has strong opinions, strong beliefs. Gives his word, sticks to it. Honorable. I confided in him a few years back on a business deal, and he gave me some advice and told me his door was always open. It meant a lot to have someone like Greg Norman say that to someone like me."

Unhappily, Spearman's advice effected no miracle transformation in Norman's game. When he missed the cut at Augusta for the second year running, Laura put him on a plane back to Australia for a couple of weeks. "He was so down," she said, knowing that, in spite of everything, Norman still loved and missed his homeland enough for a holiday there to be healing. "That was the one time I've really seen him let down and relax. He saw his friends, saw his parents—no phones, no demands."

It was there that Norman's simmering relationship with his father, his need to make Merv understand why he lived the life he did, to make Merv

175

acknowledge that he had made something of himself after all, came to a head. "Hold on a second, Dad," Norman said as Merv headed into the house one day. "We argued, we discussed, I told him what I thought," Norman told *Sports Illustrated*. "He told me what he thought. It was good. We both needed it."

Norman was riding the agony-ecstasy roller coaster yet again. On the first Sunday of July, he found himself leading the Western Open by five shots, having played the first ten holes in six under par. Reams of joyous "comeback victory" copy were already rolling off the typewriters when Norman made his first bogey. He made another for good measure, then another and another, finally finishing with a flourish by bogeying five of the last six holes. Two balls homed in on deep bushes, with one unplayable. Once Norman emerged from the woods with leaves and twigs in his hair, and once he found his ball under a woman's purse. The end result was that left-hander Russ Cochran made up seven shots to beat him by two and achieve his first victory in nine years. Norman's misfortune was almost always someone else's good fortune.

"If somebody told me when I made the turn on Sunday, 'In two hours' time, you aren't going to win this tournament,' I would have called him a liar," Norman said. "But life's a humbling experience. I made a major blunder there, and I didn't win."

"That collapse, it's added another chapter, hasn't it?" said Weiskopf at the British Open the following week, where Norman bounced back with a tie for ninth. But he added, 'Thank God there is a Greg Norman. He's made a lot of people in golf happy. He's exciting, he's a great personality, and he's a nice guy, too, but one of these loners."

Unfortunately, the constant dashing of his hopes and seesawing of his emotions were having a detrimental effect on Norman's personality and his relationships with other people, in particular Bruce Edwards, who felt he was the cat to be kicked on the course.

"He really disappointed me," said Edwards, his dark, strong face tense as he described the events that led to his leaving what should have been the best job in golf. "I found he was very fickle. I found he was very moody. I found that professionally, on the golf course, he had a hard time dealing with adversity—bad bounces, bad breaks—which is part of the game. I tried to bring him a calmer attitude, but in the end I felt that there was nothing I could do."

According to Edwards, one of the PGA Tour's most respected caddies, his attempts to help Norman achieve a more relaxed approach on the course failed signally. "At first, he didn't really blame me, but he would be so negative," he says. "There would be two balls in a bunker in our group. One would be buried, one wouldn't. He'd walk up and say, 'Well, you know which one mine is.' I'd say, 'Come on, Greg. Prepare yourself. Even if it is the one that's buried, you've

ONCE NORMAN EMERGED FROM THE WOODS WITH LEAVES AND TWIGS IN HIS HAIR, AND ONCE HE FOUND HIS BALL UNDER A WOMAN'S PURSE.

still got to play it. There's nothing you can do about it.' I mean, Tom had the ability to gut it up and carry on, and if that meant hitting it to thirty feet, if that was the best he could do, well, he'd go ahead and try and make the putt.

"Greg, it seemed to me, if he got in a bad mood or got really pissed off about the result of a shot, would carry on for the next hour. I'd find myself wondering how we'd get through it. When he'd come off the eighteenth on Sunday, I'd think, 'Gee, if he'd just kept his wits about him back there on Friday or Thursday or whenever that one hour happened, we wouldn't be one behind.' In other words he threw shots away because his temper would get the best of him."

Edwards's portrait of Norman contrasted sharply with Norman's view of himself. The Shark claimed that he had "never been a negative individual." Never. "Let's say I'm playing my bunker shots poorly. Instead of going out there and practicing my bunker shots hour after hour, I'll go and chip or hit my five-iron, something I can be positive about. Then, after four or five days of not even touching my sand wedge, I'll say, 'Okay, let's go to work.' Boom! It comes back very quickly."

To Edwards, Norman was the greatest talent he had ever seen, but when the special player-caddie teamwork crucial to success disappeared from their relationship, he began to find his job a struggle. He built a house on Norman's generosity, but he was always on edge, worrying that Norman might fly into a rage, make biting comments on his prowess as a caddie, send a club winging toward the bag, or criticize his yardages or his club selection.

"Maybe tomorrow we'll pull the right club," Norman would snarl.

"Did you hit that fat?" Edwards would query.

"I hit it right on the screws," Norman would snap back.

"I made him a bet in Australia one year," grins Edwards. "I said, 'Greg, I'll buy you dinner anywhere in the world if you can go four days without moaning or groaning.' And he agreed to it. And it was very funny because we got to Saturday and he hit this shot and it went left down the hill. He said, 'You can have the god—— dinner. Fuck the dinner.' And he exploded. I thought, 'You can't even go four days.' "

Edwards had his own theories about the times Norman had snatched defeat from the jaws of victory and on several occasions he unwisely communicated them to his boss. "I felt like his ego would get the best of him," says Edwards, who is not without a degree or two of arrogance himself. "Sometimes thirty feet right of the pin is an excellent play in the hunt. You don't always have to hit it in close. If Tom said to me, 'Do you like a three-wood or a four-wood?' and we're playing a green where the pin's five feet on and there's a bunker in front, I'd say, 'Well, do you mind being in the bunker?' In the same situation, Greg would say, 'What do you think, three-wood or one-iron?' and I'd say, 'Well, do you mind being in the front bunker?' He'd say, 'I don't want to be in the bunker, I want to be by the pin.' And I'd think, 'Greg, the game's not that easy.' There's no guarantee that a certain club will get you pin-high every time. But that was his thinking."

Gradually, his relationship with Norman broke down to the extent where they rarely spoke away from the course. He claims that the Shark would stride out of the locker room in the morning, slam the bag down, and depart to the range without a word. Edwards felt that he was becoming a bad caddie because he was too afraid to say what he thought. "I also felt that the novelty of him having me wore off, and once that wore off he was treating me like I'd heard he'd treated all his caddies in the past. . . . It's sad because I truly liked him when I started working with him, but I think he misread me and that's when he changed. I was no different than anybody else who gets chewed up and spit out and discarded."

Edwards quit before he could be fired. "Once you get on his bad side, that's it. Once you're on that four-letter list, once you cross that line in his mind, that's it, you're done. I saw that all the time."

On a clear November day in 1991, Norman stood pounding balls at the TPC at The Woodlands, outside Houston. He had not won a tournament for eighteen months—the longest dry spell of his career—and after two days of play, it was clear he was not about to win the Houston Open. Instead, he was headed for fifty-third place on the money list, his worst position since joining the U.S. Tour, and he was ready to give Ballesteros lessons in how not to hit the fairway. When he set up to hit a fade, he came up with a hook. When he set up to hit a hook, he managed a banana slice. Hitting it straight was not on the menu.

The hip injury that had caused him to pull out after twenty-seven holes of the U.S. Open was a nagging ache. That had been another black spot. Reporters and sundry officials had surrounded the fitness trailer at Hazeltine and refused to leave him alone until he explained himself. "It was like somebody had died in the thing or something," Norman said incredulously. "These guys didn't realize the pain I was going through, and yet they wanted to rip me for withdrawing. I wanted to keep playing. My physiotherapist made me withdraw. . . . But God almighty, it was like something major, a catastrophe. It was ridiculous, total stupidity for that much attention to be thrown on the situation. I mean, I get injured, and I get nailed for it."

REPORTERS AND SUNDRY OFFICIALS HAD SURROUNDED THE FITNESS TRAILER AT HAZELTINE AND REFUSED TO LEAVE HIM ALONE UNTIL HE EXPLAINED HIMSELF.

Five months later Norman felt about as desperate as he had ever been. He took a deep breath and went to see Steve Elkington, who had been urging him to talk to his coach, Claude "Butch" Harmon, son of the 1948 Masters champion Claude Harmon and head pro at Lochinvar in Houston. Norman had wanted to try to work things out on his own.

"Elk," Norman said hesitantly, not used to eating humble pie, "do you think Butch would take a look at me?"

Harmon, now famous as Woods's coach, was a pragmatist with a flair for applying sound, traditional techniques without detracting from natural artistry. As well as Elkington, who was universally regarded as having the most flawless swing in the game, he had worked with Love and Jeff Sluman. He was stockier than Norman, but they had the same superconfident, outgoing personalities and the same tanned, half-genial, half-cynical faces. He had known Norman since the late eighties when they had both participated in a tournament to raise money for a children's cancer hospital and over the years they had developed a mutual regard for one another. Harmon was a fan of Norman's intensity and ability with the driver. While watching him lose majors with iron shots that wandered right, he had always wished he could help. "The funny part about it is I was totally prepared when he asked me," Harmon says. "I'd studied so much film of his swing, I knew exactly what avenue of approach I would take if I ever had the chance."

On the range in Houston, Harmon watched Norman hit a few balls. "You need to read your own book," Harmon told him, referring to *Shark Attack!*.

Norman stared at him. "You need to go back to basics," Harmon said firmly. "Your fundamentals are bad, and you're not doing any of the things in your book."

He remembers thinking how steep Norman's swing had become and how narrow his arc: "His arms got trapped behind him on the way down. Most of the time he could square the club from that position with his hands, but sometimes, especially under extreme pressure, he wasn't able to. I wanted to put more rotation in his body and get him to where he wouldn't have to use his hands so much under pressure."

He handed Norman a two-iron. "Stand closer to the ball and swing as hard as you possibly can," he ordered. Norman took the club uncertainly and swept the ball away. Harmon didn't say a word.

Norman smashed another ball over the horizon, then another and another. Into his hands and his heart crept a feeling he had almost forgotten— a feeling of freedom, of standing young and strong and carefree on the fairways of West Lakes, smashing the ball into the blue. All of a sudden he remembered why he had always loved practicing so much, why nothing gave him as much pleasure as being out in all kinds of weather, exploring golf's nuances, hitting the full six hundred balls he believed a player should hit daily in order to groove his swing.

Harmon sent him right back to basics—altering his grip slightly, improving his posture, shortening his swing slightly, encouraging him to use his lower body more and to rotate his hips faster, and removing his famous slide. "That was the first thing that went and that took the use of the hands out except where they should be," Harmon says. "He was relying on his hands for everything. That's not to say you can't play well from there, because he did play very well from those positions, but it just seemed that every time he got under the most extreme pressure, that swing failed him. I wanted to get that shot that he hit to the right out of there, and we did a good job of doing that."

NORMAN SMASHED ANOTHER BALL OVER THE HORIZON, THEN ANOTHER AND ANOTHER. INTO HIS HANDS AND HIS HEART CREPT A FEELING HE HAD ALMOST FORGOTTEN—A FEELING OF FREEDOM . . .

"Butch just said the right words to me—positive words—at the right time," says Norman. "I could relate to what he was talking about."

One morning Norman caught sight of himself while he was shaving—sallow, discontented, unhealthy, verging on chubby. He had succumbed to burnout, had allowed himself to take it easy. That summer he had seriously contemplated packing it all in and buying a cattle ranch. "I didn't need what was happening to me." He had gone so far down that untrue rumors were going around that he was on drugs. When he picked five-year-old Gregory up from school one afternoon, the boy had been taunted by the other children and was in tears.

Laura had persuaded him to face up to the fact that Mize's chip-in had wounded him more than he realized. "I learned that the longer you hold something inside, the worse you are going to react to it," Norman said. "You might find yourself at the pub having had a few cocktails, and if someone hits you the wrong way with something in conversation, you just pop. It makes you look like a jerk."

And now his pride had begun to hurt.

"I had to look myself in the mirror and ask, 'Do you want to do the work to get back on top again?'" Norman told author John Feinstein. "It would have been easy to walk away, but that would have been quitting and I've never thought of myself as a quitter. I knew climbing back up the mountain wouldn't be easy, and it wouldn't happen fast, but I knew I wanted to do it. I missed Sunday afternoons. I missed that feeling of being back in the hunt. Even if you don't win, being there feels so great. I wanted that back again. But I knew it would be hard. I also knew if I did it, it would be the best feeling I've had in golf. That's what makes failure so great. You can't really appreciate success—I mean really appreciate it—until you've failed."

12

KING OF THE HILL

"It was like somebody put a coin in the jukebox and the right
song started playing."

Greg Norman on his Canadian Open victory, 1992

It was Norman's expression that was unforgettable. His fists were clenched
and his hands were reaching to the sky in a triumphant celebration of his
Canadian Open victory, his first in twenty-seven months, but it was his face—
awash with joy and a profound, almost grateful, relief—that imprinted itself on
the memory. "I knew it was coming," he said. "I could feel the incline."

It was September 1992. Two months earlier, playing the British Open,
Norman had felt the old hunger stir in him again—that once familiar but
long forgotten feeling that had made him compare golf to making love.
While Faldo stood on the eighteenth at Muirfield, kissing and cuddling the
claret jug for photographers for the third time in his career, Norman indulged in an entirely new experience—that of savoring a top-twenty finish.

"I came off the seventy-second hole and said to my wife and Butch
Harmon, 'We're back. I've just put on a clinic out there for seventy-two
holes. Nobody'll know about it, but I did.' And that was it. Muirfield was
the turning point," Norman said.

At the Canadian Open, Norman used a putter he'd first picked up at
age seventeen to try out tips given to him by a club pro in Florida and by a
friend at Glen Abbey in Ontario. "They just said to swing the putter, to feel
the weight of the putter head. That's all putting is, but I guess I've been too
confused about trying different positions." The resulting rush of confidence
helped him overcome Bruce Lietzke on the second extra hole of a play-off.

"That did more for me than winning by three or four shots," Norman said afterward. That told me I could play tough shots under a lot of pressure."

Looking at her husband's proud, happy face as they jetted off to Japan, Laura experienced as much relief as Norman had when the winning putt dropped. "It's nice to have you back," she told him gently. Lietzke had said exactly the same thing.

In the space of a season, Norman's life had undergone a quiet revolution. Thanks to Laura's Fit for Life diet, Harmon's coaching, and Pete Draovitch's fitness expertise, his sallow face and hangdog body language had given way to hard bright focus and the taut nut-brown physique of an athlete. He had lost fifteen pounds by giving up soft drinks and eating more fruit, and he no longer had headaches after a day of golf. "And," he told the *Australian*, "you can still have as many beers as you like and wine at mealtime."

His bedtime reading was *Zen of the Martial Arts*, a book he said he would probably read a thousand times before he died. His favorite lesson in it was the part where the Zen master tried to convince his student that he needed to start all over again. "He takes a cup and starts pouring tea into it," Norman told Feinstein. "And just keeps pouring and pouring until the tea is all over the floor. The student says, 'Master, the cup is too full, the tea is all over the floor.' And the master says, 'The cup is exactly like your mind—it is too full.' And he takes the cup and empties it. 'When your mind is empty, you can begin to refill it,' he says, 'but not until then.' "

Having soothed his soul, Norman began reconditioning his rundown body with the help of Draovitch, a physiotherapist who had healed his shoulder problem. Ten minutes with the Shark persuaded Draovitch that "he worked hard but not smart," so he designed five fitness programs, ranging from postural training to explosive training with medicine balls to boxing drills, that would improve Norman's health and help his aching back without adding to his stress. The weight-room program, for example, involved thirty to forty minutes of cardiovascular work, plus stretching, medicine ball training, abdominal and lower back exercises, weight training, and step-ups, all of which took around two hours. Since Norman lost up to five pounds when he played continuously for a month, Draovitch also advised him on nutrition.

He traveled with the Australian most weeks and found him very family-oriented and kind, likening the atmosphere on Norman's jet to being in a locker room. He had already been the butt of Norman's practical jokes, one of which involved a nurse with a twelve-inch hypodermic telling him he needed shots if he wanted to leave the plane in Johannesburg, South Africa. "The unfortunate thing about Greg the golfer versus Greg the person, I think, is not a lot of people get to know Greg the person," Draovitch says. "And I think if they did, they would be a lot better to him."

Draovitch's exercise plan for the Shark was so grueling that Love, reaching out to catch a medicine ball Norman had tossed him, was almost bowled over. "It was like in cartoons, where the guy throws you the ball and it throws you through the wall," he said. "I knew Greg was in shape, but I didn't really know just how strong he'd gotten."

Financially, Norman had entered another stratosphere. If his slump had shown him anything, it was that his passion for business and the adrenaline buzz that accompanied the successful conclusion of a high-risk deal was easily the equal of his passion for golf. In 1990 he had put his trust in Tom Crow and Cobra, when he invested two million dollars of his own money into a 12 percent stake in the equipment company, becoming an equity partner. At more or less the same time, IMG negotiated a contract for Norman to represent Cobra and carry its bag.

Crow had known Norman since 1977 when the Australian telephoned Crow out of the blue and said, "My name is Greg Norman. You don't know me, but I've seen a set of your mild steel clubs. Would you be prepared to make a set for me?"

"Actually," said Crow, who had seen Norman win the West Lakes Classic, "I do know you. And I'd be happy to."

"THE UNFORTUNATE THING ABOUT GREG THE GOLFER VERSUS GREG THE PERSON, I THINK, IS NOT A LOT OF PEOPLE GET TO KNOW GREG THE PERSON."

Norman loved the clubs so much that Crow made him a backup set nine weeks later, but when Norman signed with IMG, they negotiated a deal with Spalding. "I didn't have any business affiliation with Greg, so I respected that," Crow said. "He wanted a contract that paid him a lot of money. He needed money at that stage. In retrospect I think the Spalding ball cost him two majors. But that's only a personal opinion."

Norman, who learned to make his own woods and irons as part of his training under Earp, was actively involved in the club-making process. "He has his own ideas of how a club should look," Crow laughs, "which are not necessarily the same as anyone else's, but he's got a great eye and an incredible feel for the weight and balance of a club."

The exercise, the diet, the business, and the Zen all helped revive Norman's zest for life, but it was the soundness of his swing that boosted his confidence. "I now trust my swing totally under pressure," he said. Aided by his new caddie, Tony Navarro, a taciturn man with twenty years' experience, Norman was inching toward greatness again. There were runner-up finishes in New Orleans and the Western Open, and half a dozen top tens. In December he shot a closing 63 at the Johnnie Walker World Championship in Jamaica to catch Faldo, but then lost on the first extra hole.

In March 1993, Norman blazed a fiery trail around Doral, tying his own course record with a 62 in the third round and ending with a 70 that spread-eagled the field. He had devised a secret seven-year program of psychological and physiological improvement to carry him through to the year 2000, and this was its first reward.

"I played the best golf I think I've ever played and I lost by four shots," said Azinger, not sure whether to be annoyed or impressed.

"Mark it down, folks," wrote Gary Van Sickle of *Golf World*. "The sulking, frowning, irritable, sensitive Norman of the last two years is history. The often spectacular, fun-loving, outgoing, happy-go-lucky warrior, the Great White Shark who was a dominant force in the late eighties, is back."

Norman was pretty emotional himself. "For twenty months I was my own worst enemy," he said. "I got frustrated and down on myself. I re-evaluated what I wanted. I could have walked away, but I didn't want to. I wanted to get back to playing good golf. To do that, you have to practice hard. And to do that, you have to prioritize."

Balanced like a gymnast about to execute a handspring, Norman stood on a tawny slope at the far end of the range at Royal St. George's and clipped the ball off the turf above his feet. In practice rounds his swing had not been in sync. The steepness had crept back into it, and Harmon had just spent ninety minutes using the slope to help his pupil get the feel of a flatter plane. It was the best ninety minutes Norman ever spent.

"It was just that little bit of work that made everything fall into place," Harmon says. "It was funny because the R&A didn't like it. They were very upset that we went out of the driving range and hit the ball back over. They criticized him quite a bit for it, told him he couldn't do that again. But that hour and a half was all we needed."

For Norman, who leaned heavily on adrenaline, inspiration, and the preround preparation that would tell him how he would play that day, there were no signs that this British Open would be any different from the rest. Quite the reverse. Nothing was going according to plan. At Augusta he had opened with a 74. "What is it that happens to me in the first round here?" he fumed to Laura. He scraped through the cut with a 68, but a last-round 77 left him thirty-first. At the U.S. Open, he had missed the cut.

He dreaded performing as poorly at St. George's. "The strange thing is, there are tournaments we've gone into that you just feel so sure this is going to be the week," Laura says. "We never felt that, that week. Neither one of us. You never know, but things were not all on sync like they had been at other places."

The first round was wet and overcast. Norman started inauspiciously, carving his tee shot into the high rough to the right of the first tee and racking up a double bogey six. He managed a birdie at the second. "He was playing shit," remembers Gary Evans, a young Englishman. The experience of partnering the Shark for the first two days at St. George's left a strong impression on him. "He attempts to intimidate you. Whether that's because he's such a good player, I don't know, but it didn't faze me at all." He recalls Norman, usually a quick player, deliberating painstakingly over every shot. "He made a few comments during the course of the first round which I thought were sort of peculiar. I mean, I laughed at them but . . ."

Evans started birdie-par, so it was Norman's honor when they stepped onto the third tee. "He pulled a two-iron and nearly shanked it. It was such a bad shot. I had my hand on a three-iron. I was just pulling it out. He walked past me and he said to his caddie, 'Jesus, Tony, I got all of that.' I just thought, 'Why try and put me off the club I want to play?' Anyway, we played on and we get around to twelve. I'm three under and he's one over. We've both got seventy-yard pitch shots. The pin is cut on the front shelf. He hit a lovely shot, pitched it about three feet past the flag and it ran away to about twenty-five feet. I pitched it about three feet short of the flag, and stopped it a foot from the hole. And he made a comment along the lines of, 'Was my sand wedge legal?'

"Anyway, one of the biggest lessons I've ever learned was on the golf course that day. I was four under and he was one over after twelve holes, and he made a good birdie at thirteen to go back to even. He hit driver, eight-iron to five feet. We get to fourteen, the long par-five, and he hit it left into the crap, then he hit his second in the crap, and then he left his third shot twenty yards short, right of the green. I've hit driver up the middle, three-wood up the middle, wedge to eight foot. He hit this pitch and it was too hard. It bounced twice, hit the flag about a foot up and dropped into the hole. And from walking around the golf course with his face on the floor, miserable as sin, playing very averagely, he's gone birdie, birdie, and all of a sudden he's bounced onto the fifteenth tee, hit driver, five-iron to three foot—in. Sixteenth tee, he hit a seven-iron to forty foot for birdie, then stood on the seventeenth tee, hit driver, six-iron to four foot—in, then parred the last. I shot 67 and played great, and he shot 66 and played crap all the way around to thirteen. It taught me a big lesson. It doesn't matter how badly things are going, they can turn around. On the second day he played great and there was no stopping him."

After one round Norman shared the lead with fellow Australian Peter Senior and two ghosts from his past, Zoeller and Calcavecchia, over one of the toughest fields ever assembled at a British Open. With the exception of Ronan Rafferty, Lietzke, and Jumbo Ozaki, the top fifty players in the world rankings were competing, and the best of them were at the top of their games. Some forty-seven players delivered scores in the 60s, a first-day record, on the rain-softened course.

Norman, greeted the next morning by "Jurassic Shark" headlines, had not allowed himself to be rattled by his opening six. "I guess I had to eat humble pie on the first," he said. "As I walked off the green, I said to myself, 'There are seventy-one holes to go. Be patient.' I was just thinking about getting a couple of birdies quickly."

Ballesteros was all smiles after a 68 that was vintage Seve, full of sensational drives and miracle shots. "When you go under par, you feel young," he said.

Friday belonged to Faldo, the defending champion. On a blustery day with swirling crosswinds he made seven birdies in a course-record 63, equaling the championship record. "That's as good as it gets," said Faldo, who, twelve months earlier, had used a second-round 64 as a springboard to victory at Muirfield. He holed a fifty-yard pitch from the rough on fourteen from virtually the identical spot Norman had done in the first round. The roar that greeted Faldo's effort was so loud that Norman, standing over a par putt on seventeen, backed off and then missed. He was now two shots behind and had to sink an eight-footer on the last to stay that way.

Told that the bookies had installed Faldo as 2-to-1 favorite to win the Open, Norman said curtly, "What do they know about golf? I don't pay any attention to them."

Norman is not a superstitious man, but when fifteen-knot winds toughened Sandwich on Saturday, he joked that he'd be taking his good-luck pills each morning. Navarro already had his. His entry pass for the last two days was numbered 0001. Both men were helped by Norman's driving, which was superlative all week.

"Greg is the best driver of the last couple of decades, without a doubt," Harmon says. "I think Tiger hits the ball farther than Greg, but he's a little wilder than Greg, and Tiger doesn't really yet have the command of his shots—the draws, fades, high, low—that Greg has all the time. That was the thing that impressed me most about him."

Norman, who uses a King Cobra metal driver with nine degrees of loft and a shaft flex of X400, attributes his prowess with it to his physical stature. "I have small hips and a fairly good upper body from surfing and stuff. Look at Tiger Woods. He has a big upper body and a very tiny lower body, so he gets that out of the way quicker."

A third-round 69 left Norman a stroke behind Faldo and Corey Pavin at seven under par. Langer shared third place with Norman, and Price and

Peter Senior were at six under. "This," Norman said, "is going to be one of the greatest British Opens ever." He refused to accept that Faldo would be the main threat in the final round. "He's not infallible," Norman said sourly. "If I admitted he was the number-one guy, it would be admitting he was better than me. I don't think that, ever. He's a great player, but he can be beaten."

NORMAN EMERGED IN A CERISE, BLACK, AND BLUE SHIRT. . . . IT LOOKED LIKE AN ACID TRIP OR SOMETHING A SNAKE CHARMER WOULD WEAR.

On the final morning Norman emerged in a cerise, black, and blue shirt not quite as flamboyant as a circus marquee. It looked like an acid trip or something a snake charmer would wear. All week Norman's dress sense had provoked a mixture of amazement and despair. "The striped shirt was fine," said the *Guardian*'s Mike Selvey of one outfit, "but the sleeveless jumper—a fluorescent punky pink with green trim on the front, and a back that might once have been white but looked as if he had spent the night on a park bench without checking if the paint was dry—made him look like a cross between a particularly nasty migraine and Bertie Bassett on psychedelic drugs."

Describing another creation, David Miller wrote, "Tom Watson would not be seen dead in it; an ice hockey umpire's stripes at the back, a Mexican second-division football shirt's peacock mauve at the front. Only money, surely, could persuade anyone to walk about in public in such a garment."

On Sunday, Norman was not wearing the cursed hat, and his face beneath his overlong hair looked chiseled and intent. When he strode onto the first tee, he was wearing a sweater with a black front, a blue back emblazoned with a Technicolor shark, and one black-and-white-striped sleeve. It looked like an economy-saving measure from Yoko Ono. But it was the last time anyone spared a thought for Norman's fashion crisis. Minutes later his drive pierced the blue and the crowd roared. One of the greatest final rounds in British Open Championship history had begun.

Norman and Langer quickly birdied the first to join Faldo and Pavin at eight under. On the tee behind them, a raucous and enthusiastic crowd sang "Happy Birthday" to Faldo. Norman played as if he were cocooned in a heavenly bubble. Nothing entered it—not the colorful walls of spectators or Langer's immaculate iron play or Faldo's creeping methodically up the leaderboard. At the third he rattled in a twenty-five-footer for birdie. At the par-three sixth he slipped his tee shot to twelve feet for another. At the ninth he pitched a nine-iron to a foot to go out in 31.

"I remember watching him in that last round, and he was just so calm," Laura says, "out there having a good time. Greg has such high expectations of himself, you know. I think he just played within himself that day. Sometimes he has a hard time doing that. He tries to play to please the people who expect him to win, and you can't do that because you put too much pressure on yourself. That day he just played for Greg."

After ten holes Norman was eleven under for the tournament and led by two over Faldo and Langer. At the eleventh he saved par from seven feet and bounced back with a perfect sand wedge at twelve. Pavin, Senior, and Ernie Els, who would become the first man to break 70 in all four rounds of the Open, were lurking in the wings at six under.

Then came the dangerous fourteenth, the kind of hole where Norman, if the jinx was on him, would take out his driver and carve a completely unnecessary, overaggressive tee shot out of bounds right. Langer, who had just birdied two holes to draw within two strokes of Norman, did that very thing, steered there by a left-to-right wind. A red flag signaled disaster in the distance. Norman took out his driver. He could not have been more confident of the outcome if it had been carved in stone beside the tee box. He was so focused that he never saw Langer go out of bounds.

After a textbook drive down the fairway, Norman fashioned a beautiful three-wood just short of the green, then pitched to ten feet for another birdie. At the short sixteenth he delivered a flawless tee shot to five feet and sank the putt to stay out of range of Faldo, who birdied fourteen, and Langer, who birdied fifteen and sixteen. "Well," said a TV commentator in an awed tone, "sometimes you just run out of superlatives."

Throughout the day there was the feeling that something magical, almost spiritual, was taking place, that the game of golf was being taken to a new level.

"It was chemistry," Norman says. "Every top player knew that the other players were at the peak of their games. Every player knew that if you made a bogey, you'd lost two shots, not one shot. We were so finely tuned, we were like violin strings. We were at the perfect pitch. And to come out of that beating all those guys—outside the West Lakes Classic, that was my best feeling ever."

Langer's three-wood approach at the seventeenth hit the flagstick. "This championship really does have a touch of the Steven Spielberg's about it," the

THROUGHOUT THE DAY THERE WAS THE FEELING THAT SOMETHING MAGICAL, ALMOST SPIRITUAL, WAS TAKING PLACE, THAT THE GAME OF GOLF WAS BEING TAKEN TO A NEW LEVEL.

commentator breathed melodramatically. Norman looked at the leaderboard for the first time and immediately missed a fourteen-inch putt, making his only bogey of the day.

Millions of viewers swallowed hard collectively. Norman seemed unperturbed. "My stomach fell, more from embarrassment than anything. But it was a blessing in disguise because it kicked me into gear." Counseling himself to trust his swing, he launched a huge drive down the eighteenth fairway and strode majestically toward it, blond head held high. He hit a 198-yard four-iron to eighteen feet to set up his eighth birdie chance of the day. As the roar of the gallery rose like thunder into the evening air, and Australian flags and inflatable sharks danced, Langer crossed the fairway and said to Norman, "That's the greatest golf I've ever seen. You deserve to win."

In the crackling silence Norman holed out for a 64, the lowest final round ever scored by a champion and the lowest aggregate score in British Open history—267. Afterward, he sat stunned in the scorer's hut while his friends and family cried and hugged each other outside, afraid to believe that he had just played the greatest round of his life to win the Open. He didn't smile. He just sat stoically watching the television, waiting for Faldo, who had birdied seventeen, to do something marvelous to overtake him. It was not until Faldo holed out for a 67 and a second-place tie with Langer that Norman allowed himself to feel the heady rush of achievement.

"I'm not a man who tends to boast," he told reporters, "but I was in awe of myself. I have never before gone around a course and not had a single mis-hit. Every drive and every iron were perfect. I only screwed up on

Norman, who has been called the greatest driver in the history of the game, powers his way to victory at the 1993 British Open. (© Phil Sheldon)

that one little putt at the seventeenth, but that was probably the kick in the backside I needed. It was like playing a game of chess. I had an angle to every flag."

Speaking at the prize-giving ceremony, ninety-one-year-old Gene Sarazen, winner of the 1932 Open at Sandwich, described Norman's performance as "the most awesome display of golf I have ever seen." Player called it "the best golf I ever saw played at the British Open," and Evans, Norman's partner on the first two days, agreed. "That last round was one of the best I have ever seen, no question," he said.

Harmon goes so far as to rate Norman's last round at Royal St. George's above Tiger Woods's twelve-shot victory at the Masters, "when you consider the conditions—the wind blowing thirty to thirty-five miles an hour, and when you consider that all the contenders played well—Faldo shot 67, Langer shot 67, Couples shot 66. I mean, everyone who was there to win played fantastic, and Greg just played that much better and won the tournament. He played as well as anybody can play. I don't think you could play a better golf tournament than he played that week."

His arms wrapped around the silver claret jug, Norman told the cheering galleries, "To say I've won the British Open, which is the open championship of the world, the number-one championship major, the best major, to win it once was great but to win it twice gives me twice as much pleasure." His 64, as perfect a round of golf as has ever been played, would rank forever among the greats: Hogan's 67 at Oakland Hills, Arnold Palmer's 65 at Cherry Hills, Nicklaus's 65 at Augusta, Miller's 63 at Oakmont. Only one player had ever finished under par over four rounds at St. George's in an Open—Bill Rogers in 1981—and Norman demolished his record by nine shots.

On his way to the prize-giving ceremony, Norman was embraced in a bear hug by Faldo. "Great job," he said. "Well done. You finally stuck your fingers up to them."

Norman burst out laughing. "Yeah," he said. "Fun golf, wasn't it?"

"Greg was always out of my range," Faldo said. "I needed every birdie, but when you are staring at these opportunities in this kind of pressure, it's difficult to get the thing in the hole."

Afterward Norman, showered and relaxed in jeans and trainers and so happy he could have wept, climbed into a red Rolls Royce with Laura and rode away into the sunset to a champagne party. "This makes me feel so good," he said. "For myself, my friends, my family. They've seen what I've gone through, and they see what I want to achieve. I did it today."

A month after his British Open triumph, Norman was climbing from his car on the final morning of the PGA Championship when he was accosted by a well-meaning spectator. "When you win today," the man said, "I want you to take your hat and throw it in that bunker. You throw it in the exact same spot where Tway made that shot."

From the moment he signed his scorecard at Sandwich he had been thinking ahead to the PGA, which was returning to Inverness, the scene of Tway's implausible bunker shot. "I am ready for another major win," Norman said confidently. "My game is strong right now." But even he couldn't ignore the possible implications of karma. "It seems unbelievable that I'm going back to Inverness as Open champion," Norman said, ". . . a flashback of 1986. That's a mind-boggling coincidence."

Now, standing on the eighteenth tee at Inverness, minutes after he had ended the 1993 tournament tied with Paul Azinger, Norman was trying very hard not to think about coincidences. He didn't want to picture Tway popping ecstatically out of the bunker, or see the surprised, elated faces of Mize or Calcavecchia or Frost or Gamez as fate handed them aces. And he certainly didn't want to dwell on the double bogey he had chalked up by leaving his ball in the bunker at the sixth that afternoon, or the bogey at the seventh. After all, he'd recovered with four birdies that took him past Faldo, Singh, and Watson, and left him tied with Azinger at 272. And his 69 made him the first man in history to shoot eight rounds in the 60s in successive majors.

"WHEN YOU WIN TODAY," THE MAN SAID, "I WANT YOU TO TAKE YOUR HAT AND THROW IT IN THAT BUNKER. YOU THROW IT IN THE EXACT SAME SPOT WHERE TWAY MADE THAT SHOT."

Azinger was a nervous wreck. His sinewy forearms were tense, he was having trouble breathing, and he was worried he might throw up. He was beginning to think that "the best player in the world not to have won a major" was a tag that should never have been applied to him. Maybe there was a reason he had bogeyed the seventy-second hole of the 1987 British Open to lose to Faldo—that his game went south on the back nine at majors.

Beside him was his caddie Mark Jimenez. Now that really was a coincidence. Jimenez was the man who had carried Tway's bag to victory at Inverness in 1986. Azinger breathed in deeply and hit his tee shot. Both men were on the green in two and the Australian had an eighteen-footer for birdie. Azinger watched as Norman, strong and charismatic, crouched down to inspect his lie.

For Norman and everyone who watched him, there was something fitting about the scene, almost as if destiny had come full circle. When the ball left his putter, it rolled unerringly toward the hole and started to tip in, so that joy was surging across his face and his putter was thrusting upward in anticipation of triumph, when, defying every law of gravity and nature, the ball reappeared. The crowd gasped. Norman's putter flew into the air and his hand covered the shock and pain on his face.

"Two feet from the hole, there was no doubt in my mind that putt was in," Azinger said. "That was as perfect a putt as I could have hit," said Norman.

There was a palpable feeling of doom as they proceeded to the tenth. It was hard not to believe some kind of hex was in operation, and, not altogether unexpectedly, Norman hit his approach to eighteen feet and three-putted, missing a five-footer that would have kept his hopes alive, to give the American his first major victory.

Head bowed, Norman ran the gauntlet of the gallery on his way back to the clubhouse. His son, Gregory, held his hand. "I'm proud of you," the boy told him.

"He was unlucky in that his ball ended up just in the rough," Azinger says, "and you know you're in a play-off and you've got to go at the flag. . . . He had no chance really. . . . The first putt he had was nearly impossible. People say that the second putt was a three-footer. It was a four- or five-footer and it had a significant amount of break. But if he had hit [the first

196

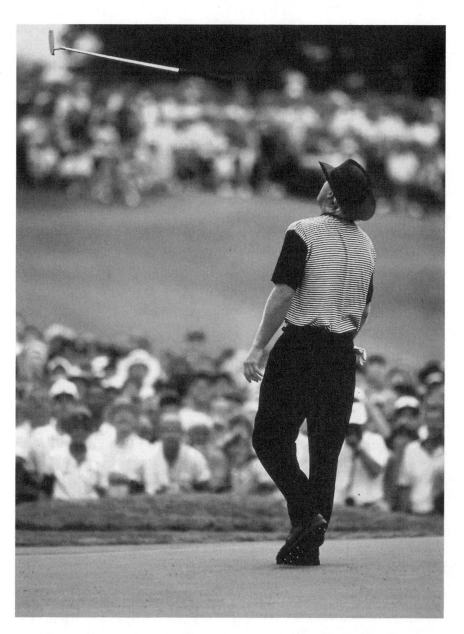

Norman tosses his putter skyward in disgust after a three-putt on the second play-off hole saw him hand the 1993 PGA Championship to Paul Azinger. (© Phil Sheldon)

putt] hard enough to go three feet farther, it might have reached the hole and then gone ten feet by. It was a hard putt."

Norman wasn't the first player to achieve the ignominious distinction of losing play-offs in all four majors, but he was the second; Craig Wood had managed it in the thirties. Norman had now finished runner-up six times in a major. "Well," Norman said, "at least I was there." He refused to accept that he might be jinxed and graciously acknowledged Azinger's achievement. "It wasn't meant to be, it's as simple as that. I walk away from here with good feelings. I'm still proud that I've turned my career around in a phenomenal way this year. I'll have a couple of beers and I'll be fine."

"That week was an incredible ball-striking week for me," Azinger says. "Statistically, I was first in greens in regulation, I was first in driving distance, and I was second in fairways hit. I didn't have a three-putt the whole tournament, and when I think about how good I hit it and the fact that Norman's putt could have lipped in on eighteen instead of lipped out, wow! I could still not have won a major. How much luck is there involved when you think about it?"

Jim Gallagher Jr. had just been the recipient of the largest dollop of good fortune he'd seen in ten years as a PGA Tour player, but he was uncertain whether to do cartwheels or apologize. For sixty-five holes the Tour Championship had belonged to Greg Norman. Serene and powerful, he had strolled the fairways as if every inch of San Francisco's Olympic Club, from the cypress trees to the $540,000 prize that would ensure he won the money list, were his by divine right. Then, inexplicably, he bogeyed four of the final seven holes to plummet into second place. "Norman wasn't so much mishitting as misplaying—unnecessarily forcing the ball at the pin with efforts that were poorly conceived and inappropriate to the situation," Jaime Diaz observed in *SI*. "Norman went from being a tank rolling inexorably and triumphantly toward Olympic's stately clubhouse to a cable car careering down Hyde Street toward disaster."

In rapid succession Norman missed the twelfth green with a 131-yard nine-iron, hit a poor chip from behind the green at the thirteenth, plugged his ball in the bunker with an aggressive sixty-degree-wedge shot at sixteen, and hit an ill-advised eight-iron shot directly at a pin cut on a severe slope at the back of the eighteenth green.

"I didn't physically put on a bad performance; I just mentally put on a pathetic performance," Norman said frankly. He was striding crossly from the scoring hut when he bumped into Gallagher, the thirty-two-year-old who "backed into" the third victory of his career playing the last four holes one over par. Caught on the hop, Gallagher was unsure what to say. "Sorry about that, Greg," he said sheepishly.

Norman was not exactly devastated; it had been too good a season for that. He had finished in the top ten seven times in fifteen appearances in the United States. But he was frustrated to have fallen at the last ditch and to have lost the chance to compete for Player of the Year honors. He had forgotten his own formula for playing Olympic—aim for the middle of the greens and forget the flags—and he had no one to blame but himself.

"When you look at Greg Norman, his strengths and his weaknesses are almost one and the same," Harmon says. "Greg Norman's strength is that he's not afraid to try any shot in any situation, and sometimes that's a weakness in that he gets too aggressive when he should maybe be a little more conservative. But then again, that's how Greg plays, and he wouldn't be the great player that he is if he didn't play like that."

In December, Norman flew to Melbourne for the Australian Open, arriving pale and distressed and ill. Throughout the twenty-one-hour flight from Los Angeles, via Hawaii and Pago Pago, he had been running a high fever, and he had been ill several times. Norman suspected food poisoning; Raymond Floyd, who had been with him, was convinced it was exhaustion. "I think Greg is just run down. He's been doing so many things in such a short period without time even to take a breath."

There was plenty of evidence to support this assumption. Prior to the Tour Championship, Norman had been in Japan. Having finished second in San Francisco, he flew to Cairns, Australia, for a fishing holiday, returned to Japan and holed an eagle putt to win the Taiheiyo Masters, flew back to the United States and won the Grand Slam of Golf, jetted to California to play in his own charity event, the Shark Shootout, and was on the plane to Melbourne for the Australian Open within an hour of finishing.

"If I'd been in America, I would have pulled out," said a gray-faced Norman. "But down here it would have hurt everybody, and I just figured I'd rather hurt myself."

"How he is able to play golf at his level is beyond me," said Frank Williams, IMG's man in Melbourne. "He gets up at the crack of dawn and keeps going till he flops into bed at ten or eleven at night, and then he gets up and does the same thing again."

It turned out that Williams, like Norman, was an incorrigible practical joker. At the Australian Skins earlier in the year, the Shark was autographing programs and shirts for the television cameras when he was asked to sign a glove for Boris Yeltsin. "Screw Yeltsin," grinned Norman. He thought it was a joke.

Williams smiled quietly to himself. When Norman came off the course, worrying about his performance, he decided to teach him a lesson. "Greg," he said sternly, "that's the least of our worries. We've had to close down the switchboard at Sanctuary Cove because of all the complaints. Why would you say, 'Screw the Russian president?' "

"What are you talking about?" asked Norman, alarmed.

"Look," Williams said angrily, "how many times have I told you that when you've got your mike on, you must put your hand over it if you don't want to be heard."

Norman paled. "Oh, my God!" he cried. "What am I going to do?"

At first Williams pretended to be completely unsympathetic, but finally he relented and helped Norman concoct a story whereby Yeltsin was actually the name of a boatbuilder from Detroit who was hassling him over the purchase of another yacht.

In the interview room Tom Ramsey had been primed to ask the leading question. "Greg," he said, "Rupert Murdoch has phoned me personally and he wants to know why you said fuck off to the Russian president."

"You always believe what you want to believe," Norman said. "There's a boatbuilder in Detroit called Yeltsin—"

He stopped. The journalists were collapsing with laughter. He looked around for Williams. "I'll get you," he said. "No matter what, I'll get you."

A week later Williams was holding a player party at IMG's Melbourne office, when five policemen came to the door. He apologized for the noise, but they ushered him into a quiet room. "We've got a warrant for your arrest," one told him.

Williams beamed. "Oh, yes," he said. "Who's arresting me? Greg Norman?"

The policeman scowled. "If you think we've got nothing better to do than come here on the whim of some adolescent golfer, you're very much mistaken," he said and handed Williams the warrant. Williams cast a glazed eye over the official emblem and list of charges, including tax evasion and illegal transference of money. He began to panic. "I thought to myself, 'No, it's got to be Greg,' but I can't see Greg anywhere to pounce on him. Then I look across and see my wife crying. I thought, 'Oh, my God, this could be for real.' "

Before Williams could utter another syllable, the police were bundling him into the paddy wagon. He was taken down to the station, fingerprinted, read his rights, and locked in a cell after having his belt and shoelaces removed. "Jesus Christ," Williams thought as he sat on the prison bed with his head in his hands. "My whole life is falling apart." With trembling fingers, he reached for the envelope he had been told would inform him of his legal position. There was a note inside. It read, "Paybacks are hell, you asshole!!!!"

13

POWER STRUGGLE

"There's no doubt in my mind that Greg will end up a billionaire."

Frank Williams, June 1997

In a hotel suite in downtown Sydney, Hughes Norton was staring goggle-eyed at Greg Norman. Norton's face was gray and sweating, his body paralyzed with disbelief. In the space of five minutes, life as he knew it had ended. Divorce had been hard enough on him, but this caught him right in the solar plexus. Outside the sun was shining and the crowds were flocking to the fairways of the Greg Norman Holden Classic, but Norton felt chilled to the bone.

"The guy I'd done enormously wonderful things for, in the end, forgot them," Norton said. "I guess it's the way life is in our business."

It was December 1993. Norman had summoned Norton; James Erskine, IMG's Australian kingpin; and Frank Williams, the regional manager for IMG in Melbourne, to a meeting. There were no preliminaries. Norman simply stood up and said bluntly, "As you all know, I've not been happy for some time, so I've decided that I'm now leaving. Frank has accepted a position with me and he will also be leaving."

Norton and Erskine slumped in their chairs like stunned mullet. Norman had been without a contract at IMG for more than a year, during which time Williams repeatedly had warned the company that Norman hated being leveraged with other clients (packaged with lesser players to help boost their value) and did not feel he was getting the service he deserved; but somehow Norton didn't have the slightest inkling he might go. He either didn't see it or did not want to see it.

"Let's make this friendly," Norman said brightly.

"Hughes was devastated," Williams recalls.

Depending on whom you talk to, McCormack, Erskine, and Norton himself are all variously blamed for Norman's decision to walk away from IMG, but his actual reasons were more specific. Williams believes that one of the most critical was Laura. "He considers his wife and himself a partnership, and I think James made the mistake of not including his wife as part of the partnership. He never consulted with Laura and Greg. She's a very important factor in [Greg's] life. She's the single most important person in his life, along with his children. I think they deliberately tried to keep her out of the loop and I think Greg resented it."

To Norton, who had without prompting described Laura as "one of the greatest people I've ever known," this statement was extraordinary. "That's the first I've ever heard of that," he said. "She was always around for discussions on important issues, so I'd be amazed if she thought she wasn't involved in decisions."

Bev Norwood, a friend of both men, supported this view. "Having seen the interaction between the two, I can tell you I have never to this day heard Laura Norman's name mentioned by anyone at IMG in a negative context."

The whole split was traumatic. Norton considered himself to have been "fired," a statement Norman views as "extraordinarily rash. Hughes Norton was never fired. My contract expired with IMG, so I didn't fire anybody. Matter of fact, during the time of the contract running out, I'd asked for certain specific things to be done by IMG, and they totally ignored them. They didn't recognize that I needed extra help because of the way my business was. It had nothing to do with Hughes Norton; it had a lot to do with IMG because they didn't fulfill the wishes of their client."

Price, who, along with Faldo and a host of other top players, would soon leave IMG, totally supported Norman's decision. "We spoke a lot about IMG over the years," he says, "especially on the golf course. At that stage, I felt that [leaving] was the best thing for him. Don't get me wrong: IMG is a good company. But it is archaic, to say the least. The company was structured in the sixties and it hasn't changed, and I think it's been to their detriment. They're going to have to change their tactics if they want to survive in the next decade, because sure as hell there is going to be somebody behind them that is going to challenge their position. I think Greg and myself and Faldo would still be with them if they had listened to us."

The fallout from Norman's departure was tremendous. Personally, it was as painful a blow as Norton had ever experienced; professionally, it cost him dearly. Rightly or wrongly, he held Norman completely responsible for his demotion as head of IMG's golf division.

Norton, who is liked as much as he is loathed in the golf world, has few regrets. "I could be wrong, but my feeling after the fact, analyzing it, is if Greg had allowed or I had pushed more to have [people like Ian Todd, who runs our European operation, and Alastair Johnston, who he thinks the world of] involved, that we would still be together. As I say, that's not the way Greg wanted it and I didn't realize then, as I do now, how important that is. That would be my one regret. But, in terms of the job that I personally did or that IMG did, you know, we made this guy $100 million."

THE FALLOUT FROM NORMAN'S DEPARTURE WAS TREMENDOUS. PERSONALLY, IT WAS AS PAINFUL A BLOW AS NORTON HAD EVER EXPERIENCED; PROFESSIONALLY, IT COST HIM DEARLY.

"They wouldn't have made a lot of money if Greg wasn't winning," Laura said dryly.

Norton claims that the Australian pleaded with him for years to quit IMG and work for him. "I would always say to him, 'That's very flattering and it would be great for me, but it's not in your best interests.' But I always felt that he wanted loyalty and I gave him 110 percent. He'd say, 'You're not loyal because McCormack signs your checks, not me,' and I'd tell him, 'Yes, Greg, but you're doing much better with me at IMG than you would with me as your Great White Shark guy.'"

The breakdown of the relationship between Norman and Norton had as its roots the Cobra deal. In September 1993, Norman, an equity shareholder in the company, had relinquished some of his shares in the first public offering. The second offering was a year later, and then on January 1, 1996, when American Brands bought Cobra, Norman realized on his investment, earning some $44 million in total from his $2 million stake.

When Norton approached Norman around the time of the initial offering and asked him to pay him $1 million of that money, Norman was absolutely appalled. Was Norton really suggesting taking money due his employer? If he was capable of that, what might he do to Norman?

Incredibly, Norton did not flinch when this allegation was put to him.

"Do you want to know the truth of the matter?" he asked. "And it's never been said before. I did the Cobra deal with Greg and for Greg. Greg tried, at the end, to withhold commissions on the deal which we felt were very much due and proper. Greg's thing had been that he had enormous personal affection and respect and loyalty for me, but less for IMG the corporate entity. At the end I felt that the only way to get for IMG what was duly ours was to appeal to him on a personal basis. And that's the absolute truth of that scenario. He chose not to do that either, so . . . "

Asked whether he thought that Norman might have gained the impression that Norton wanted the money for himself rather than his employer, he replied, "Oh, I'm sure he did. Obviously. That's what he said."

But according to Norman, "IMG had nothing to do with the Cobra contract." He smiled cynically. "Very interesting, isn't it? I'll leave it at that."

"IMG could never have been entitled to any of the Cobra money because they didn't make an investment," Crow says. "It was Greg's name on the check, it was his money. Hughes Norton negotiated the representational deal, the deal for Greg to represent Cobra clubs and carry the bag. The other deal had nothing to do with Hughes Norton. He didn't put his name on the check. Without question, Hughes Norton has and had absolutely no entitlement to the money."

Norton sticks to his story. "I came up with the concept, I created the value," he says emotionally. "And it's not the money, it's the principle. It's ethically, morally, and logically wrong that he would not have paid me for the creative work of what turned out to be the greatest deal of his career."

Since 1996, Norton has been more famous, or infamous, as Tiger Woods's manager. He avoids contact with the man who was once his closest friend. When Williams suggested that the three of them have a conversation about what happened, Norton retorted, "We just had it."

"It was just like a lovers' quarrel or something," Laura says. "Hughes took it personally and it wasn't anything personal. It was simply business."

Three years later Norton still finds it distressing to talk about. "To yell and scream about loyalty and then do what he did to me on the Cobra deal alone is unconscionable," he says shakily.

He admits he is saddened by the situation. "We all have our flaws and Greg has his and I have mine, but he's basically, deep down, a really good, giving, caring person, and I miss that. But I'm also the sort of person,

205

whether it's my divorce or my divorce with Greg, I'm not a great one to chase him around after I've been fired and say, 'Let's be buddy-buddy and hang out and be pals.' I'm just not that way. I'm more of a black and white loyal person."

"IT WAS JUST LIKE A LOVERS' QUARREL OR SOMETHING," LAURA SAYS. "HUGHES TOOK IT PERSONALLY AND IT WASN'T ANYTHING PERSONAL. IT WAS SIMPLY BUSINESS."

Fuzzy Zoeller was waving the white towel again. In a tongue-in-cheek echo of Winged Foot, he took it out of his bag as he walked toward the eighteenth green at the 1994 Players Championship and raised it in admiration, causing Norman to burst out laughing and place his hat affectionately on Zoeller's head. For four days Zoeller had ambled his way around the Stadium Course at Sawgrass and never once scored worse than 68. He had shot twenty under par on a course so wicked that Weiskopf described it as "Donkey Kong" golf, and lost by four shots. "That's the best I've ever played and had absolutely no chance of winning," Zoeller said wryly.

Instead, the honor went to Norman. He shot three 67s and a record-equaling 63 for a twenty-four-under-par total of 264. His only bogey came when a leaf blew across his line as he prepared to hole a nine-footer at the thirteenth. It was his first for sixty-six holes and the first for ninety-two stretching back to the Nestle Invitational the previous week. "I really wanted to go bogey free," Norman said. "There are things you have an opportunity of doing in life maybe once or twice. And seventy-two holes without a bogey is rare."

For once no carefree rookie recorded a double eagle or some such to beat him on the eighteenth, and for once Norman didn't beat himself. The only hint of his old lunatic bravado came at the narrow, water-logged sixteenth in the final round, where he decided he was swinging well enough to hit a sliding three-wood into the green. Tony Navarro clung to the club.

"Let's just lay up," he pleaded, fear of failure moving him to say the four words Norman hated most in golf. Norman fumed and fretted and champed at the bit, but he saw reason. He laid up and made par. "A play like that might help us out in the future," Navarro said optimistically afterward.

Since missing the cut at the 1993 U.S. Open, Norman's finishes read second, first, third, second, tie for fourth, tie for seventh, tenth, second, first, tie for eighteenth, tie for seventh, tie for sixth, and first, and yet he was about as far from being a happy man as it was possible to be. Sitting in the locker room after his first-round 63, picking irritably at his orange workout shorts, he responded to a question on why he was no longer gregarious but world-weary and withdrawn, with hurt and anger. "I'll tell you what happened," he burst out. "You become cynical. Why did Michael Jordan retire? Because of all the badgering. Why do athletes go into a shell after a period of time? Because of all the constant badgering. Unfortunately, that's the nature of the beast. We do it to ourselves, and the media is such now that it focuses on whatever it can get its hands on. I was never a cynical person. Never have been. But I am now."

Behind the scenes Williams had moved in as managing director of Norman's new company Great White Shark Enterprises, not without a certain amount of sniping from IMG. When Norman dared to suggest that the Australian Masters had lost its magic, Erskine snapped, "What do you want? Gold [toilet] paper?"

"That's the stuff you use, right, James?" Norman retaliated.

"Yes, Greg, I got it from your private jet," Erskine said sarcastically.

The vilification heaped on him during his slump was a thorn in his side even the British Open trophy hadn't soothed. It rankled that other players could make eleventh-hour screwups or offensive statements without being crucified the way he was. On the Monday of his Open defense at Turnberry, he stood on the edge of the putting green glowering at John Daly. "What the hell could you have been thinking?" he burst out. Daly, who had thoughtlessly alleged to a British tabloid that some players took drugs, looked up in surprise. When Norman repeated the question, he became defensive and said he was tired of being portrayed as the only black sheep on the tour.

"I was livid with the guy, absolutely livid," said Norman, who was tempted to follow Daly into the locker room but didn't want to do something he would regret. "How dare he say any of us are on drugs. I'm not the one who is an alcoholic; I'm not the one who tears up rooms. . . . If I had done the things he's done, I'd have been ostracized so fast it would have been ridiculous."

The needles were coming in again, and they were much deeper and more painful than Norman's worst nightmares could have led him to believe. Even Davis Love, the moon-faced, likable former Players champion, was in on it. "If he walked out here now, he'd get attacked," he told *Golf Digest*, suggesting that the Shark needed to add a bodyguard to his staff. "Guys would pin him in a corner and scream at him."

The cause of this outrage was the bombshell Norman had dropped at the Shark Shootout on November 17 when he announced a $25 million World Golf Tour, a series of eight $3 million super-events, featuring the top thirty players in the rankings and ten invitees.

The background to this was simplicity itself. The Montgomery brothers, John of Executive Sports, and Scott who ran the Doral-Ryder Open, had approached Norman and asked if he would be prepared to put his name behind a world tour in 1995. Norman, who had always been a big fan of the idea, said he would, but only if the difficulty of individual circuits protecting their power bases could be overcome. The Montgomery brothers went away and came back with a plan whereby existing events, such as Norman's own Shark Shootout, could be used. Norman was convinced; Rupert Murdoch, the Australian media tycoon, weighed in with a $120 million offer from his Fox television network over five years; and it was decided that John Montgomery should announce it at a press conference at the Shark Shootout.

"John got up in front of the microphone and froze," Williams recalls. "So Greg stepped in and said: 'This is the deal . . . ' And the shit hit the fan."

Nothing—not fame, not abuse, not wealth, not suffering—had prepared Norman for the scale of the fury that came his way as the news exploded around the golf world. "Greg's Golf War," declared the *Evening Standard* in London amid reports that Tim Finchem, the U.S. Tour commissioner, who was diplomatic and reasonable in the immediate aftermath, had hardened his stance considerably when his players rallied behind him. The

U.S. Federal Trade Commission was already investigating the Tour for possible restraint of trade, but for the sake of protecting his $82 million circuit, Finchem was prepared to resist them, suspend any players who joined the rebel tour, and fight all the way to Congress if necessary.

NOTHING—NOT FAME, NOT ABUSE, NOT WEALTH, NOT SUFFERING— HAD PREPARED NORMAN FOR THE SCALE OF THE FURY THAT CAME HIS WAY . . .

The player reaction was even more extreme. Arnold Palmer put his face inches from Norman's and warned, "Greg, slow down," and the *New York Times* ran a poll showing that not one of the top thirty players (other than Norman) supported Norman's plan. To Norman, who had canvassed player support—starting with the major champions of 1994: Price, Els, and Jose Maria Olazabal—and believed he'd gotten it, it was devastating. "Nick was the first guy I spoke to," Norman said. "If he didn't think the idea was any good, I wouldn't have proceeded." But Price, like Els, was cagey. "If the PGA Tour doesn't give its blessing, then I'm not going to be able to play," he hedged. "Greg asked for my support and I gave it, but there's a big difference between commitment and support."

"He was supported by a lot of his friends and then when it went public, they didn't support him," Laura said. "And that really hurt him."

Olazabal was a lone voice in a wilderness of criticism. "Please feel free to use my name as a strong supporter of the idea," he said in a fax to Norman.

The reaction of the golf community to "Norman's World Tour" was outrage. While it was generally agreed it would provide a much-needed wake-up call to the smug complacency of the other tours, most people believed that greed lay at its heart. Any way you painted it, it perpetuated the wealth and success of an already elite minority, glorified Norman, damaged the other tours and the image of the game, and cheapened the majors and the competition. As Jerry Tarde said in *Golf Digest*, the events would be "little more than glorified Skins Games."

Thomson concurred. "The potential to damage and even wreck the U.S. and European Tours is real. That's not to say they don't need a good shake-up. But the tours are professional golf's nurseries, and they need to be nurtured by those who've come through the system to become famous and wealthy. That particular lucky elite would not be in clover today had those tours not been in place for them to get started. Before they leap into the beyond, I hope they consider those they leave behind."

Norman, meanwhile, felt his motives had been completely misinterpreted. "The perception with me with the World Tour was just ridiculous," he says.

"It came out that he was trying to do something for Norman rather than for the good of golf," Williams said, "and he really was trying to do

THE REACTION OF THE GOLF COMMUNITY TO "NORMAN'S WORLD TOUR" WAS OUTRAGE. . . . MOST PEOPLE BELIEVED THAT GREED LAY AT ITS HEART.

something for the good of golf, or what he perceived as the good of golf—whether that's right or wrong. He took a helluva hammering from his peers and from the golf world at large. I remember John and Scott and I sitting with Greg in his old office and we said, 'You know you're going to get a lot of flak from this? They'll put their own twist on it and the twist it'll be is that, "Wealthy guy Greg Norman's getting even wealthier." ' He said, 'Oh, I don't think it'll be that bad when I explain it all.' 'Course, he never got the chance to explain it. It was like everything in Greg's life, done on the run and in a hurry."

Price was of a similar mind. "I think the mistake that he made with the World Tour was he tried to put it together too quickly. But other than that, I think his intention was to do something for the betterment of the game. I don't believe for one minute that he was doing it for financial gain because the money that he stood to make out of it was negligible. And he was absolutely right. He made the respective tours think about golf on a global scale, especially in the U.S., which tends to be insular. It was probably the biggest step forward that we've ever seen."

To Norman the most upsetting part of the entire incident was when he started getting letters from PGA club professionals who wanted to stop carrying his clothing line because he was "ruining the game" with the World Tour. "I was devastated by that," says Norman. He phoned every pro individually and persuaded them to restock.

Since then Finchem and the other circuits have moved inexorably towards a mini-World Tour of their own. "Are they ruining the game?"

210

says Norman, who had eleven top tens to finish runner-up on the money list despite undergoing hemorrhoid surgery after the World Series. "Of course not. Those people are doing it because they can see how much money there is on the table to be made."

By February 1995, Norman's World Tour was dying on its feet and he had two new worries to contend with. At the Alfred Dunhill Challenge, the Southern Africa vs. Australasia match held in Johannesburg, he had received more bad press after his singles match against Price. At the sixteenth hole he and Price were, respectively, fifteen and nine feet from the pin and all square, when Norman suggested that they concede each other's putts. The Zimbabwean readily agreed and went on to win the last hole and the match. But afterward both received a hostile reception from officials and other players for taking friendship too far and making a joke out of a serious event.

"Greg's got to understand he deserves better than that," Schofield said. "He let the game down, he let the team down. Unfortunately, Nick Price conspired with him. That's not what golf is about. . . . This was supposed to be a special addition to the calendar and there were players trying their guts out, but what happened between Norman and Price was absurd. Both men made an error of judgment. If the show is more important than the result, then it's not worth having."

It was not the first time the European Tour's executive director had turned on Norman. At the Johnnie Walker Classic in Manila that month, he had confronted the Australian on the subject of the World Tour and was persuaded by Norman that he had been "used" and that "it really wasn't his game show." That hadn't stopped Schofield from writing to the sponsors of the Dubai Desert Classic, the Irish Open, and the European Masters to complain about another matter—the $300,000 appearance fees Norman was supposed to have received in 1994.

"A guy in my shoes has to be pro prize money and against appearance money," explains Schofield, who has adopted a sort of Band-Aid regulation in Europe whereby incentives must not be more than 25 percent of the prize fund. "And many sponsors would go to any apparent lengths to skewer Greg Norman."

Norman was furious. "To single me out in three tournaments I played in put me in a very awkward position and I don't forgive Ken for that," he said after a heated debate with Schofield in early 1996. "Ken and I had known each other, basically, for twenty years, and the twenty-year relationship ended right there, as far as I was concerned."

" 'Why me?' That's what he said," Schofield reports. " 'Why do you pick on me? What about all the other guys?' I just said, 'I'm sorry, Greg, but the issue appears to be you. It always seems to be you that's in the headlines—or people close to you—wishing to ram down people's throats that you can command and receive on our Tour sums that appear to break our regulations.' "

On the golf course Norman used these conflicts to drive himself forward, with spectacular success. A chance to steal Crenshaw's thunder at the Masters only ended when he pulled a sand-wedge shot seventy feet left of the flag on the final hole and three-putted. "I had 106 yards to the hole," Norman explained, "and I don't like hitting a sand wedge that far. I like 104 yards. It was a little uphill, there was a breeze coming out of the right-hand corner, and I was on a hanging lie. It was one of those deals. . . . I was between yardages."

In 1986, the Year of the Shark, he had told a reporter, "When everything is going in the right direction . . . my caddie gives me half yardages . . . he'll say 131.5 yards instead of 132. He knows that if I'm really playing well, I can put it to within that half yard."

When back spasms forced him to pull out in the second round of the Heritage Classic in 1995, he took a five-week break, relaxed, spent time with his family, and didn't touch a club until the Memorial Tournament. "You're lucky to see me this week," joked Norman, before sweeping majestically to victory at Muirfield Village. A final-round 66 included one-putts on six of the last seven greens and birdies at seventeen and eighteen.

At the U.S. Open it was business as usual, and this time it was Corey Pavin who pipped him to the post. "You could call it another shot heard 'round the Greg Norman household," Jenkins said wryly as Pavin's magnificent four-wood to the eighteenth at Shinnecock consigned the Shark, who had shared the fifty-four-hole lead, to second place in yet another major.

In August he caused a huge fracas when he accused Mark McCumber of illegally repairing a spike mark on the seventh green in the first round of the World Series, effectively labeling him a cheat. In golf there is no mud that sticks like cheating, and therefore most players, even when they are 99.9 percent certain that a partner has knowingly violated the rules, tend to confront them in private. Norman was having none of it. He refused to sign McCumber's card after the round and, when McCumber insisted he had merely removed an insect, threatened to withdraw from the tournament. "An ugly scene ensued in the scoring trailer," reported *Golf World*.

"I didn't sign the scorecard for a reason," Norman fumed after the Tour's senior director of rules signed McCumber's card on his behalf. "What I saw is what I saw. I'd say it again if I saw a violation that blatant. I was furious because I was disappointed in what I saw. I could've bench-pressed five hundred pounds, that's how mad I was."

While McCumber went home with his reputation in tatters, Laura, Navarro, and Finchem persuaded Norman to stay. "They told me, 'Don't compromise yourself,' " Norman said. "They were right. Why compromise Greg Norman's chance to win?" Three days later he holed a sixty-six-foot chip to beat Price and Billy Mayfair on the first play-off hole. "The golfing gods were good to me today," Norman said.

THERE WAS A THEORY IN SOME QUARTERS THAT NORMAN HAD DELIBERATELY HUMILIATED McCUMBER TO EVEN THE SCORE FOR McCUMBER'S OUTSPOKEN OPPOSITION TO THE WORLD TOUR.

There was a theory in some quarters that Norman had deliberately humiliated McCumber to even the score for McCumber's outspoken opposition to the World Tour. "Who does Norman think he is, God?" McCumber had been quoted as saying. But Price thought the World Series was Norman's moral reward. "Greg is a man of high principles," he said. "He is extremely adamant about what he saw."

In October, Norman arrived at the Dunhill Cup, his first event in six weeks, fresh from a holiday in Belize with Nick Price. He had gone there to recover from a bout of chemical poisoning, possibly from lettuce or fruit, which caused him to lose thirteen pounds in six days and spend ten days in

Norman demonstrates the graciousness in defeat that is his most enduring trait—this time after losing the 1995 U.S. Open to Corey Pavin. (Matthew Harris)

bed. "Reports came in from Australia that I had cancer, and in the U.S. something else," Norman said. "I am fine now."

Norman finished atop the 1995 money list with a record $1.6 million, but he was robbed of the Vardon Trophy, awarded for the lowest stroke average (his was 69.06), on a technicality. Under the rules any player who withdraws in midround becomes ineligible for the award, and, by failing to complete the second round of the Heritage Classic with a back injury, Norman had disqualified himself. But there were compensations. His Australian Open victory was his first in his own country for five years. His peers voted him Player of the Year, he appeared in sepia tone on the cover of *Men's Journal* describing his life as a business tycoon, *Golf World* voted him Man of the Year, and *Golf Australia* devoted an entire issue to him.

In the early days, when Norman was taking his first tentative steps toward fame and independence, Laura was involved in every business decision. She answered all the fan mail and fielded all the phone calls. "I remember the day that Greg said he needed a secretary," she says. "I said, 'Oh, no, I don't want us to get that big.' And I fought it every step of the way, expanding, I guess. I liked the way things were."

Now, with Williams's help, Norman was expanding Great White Shark Enterprises, Inc., into a multifaceted corporation with a worldwide staff of forty-three, but Laura was still consulted on every crucial move. "He trusts her like nobody else," Norton says. "And I think any of the crunch-type decisions, he would always get her input on."

"REPORTS CAME IN FROM AUSTRALIA THAT I HAD CANCER, AND IN THE U.S. SOMETHING ELSE," NORMAN SAID. "I AM FINE NOW."

In an article entitled "Team Norman," Australia's *Sun-Herald* discussed Norman's growing entourage, people like Navarro, Draovitch, Stuve, Flash, and John Cott, an IMG chauffeur. "He's just weeded out people he's not comfortable with," Laura said.

Norman had approached Frank Williams about running Great White Shark Enterprises shortly before he left IMG. They had been good friends since 1977, and Williams had the added advantage of having absorbed IMG's knowledge while managing to avoid being cast in their mold. Born in England, he had pulled himself up by his bootstraps, starting out as a post office clerk and then selling fish on the King's Road in London. Later he migrated to Australia and worked for Electrolux, before buying a 50 percent share in the Australian Masters in 1980, developing the concept, selling it to IMG, and ultimately heading their Melbourne office.

"Frank has wonderful skills with people," Norman told Bernie McGuire in *Australian Golf Digest*. "He's very loyal." But he acknowledged that "because of our friendship, I've probably been a little bit harder on Frank than anyone else in life."

Williams gives a wry smile. "If he ever sees the error of his ways, he's always been the first to apologize," he says, "which is something I find very difficult. But he has got a temper. It'll take a long time to build, but when it comes to a crescendo—God! I could always make him angry if I didn't keep him informed on something or I made the mistake of thinking it's not important enough for him to know. He hates that, hates it with a passion. So our differences of opinion—and there have been a few—are usually a lack of communication, sometimes caused by him being so damn busy and giving me ten minutes when he should give me an hour. He's always on the go. He lives life at a hundred miles an hour. Never stops. . . . I wouldn't be him for the world. But he doesn't complain about it. He just gets on with it."

Asked if he considered Norman a principled person, he said cautiously, "On some things."

To Norman, no attribute in life is more valuable than loyalty, and friends and employees found to be lacking in it are ruthlessly expelled from his circle. "I'm so much better now because I control my entire office," he says. "People that work for you, you sign their paychecks and you have the loyalty, you have the trust. I'm extremely loyal to people. I'll throw a blanket over people and give them anything they want if they just show me the loyalty back."

In the eighties Norman used to fall asleep in business meetings, bored rigid by the plotting and planning he paid others to do. When one or two expensive mistakes were made with his money, he began to sit up and pay attention. He found, to his surprise, that he loved high-risk wheeling and dealing, loved to spend days threshing out deals over boardroom tables, loved dreaming of taking his company to "the next level." Gradually, he learned to trust his instincts. The Cobra gamble paid off handsomely, and the Greg Norman Collection—the clothing company that grew out of his deal with Reebok but is now separate—is riding lucratively on the coattails of the Tommy Hilfiger, Ralph Lauren sportswear-as-fashion boom, to the tune of some $200 million in annual sales by 1996. Even his cars were big business.

"I have one Ferrari I drive, the others are for investment," Norman told the *Sunday Express* in 1989. "People say I should invest in art. Bull. I understand art, not paintings. Instead of Mona Lisas on the wall, I have Ferraris in the garage."

"His father is very clever and Greg's become that way," Toini Norman says. "Even Greg himself says that he's more like his father these days."

"To me, he was always what we call street-smart," Norton says. "In the case of his Ferrari collection, he had a knack for knowing when it was the right time to buy, and it's a very fickle sort of market. He wasn't a classic businessman, traditionally trained, or what you would call a great business mind, but he had wonderful savvy."

IN THE EIGHTIES NORMAN USED TO FALL ASLEEP IN BUSINESS MEETINGS, BORED RIGID BY THE PLOTTING AND PLANNING HE PAID OTHERS TO DO.

Norman agreed. "I'm not saying that I'm some Harvard Business graduate," he told McGuire. "I'm not anything. But all the people I've got to know on Wall Street, well, I would say that the majority of them are street-smart. They're not Harvard graduates. They've learned the hard way."

He told McGuire that Kerry Packer had given him "a wonderful piece of advice in 1985 or 1986 [when] I was asked to get involved with a business. I knew he was in the media. I walked into his office and said, 'K. P.? I need to see you. I've had this proposition. Someone has asked me to be the figurehead of something, and I'm really not too sure about it.' K. P. said, 'Son, you keep out of my business and I'll keep out of your business.' I said, 'K. P., that's all I needed to hear.' "

"There is no doubt in my mind that Greg will end up as a billionaire . . . because he's very innovative," Williams says. "A classic example is when we bought the sod farm. We were just walking around and he said, 'Isn't it silly, we build golf courses, but we buy the sod from another company. Why don't we buy our own sod farm?' So I went up to Avon Park, Florida, got the world rights to [Australian turf farmer] Hugh Whiting's grass and re-named it GN-1. Then we used it at the Medalist [Norman's first U.S. course, codesigned with Pete Dye in Hobe Sound, Florida] as a marketing ploy. Currently, we can't buy enough of it."

It is successes like these that have helped to quadruple Norman's fortune in the four years since he left IMG. In 1995 he made a reported $11 million in endorsements alone. Along with the Shark Shootout in California (which has raised more than $10 million for charity), he has the Greg Norman Holden International (formerly Classic) in Sydney and his own boat-building company, Norman's Yachts, Inc. He has more than twenty-five course design projects either open or under development, each of which pays him one million dollars. Two days after the 1997 BellSouth Classic was held at the TPC at Sugarloaf—his 7,259-yard Atlanta design—his office received eighteen requests for course designs.

"The homage is unmistakable," *Golf World* said of Sugarloaf. "It's Augusta National-meets-Royal Melbourne." Ron Whitten concluded, "It could be the best thing to emerge from the hills of Atlanta since Bobby Jones."

"Greg is just a product now of twenty-five years of hard work," Grady says.

"He's an excellent businessman," Crow says. "He has the same focus in business as he has in golf. He has the same energy."

But Marshall was not alone in believing that Norman's blossoming empire and extracurricular pursuits had detracted from his focus on the golf course. "He knows that, rightly or wrongly, to be judged at the top level of golf, you have got to be successful in the majors, and I think that to achieve that you've got to be single-minded. For somebody like Greg, who has always been incredibly materialistic, who has always wanted to be in the limelight, it is difficult to bring all of your energies to bear and shut out all that other stuff and concentrate on winning."

"I guess at some stage you make a choice about whether you want to fly all over the world, building golf courses and running huge businesses, or whether you just play golf," Clayton says. "Faldo just wants to play golf, it seems to me. I'm sure he does some of the other stuff, but golf is a major priority, whereas with Greg, I'm not sure golf is a priority. But how do you criticize the guy for not being so one-dimensional—he's got no room in his life for anything else?"

As his empire has grown, the size of Norman's toy collection has increased proportionately. By the end of 1996 his Internet site was declaring that he had no idea how many Ferraris he owned (it was believed to be six). He also possessed a custom-built $18 million Gulfstream IV jet, a $4 million Bell 230 twin-engine helicopter, his eighty-seven-foot fishing yacht *Aussi Rules*, a couple of smaller boats, three Harleys, two Jet Skis, a Rolls Royce, a Bentley, a Mercedes, and six Chevrolet Suburbans, not to

Speed merchant: Norman tests the horsepower on his beloved Harley Davidson. (Allsport)

mention the mansion with housekeeper, house manager, groundskeeper, etc., on Jupiter Island, Florida. The scale of his wealth and his perceived flaunting of it had a lot to do with the envy and hostility he aroused on the Australian and U.S. circuits.

"I've never wanted to be the guy with the most on the block," Norman insists, "contrary to all this bullshit you read about Greg Norman."

When it is pointed out to him that he certainly seems to have the most on the block, he snaps, " 'Course I've got a lot, but that's not what I wanted. I've got a lot because I worked damn hard on the golf course and I was pretty smart with some of my business decisions. Yeah, I've got a lot, I'm not denying that, but it was not my sole objective in life to go out and get money."

"No one has the right to judge you on how you spend your money," Laura says flatly. "Greg has probably been a little more extravagant than most golfers. He loves spending money on wonderful things and he loves having beautiful things around him. He's always had a suite when he went some place, where other people would stay in a cheap hotel. It's just the way he is and he can afford it and he's put down for it. When he first got a helicopter, he'd fly to tournaments and people would say, 'Well, it's okay for Arnold but it's ridiculous for Greg.' Well, Greg could afford it, so it wasn't ridiculous. Yet people would make a judgment on what was right or wrong, with how he should spend his money. I think it comes down to jealousy."

Norman agrees wholeheartedly. He still sees himself as the same blue-eyed country boy he was at seventeen. "People are very jealous of what I've got. You read about [how] I own all these Ferraris and two helicopters and planes and a house over here and a house over there. I don't have two helicopters, I have one. I don't have six Ferraris, I have four. I have Harleys. But I enjoy them. Is there anything wrong with that?"

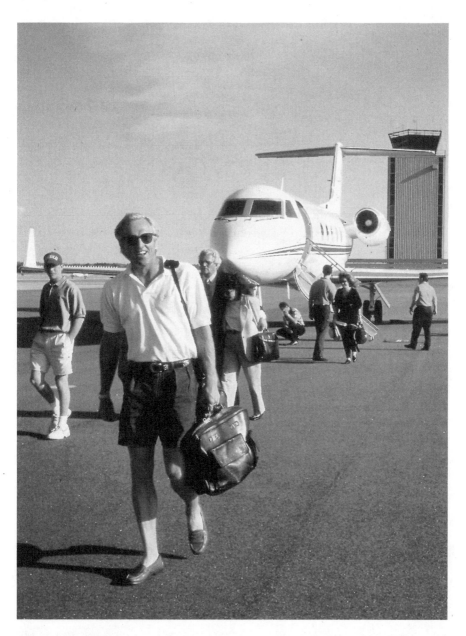

Jetsetter: The Shark and his entourage arrive at Augusta [Frank Williams is at his left shoulder]. (© Phil Sheldon)

14

DEATH IN THE
AFTERNOON

"People who talk about choking under pressure have no idea
how many things can go wrong on a golf course besides nerves
and fear."

Arnold Palmer

The fairways of Augusta National dropped away from the clubhouse in an
unblemished emerald wave, curving treacherously around the tall, spare
pines and the fuchsia splash of azaleas in the dark pools. It was early, but already the crowds were taking up their positions. Craned forward at Amen
Corner or lolling under the pines, they were dotted decoratively around the
course in that half-languorous, half-tense attitude peculiar to Augusta galleries, in any position that might afford a view of what promised to be one of
the greatest final rounds in history.

Even the hardest-boiled newspapermen agreed: Justice had never
seemed so poetic. Greg Norman, whose ardent, unrequited infatuation with
Augusta had survived some of the most wicked injustices in memory, was
leading by six strokes going into the final round of the 1996 Masters. In the
dim distance was his old adversary Nick Faldo. Phil Mickelson, now saddled
with that unfortunate tag—"the best player in the world not to have won a
major"—was lying third, and everyone else was too far back to figure.

"If I have one dream left in golf, it's to win at Augusta," Norman had
said two years earlier. "If I told you different I'd be lying, not only to you but
to myself. I love everything about the tournament: the golf course, the way

they run it, everything. It feels different than any other tournament in the world, and I've been so close to winning it that I'd be very disappointed if I didn't someday win it. But I honestly believe I've got a lot more chances to do it."

Out on the range Norman felt nervous, but as he later told Laura, "It was the right kind of nervous." He didn't feel the curious deadness that had come over him at St. Andrews in 1990, and he didn't feel as jittery and nauseous as he had at Turnberry in 1986. He felt hopeful and relaxed. Watching him, Harmon thought his ballstriking was almost perfect. A constant stream of people came up to wish Norman the best. "Enjoy yourself," Williams told him. Among the pile of good-luck notes in his locker was one from Price, "Go out and win by twelve," his friend had written. Frank Nobilo smilingly said the same thing. Norman's mouth twitched. "I'd rather have a two-stroke lead than a six-stroke lead," he told the New Zealander.

EVERYWHERE HE TURNED THERE WERE CONSTANT REMINDERS THAT HIS FAMILY, FRIENDS, AND A MILLION SPECTATORS WERE DEPENDING ON HIM TO DO HIMSELF JUSTICE.

In a way there were too many well-wishers, too many people piling their expectations on his shoulders. Everywhere he turned there were constant reminders that his family, friends, and a million spectators were depending on him to do himself justice. He tried reading *Popular Mechanics* but couldn't take in a word. There was no escape—not even in the bathroom. There, he had run into Peter Dobereiner, the ailing golf writer, who had always been one of his biggest supporters. "Not even you can fuck this up now, Greg," Dobereiner said teasingly.

Greg Norman was contemplating catastrophe, and it didn't faze him in the least. In about ten minutes all the trophies, fame, and Ferraris in the world would not be able to save him as his million–dollar swing exploded

Norman treads water as part of his brief naval training (Colorific/Robert Beck)

into pieces, but somehow Norman was not in the slightest bit perturbed. He fixed his gaze on the horizon and listened calmly to the voice that had entered his consciousness.

"Uh, Greg, we've got a little problem," said Lt. Maris "Weasel" Luters.

After a day of training, during which he had emerged with flying colors from the ejector-seat test, the water parachute drag, and the full-gear water tread, Norman was one hundred miles out of San Diego and seven thousand feet above the U.S. Navy carrier *Carl Vinson* in an F-14. Weasel, his top-gun pilot, was alerting him to the fact that the flaps wouldn't go down. It was looking ominous for them. Without the flaps it would be impossible to slow the jet sufficiently for it to hit the deck of the carrier safely, and they would have to make an emergency landing at a nearby runway. At the last possible second the flaps released and they made it to the ship. Afterward, Norman was asked if he had been afraid. "Oh, no," he said. "It just meant we got to look at the sunset longer."

At forty-one, when the average man is beginning to realize that it isn't necessary to be the first one off at the lights, Norman's relish for gut-wrenching, adrenaline-spewing activities was increasing daily. He stroked bull sharks sleeping in underwater caves; drove at 190 miles per hour in Lamborghini Diablos on desert highways; hugged the wall at 180 miles per hour in Roger Penske Indy Cars; and ran out of oxygen eighty-eight feet below the sea and rose to the surface no faster than his own bubbles, suffering from only a mild case of the bends. "Greg likes to stand right on the edge of the cliff," Elkington said.

Another favorite Norman pastime was to fly his Bell Jet Ranger helicopter—pitch-black with the word *Shark* in gold lettering on the side—at high speeds at low altitudes or weave it through the Everglades. "He has a qualified pilot with him, but he scares the heck out of some of the people who fly with him," Gary Stuve reports.

Nonetheless, Norman hotly denies that he has ever undertaken any activity that might result in death or serious injury. "I would never put myself in a position where I would be jeopardizing my life," he says categorically. "Never ever. Never have, never will. There's not one thing that I do that's dangerous. Now, when I went diving with sharks I had a cage. I wasn't out there being Mr. Macho Man saying I can swim with great whites. I was in a controlled environment. When I go up in a fighter jet, I'm in a controlled environment because I know that that pilot's not going to kill himself. Go check my driving record. I enjoy driving fast, but that doesn't mean to say that every time I get in a vehicle I drive at one hundred miles an hour. No. Roger Penske invited me to drive an Indy Car at the racetrack. I got in there and I put that pedal flat. But you couldn't hurt yourself even if you spun out because it's got protection. And I'm not the type of driver who goes beyond my capabilities. There's never been a situation, I can honestly say, where I've jeopardized my life or anybody else's."

In contrast Norman was finally learning to throttle back on the golf course, to use his vast resources more intelligently and manage his game more professionally. When the core of his driver caved in shortly before the final round at Doral, he called Laura and had her rush a pile of clubs to him in his helicopter. He selected a titanium-headed Cobra and played his way coolly and methodically to a two-stroke victory. "Greg is where he is now because of maturity and learning from mistakes," said Harmon, who had checked Norman's swing for the first time since the previous August. "He is more aware of his capabilities and not so gung ho about always hitting the perfect shot. He has learned how to come down the stretch and win."

Standing in the sunshine with Norman minutes before the start of the final round at Augusta, Harmon had no idea that those words would come back to haunt him. He watched the balls climb sweetly into the blue and savored the fruits of their hard work. There had been a few small hitches. They had fallen out briefly over, among other things, Harmon's general unavailability, and Norman had missed back-to-back cuts at Bay Hill and The Players Championship. But they made up, and Norman bounced back the way only Norman could, with more heart and fight than ever. Harmon watched Norman's square brown hands clip another ball off the manicured turf of the practice range. He was, Harmon thought, as ready as he ever would be.

Every April, Norman walked out onto the clubhouse lawn, where Green Jackets and ordinary folk basked in the spring air and tucked into clam chowder and toasted tuna sandwiches, and fell in love with Augusta all over again. He even loved the color of it. "It's the only pure golf tournament we play in," he told reporters on Tuesday. "It's just pure golf. Over the years, you get to know the people and where they sit. You see the same face at the corner of sixteen, off the seventeenth green, on eighteen. Those are the type of traditions that you really love to play with and understand."

Everybody knew Norman's feelings about Augusta, how much the Green Jacket would mean to him. In *Augusta: Home of the Masters Tournament*, a club member tells author Steve Eubanks, "I remember one time I was sitting on a golf cart with my green jacket on and Greg Norman popped out of the club and said, 'Sir, may I say something? I want you to know this is the greatest golf tournament in the world.' "

Asked about his game since the two missed cuts—the first time in his career he had missed successive cuts in the United States—he said his only problem was mental. "I think there's times when you just get tired," he explained, managing, despite this, to radiate an uncharacteristic aura of tranquillity and goodwill. "You go at it hard and sometimes you wake up on the thirty-first of December and think, 'My God, I've got to get through it all again.' But that's part of life." He smiled.

"Someone wrote that everyone in life tries to overcome fear," said a reporter. "We are driven by fear. What is your fear?"

"Well," replied Norman pleasantly, "one of my great motivations in life is the fear of failure. I like the idea of pushing myself to success, you know. And the way you push yourself to success is that you don't want to fail."

On Wednesday, Norman woke up with his work-stressed back hurting so badly that he was hardly able to take the club back. "He was just so frustrated," Laura said. "It hadn't happened to him in forever. He kept saying, 'Why now, of all times?' " But Fred Couples sent over his back therapist, Tom Boers, and by the following day, Norman felt like a million dollars. On a glorious spring morning he pushed himself to the most perfect first round of his Masters career, making nine birdies in a 63 that tied Nick Price's ten-year-old course record. It was his first opening score in the 60s at Augusta since 1981 and it was, as the *New York Times* put it, "the stuff of dreams."

For the first six holes Norman had made nothing but pars and a familiar tightness crept into his jaw. Then the ball started to roll for him. He was wearing an elegant cream shirt, striped sweater, and black pants, and when the crowd showed its appreciation as his 220-yard four-iron shot flew out of the woods on fourteen and landed three feet from the hole, he laughed delightedly, bowed, and doffed his hat.

Afterward he described it as one of the best rounds of his life. "It was one of those things where I just let it flow," beamed Norman, who was leading by two strokes over Mickelson and four over Hoch and Tway. "You just try to keep the momentum going that's within you. You don't let it get away from you and get too excited about it. I am happy and excited, but there's a long way to go."

The most striking aspect of Norman's performance was his composure. He was as tranquil as a Zen student trimming a bonsai tree. When gusting winds sent putts scurrying off Augusta's concrete greens on the second day, he simply "factored in" the new conditions and responded with a 69 on a day when the stroke average of the field rose to 74.43. He now led by four over Faldo and was six in front of Mickelson and Frost. "I'm very relaxed, very comfortable within myself," he said. "I'm feeling good and looking forward to the weekend."

THE MOST STRIK-ING ASPECT OF NORMAN'S PER-FORMANCE WAS HIS COMPOSURE. HE WAS AS TRANQUIL AS A ZEN STUDENT TRIMMING A BONSAI TREE.

On Saturday, Faldo entered the equation, but not even he could upset Norman's equilibrium. "Greg's going really well and I'm just trying to catch him," the Englishman had said after a second-round 67, but in the third round nothing went his way. His face clouded, his Harrison Ford fringe flopped over his eyes, and he slumped to a 73. He wasn't the unbeatable giant he had been when he went head-to-head with Norman at St. Andrews. An affair with twenty-one-year-old Arizona golfer Brenna Cepelak, a multimillion-dollar divorce, and the worst dustbin-digging excesses of the tabloids had left Faldo battered and bruised, and he hadn't contended in a major for two years.

Norman maintained his serenity even when his approach to the short twelfth was snatched by the wind and deposited on the bank between the front bunker and Rae's Creek. "I never got mad because I hit the shot solid," Norman explained. "It'd be a different story if I hit a bad shot. Then it would be, 'Why did you make a stupid mistake like that?' " Instead, he walked calmly back to eighty-one yards—a distance from which, for reasons known only to himself, he claimed he had hit fifty thousand practice shots—and hit a sand wedge to ten yards for a lucky bogey. His eventual 71 left him at 203, thirteen under par, six strokes ahead of Faldo and seven ahead of Mickelson. Scott McCarron, Frost, and Duffy Waldorf were a remote fourth at 212.

Afterward, Faldo gave the predictable "Anything's possible with the heat on at Augusta" press conference, and Norman gave the predictable "I'm just going to go out tomorrow and play as if we're all on the same number" speech. He seemed very contented and at ease. He was, as Harmon said, "finally at peace with Augusta."

When Greg Norman was named Player of the Year in 1995, he told *Golf World* that he had an actual written list of things he still wanted to achieve: trek the Himalayas, dive under the polar ice cap of Antarctica, fly in the space shuttle, cruise down the Amazon, land a jet on an aircraft carrier. Norman loves lists. On his Internet site were his seven favorite dives, ranked according to beauty, water quality, or degree of difficulty, and the four he was planning to get to—Truk Lagoon, Micronesia, the Red Sea, and Antarctica. In *Golf* magazine's column, "One Man's Total," Norman claimed that he had flown 275,600 miles in 1995, used four drivers in his career, dived to 180 feet, beaten 7,000 practice balls most weeks, and hit a tee shot 483 yards on the eighteenth hole of the King's Course at Gleneagles during an exhibition.

"Life, to him, is a checklist," Rick Reilly says. "Fly F-14 jet—check; pat shark at the bottom of ocean—check. You wonder if he ever stops and says, 'That was wonderful. I enjoyed that.'"

At the top of Norman's checklist was victory at the Masters. And there was no reason he couldn't achieve it. Only Nicklaus had a higher top-ten-finish percentage on the PGA Tour (53 percent to Norman's 49 percent). When the inevitable "karma" question was asked in the Shark's pre-tournament interview, he said he believed things happened the way they are meant to. "Sometimes you don't feel like you've got a chance to win or somebody else is running away with it and, boom, something happens and turns the whole game around just by the bounce of a ball. Why does the ball bounce that way? Those type of things you think about and reflect on. They all even out in the long run."

On Sunday morning Norman and Faldo stood on the first tee at Augusta, each lost in his own thoughts. It was hard not to feel that karma was at work, that it was finally balancing things out for its most ill-used golfer. Up on the clubhouse lawn, Crenshaw was talking to the television cameras. "He's battling a lot of demons right now," he speculated about Norman's frame of mind. "All third-round leaders battle those demons. He's said many, many times that he wants to win this one. He's prepared, his mind looks very strong. We'll see."

On the first hole Norman proceeded to pull his drive and make bogey from a greenside bunker. It was an unfortunate start, but he didn't seem rattled. He hit a beautiful chip to a couple of inches to match Faldo's birdie on the second, and they were off. Norman saved par at the third, bogeyed from the bunker at the fourth, and parred the sixth while Faldo birdied. At the par-five eighth, Norman pulled his three-wood second thirty yards left into the pines. The gallery muttered uneasily. Grimly, Norman gritted it out for par, his mouth a hard white line. Faldo birdied.

Settling down to watch the telecast in a hotel hundreds of miles away, Grady felt a sense of shock as the camera panned in on Norman, standing on the ninth tee with a three-shot lead. "You could see in his face then that he was in trouble."

Rodger Davis, who was in Bali doing a corporate day, experienced exactly the same feeling of dismay. "There're not many things I'd feel sorry for Norman about, because he's made so much money and all this, but when it came on TV and I saw his face, I thought, 'I don't believe this.' He was on the eighth and he was still four in front but you could see it in his face. . . . And his expression didn't change all day."

Trevino once observed that hard hitters like Norman needed to learn to gear down in the closing rounds at Augusta. "Once they start tucking those flags in back, you have got to sneak up on them. . . . The problem with a hard hitter is he's got to fly the ball past the hole all the time. When they put them in back, you're a dead man."

Norman was conscious only of his dwindling lead and Faldo's relentless march. On the ninth fairway he fired a ninety-eight-yard wedge shot at a pin perched on a knoll as slippery as ice. Faldo was safely on the green, some thirty-five feet away. Norman's ball paused for a split second, then spun back twenty yards down the hill. There was a little gasp from the gallery, and he seemed visibly to shrink. Faldo two-putted for par and Norman bogeyed. Two strokes separated them at the turn.

"The reason Nick Faldo is such a wonderful player is because he doesn't really care about being in there three feet," Edwards says. "He's going to put it in there where he's not going to make bogey. He won the British Open with eighteen pars which, God bless him, is how you play the game. The ninth hole at the Masters was a typical example. He didn't care that he was thirty-five feet by. He'll take his four. 'Go ahead and make your mistake. Oh, you just did.' "

AT THE TENTH WILLIAMS WAS RUSHING NUMBLY DOWN THE HILL IN THE SULTRY HEAT, PANICKING ABOUT LAURA. "SHE'S A WRECK," HE SAID. HE WASN'T DOING TOO WELL HIMSELF.

"There're certain things you've just got to do at Augusta," Rodger Davis says. "Greg is a good enough player to do them, but I think at times all he sees is the flag."

At the tenth Williams was rushing numbly down the hill in the sultry heat, panicking about Laura. "She's a wreck," he said. He wasn't doing too well himself. He covered his eyes as Norman missed his seventh green of the day, hit a weak chip to ten feet, and missed the putt. Faldo made a comfortable par. At the eleventh Norman's fourteen-footer for birdie rimmed the hole. His hand shielded his white frozen face. He missed the three-foot return and made another bogey. He and Faldo were now tied.

A sportswriter sidled up to Williams, who had separated himself from the clammy, nervous crowd and was standing beside a pine tree with his head in his hands. "How do you feel around now?" he asked cheerfully. Williams tried to disguise a murderous glare. "Great," he said. "I have every confidence." Crestfallen, the reporter scurried away. "Christ," Williams said. "How does he think I feel?"

He walked over to Laura and Morgan-Leigh, who were clinging to each other on the rise above the short twelfth like the hypnotized witnesses of a car crash. Below them, Norman pushed his tee shot into the water. He took a double bogey to Faldo's par. Wordlessly, Williams wrapped his arm around Laura. Norman's face had become a mask of pain. He drove woodenly into the pines on the thirteenth. A funereal silence cloaked the gallery, now in no doubt that they were helpless bystanders at the total disintegration of a champion's psyche. "I feel sick to my stomach," one spectator said. Another compared it to watching Old Yeller die.

In the locker room, Price turned away from the television, picked up his car keys, and drove to the airport. "I couldn't watch," he says. "I knew how much the Masters meant to Greg. I knew what was happening and I didn't want to see it."

"It was devastating," Harmon recalls. "I walked around with Laura and Morgan-Leigh, and it was one of those things where, as you watched it happen, you couldn't believe it. The man had played so well for three rounds. He just had such total control, not only of his swing but of his emotions. He had done everything right, and to see it all start to come apart was very difficult for a teacher to watch. More difficult for the hurt that not only he was going through, but his family was."

"I FEEL SICK TO MY STOMACH," ONE SPECTATOR SAID. ANOTHER COMPARED IT TO WATCHING OLD YELLER DIE.

Watching from the sidelines as Navarro persuaded Norman to lay up at thirteen, Leadbetter was eerily perky. "His routine has changed by six or seven seconds," he commented. "He's gripping the club and regripping it. He can't get comfortable." Faldo, his own pupil, was a textbook study on how to stay calm and play smart in the pressure-cooker environment of Augusta's back nine. He hit the best shot he had hit all week, a 215-yard two-iron, to the heart of the green and matched Norman's eventual birdie.

"We talked about this last night," Leadbetter said breezily. "I told him, 'Nobody's shot a low number to win the Masters since you came from five behind to beat Raymond Floyd in 1990.' "

Minute by minute the life seemed to be ebbing from Norman's body. At the fifteenth his two-hundred-yard six-iron tilted toward the water but stayed up. Jaw clenched, Norman chipped for eagle. He put everything into it. His whole being seemed to center on the hole, to will the ball toward it. Twenty thousand people held their breath as it rolled across the shiny green and slid tantalizingly close to the hole. Then it stopped cold, inches short. Norman, his putter raised in silent prayer, his face contorted with agony, fell to his knees, arched backward, and collapsed on the green.

"I hit the most perfect shot," he says now. "I put all my energies into it. I visualized it. Everything I know that I'm good at—feel, not executing till you're ready to go. And then when it didn't go in, I thought: 'Oh, shit.' Then Faldo hit a great shot, too, so I didn't even make up a shot. So that's when I

DEATH IN THE AFTERNOON

knew. And the next shot [at sixteen] was indicative of the emotions going out of my system."

From that point on Norman was, in Riley's words, "a dead man walking." On the sixteenth tee his hands fidgeted, fussed, and clenched the club like an executioner on his first day at the job. In a misguided attempt to pull off a miracle, he hooked his six-iron tee shot into the water. The resulting double bogey left him four strokes behind, tottering blindly up the closing holes, gaunt with suffering.

Faldo looked shell-shocked himself. What should have been his finest hour had become tainted and yet, as he walked up the eighteenth, acknowledging, with the smallest of waves, the muted applause of the crowd, it is hard to imagine another player reacting with more humility, compassion, or grace. Always portrayed as a cold fish—socially inept and mechanical—Faldo showed a degree of humanity in victory that brought tears to the eyes of the gallery. After holing a birdie putt on the last for a 67 to Norman's 78, he put his arms around his weary opponent and held him for a minute. "I don't know what to say," he told Norman, "I just want to give you a hug."

Afterward, Faldo stumbled toward the cameras, choking on his words. "From ten, eleven on, it was so nerve-wracking it was unbelievable, so emotional . . ."

Norman was already headed toward his fifty-second, second-place press conference, an affair of such dignity that Bobby Jones would have been hard-pressed to beat it. Throughout it all Norman was philosophical, candidly admitting that he "played like shit. . . . Call it what you want to call it, but I put all the blame on myself. . . . My thought pattern was good, but my rhythm was out." He then used gentle humor to explain the worst collapse in major championship history.

"Greg, is it humanly possible not to dwell on a day like this, at least for a while?" someone asked.

Norman smiled thinly. "Watch," he said.

He glanced up at the television screen, on which Crenshaw was helping Faldo into his third emerald blazer. "God, I'd love to be putting the Green Jacket on," he said, "but life's going to continue. I'm sad about it. I'm going to regret it. I've let this one slip away and I've let others slip away. But it's not the end of my life. I'll continue to win golf tournaments. I'm not going to fall off the face of the earth because of what happened here."

Asked if he felt like screaming, he said softly, "I don't know how I could ever convince you guys that I know I screwed up today, but it's not the end of the world for me. It's really not. I've got forty million bucks. . . .

"I AM UPSET INSIDE, BUT I'M NOT GOING TO RUN AROUND AND BE LIKE A DENNIS RODMAN AND HEAD-BUTT AN OFFICIAL. I'M NOT THAT WAY."

If I had won today and all those other championships, my life might be totally different. But I didn't win. I am upset inside, but I'm not going to run around and be like a Dennis Rodman and head-butt an official. I'm not that way. I respect the game of golf we play. I love the game of golf. It's given me a lot and it's going to give me a lot more."

"I honestly, genuinely feel sorry for him," said Faldo, who hoped that this victory would be remembered for his performance rather than Norman's loss. "What he has been through is horrible. If it had happened to me like that . . ." His voice trailed off. "Greg's a great player, a great competitor, he really is. He's a great guy, too. He's a credit to the game, and the game needs him out there all the time. I think he's fantastic. The man's got the drive and the commitment, and he'll be back."

Harmon waited anxiously in the locker room for Norman. He had walked off the course when the Shark hit his tee shot in the water at sixteen, unable to take any more. "When he came in, I just went up to him and put my arms around him and said, 'Greg, I can't tell you how bad I feel and how sorry I am for you.' And he said, 'Butchy, I just didn't have it today. My good shots weren't good enough and my bad shots were pitiful.' And that was pretty much it."

When it was all over, Norman drove out to the airport to board his jet. He was deeply touched that a small group of supporters had come to offer words of comfort and to praise him for his sportsmanship in defeat. He stood with them for a few minutes, signing photographs and chatting quietly. Then he climbed slowly up the steps to the aircraft, where his devastated family and friends were waiting. He looked at their pale, sad faces. "I'm sorry I let you all down," Norman said.

When they took off, Norman had a beer and talked to Laura. Somewhere over Florida the mists closed in on him. "Sorry for drifting off for a minute," he said to Laura. "Greg, you drifted off for over half an hour," she told him gently.

When the plane touched down at West Palm Beach, they stayed on board and got deliriously drunk. "Greg felt disappointed for us, and we felt disappointed for him, and nobody really knew what was going on or how anybody felt," Laura recalls. "We sat there for hours on the tarmac in the plane, just talking. Greg needed the support of the people around him. The loss was disappointing, of course. I know how badly Greg wanted to win the Masters. But he accepted it so much better than everybody else. I was very angry with a couple of the reporters, the way they described it like it was a funeral in our family. You know, we have such a good perspective on what's really important, and although a golf tournament is important, it isn't as important as the things that are going on in the world, people dying, people getting sick. As bad as everybody felt, we didn't think it was the end of the world."

After the agony came the dissection. In Britain, under the heading "Norman's Chokes," the *Independent* documented the seven times the Shark had led a major going into the last day, winning only the 1986 Open. The *Augusta Chronicle*, the paper that helped create Norman's heroic nickname, used it against him on Monday. "Shark Skinned," screamed a banner headline. Murray, the columnist who eulogized him when he finished fourth in his first Masters, told his readers, "There's only one golfer on the planet that can regularly beat Greg Norman in a major tournament. That's Greg Norman." The *Philadelphia Inquirer* said that the life had leaked right out of Norman. "And if you took any pleasure at all in witnessing that, then your heart is as hard as a tombstone." *Golf Digest* compared it to other catastrophic collapses—Snead's eight on the seventy-second hole of the 1939 U.S. Open and Palmer's "bizarre unhinging" in the 1966 U.S. Open when he squandered a seven-stroke lead in nine holes. In the *Times*, Mel Webb wrote, "Norman seems to be a man specially selected by Kismet to be its stool-pigeon."

Most players felt for him from the bottom of their hearts, but Chi Chi Rodriguez believed that Norman's collapse was "God's way of punishing him for what he did to Mark McCumber. I don't think you ought to destroy a man's character that way."

Callahan thought the epilogue to the Masters was more curious than the tournament. "In the pressroom postmortem, the fifth word out of Norman's mouth was scatological. But the news that went out was how 'classy' he was. 'He's a real man,' said the man from *Sports Illustrated*. 'He is more a man for it,' wrote the man from the *New York Times*. So manliness got a good going-over into the bargain. Be a man. Take it like a man. . . . A minority in the audience thought Norman took it too much like a man, too blithely anyway. His eerie smile bothered them."

On Sunday night, hours after the tournament, Norman and Laura went walking along the beach in Hobe Sound. They tried to discuss what had happened, but little came of it. "Never in my career have I experienced what happened between the tenth and fifteenth holes of Augusta last year," Norman told *Golf* the next season. "I was totally out of control. And I couldn't understand it."

"That was his worst disaster, that one," Thomson says. "There was no excuse for that, and there was no excuse of ill luck for that one. He did that himself. He just held on too tight. He has a faith in strength, whereas the real golfer is the opposite. The reason Hogan took about forty-five waggles before he ever hit a shot was to get the lightest possible grip of the club and still have it under control. He was about 180 degrees from where Greg was at Augusta. [Greg] was trying to hang on tighter and tighter in the mistaken belief that that would get him where he wanted to go. And that was his downfall. When I watched him, he was trying to crush the club. It's a wonder the shaft didn't buckle. That was the worst thing that ever happened."

When *choking*—the ugliest word in the language and the cruelest, a word denoting cowardice and chronic fear of victory—was held up as the cause of Norman's demise, Thomson refused to accept that Norman might have been eaten alive by nerves: "He's never lost because he's been afraid, which is what choking's about. That's absolutely untrue. There was never that. But he had a faith in, I think, the wrong things, like hanging on tight and using strength."

"You can't win seventy-one tournaments and be a choker," Price said flatly. "You can't win ten tournaments and be a choker. I can tell you the guys on tour who are the chokers. They are the guys who are good players but they've won two tournaments in their whole careers. Something stops them playing well under pressure, and whether that's guts or that they're afraid of success . . . Those guys are the chokers."

To Price, Norman simply lost confidence and never recovered it. "But again, when he started playing poorly, he could have started playing more conservatively."

"Greg does all right until the head comes off and the turnip goes on," Newton told *Golf Digest*. "I don't think it's bad luck. He's had some bad breaks but you make your own luck, I think. Technically, there isn't much wrong either. The biggest flaw in his game is his course management. The bottom line is, it sucks."

"Well, of course, Norman has got an awful lot of talent," Middlecoff told *Australian Golf Digest*. "But he hasn't got a whole lot of sense, I don't think, about golf. . . . What he did at Augusta this year was unbelievably bad. There are about eight or ten places on that golf course, no matter what the weather conditions, you avoid. He just made every mistake that he could make."

But sports psychologist Dr. Bob Rotella felt that to victory-motivated players, like Norman and Palmer, losing by one stroke or twenty makes no difference. "A lot of the world has trouble understanding that, because most people are embarrassed to death about shooting a high number. A guy like [Norman], he wants to win or he doesn't care. They're the kind of guys who couldn't live with themselves if they didn't go for the flag."

Everyone was an expert with an opinion. Teacher and television commentator Peter Kostis thought that Norman would benefit from a ball with a lower spin rate. Johnny Miller said there were twenty-five ways Norman could have won, but he chose the one way he could lose. Others felt that Faldo was a crucial factor. Faldo agreed. "The key was for me to play with him on Sunday. If you're right there, then he can really keep a close eye on things."

Harmon thought the eleventh, where Norman hit two perfect shots and a near-perfect putt and made bogey, was the turning point. "That, to me, was when all the air just went out of him." Callahan believed the twelfth, where Norman "went for the pin . . . which small children know not to do," was a classic miscalculation. "That's when 'good old match play' kicked in. That's when Janet Leigh went back into the shower."

"The question is, was Greg Norman playing 'Greg Norman' at Augusta or was he playing smart?" Mike Clayton wonders. "You can have the image of Superman, flying around the world, but you have to be careful that you don't start playing the part of yourself in your own movie. You've got to say, 'Well, I'm not going to be a Hollywood hero this time, I'm just going to be a regular guy.' Maybe he plays 'Greg Norman' too much. Maybe he should start pretending he's Jack Nicklaus or Peter Thomson, instead of doing what people expect Greg Norman to do. You never saw Nicklaus make one of those mistakes, never mind five in a row."

"It's one of those situations where everyone tried to put their finger on what happened," Harmon says in frustration. "David Leadbetter said that his swing wasn't sound, which was ridiculous because it was very sound when he shot 63 and 69 in the first and third rounds. I think it was more mental than physical."

"I have to say, he might never recover from the Masters," Newton says. "The Larry Mize thing was big at the time, but I think, being as resilient as he is, he got over it. This one he's got a real hang-up about because everyone, including me, has always thought that if he was going to win an American major it would be at Augusta because it's made for him. . . . He may never recover from that. He wouldn't admit that."

Eighteen months later Norman believes he has recovered, that nothing could ever hurt him like the Mize defeat. "It's just one of those things that just got away. That's the simplest way of putting it. I mean, it hurt. Tony hurt just as much as I hurt. Because it got away. There wasn't anything we could do about it. I should have been able to do something about it, personally and internally, but I couldn't. It was just one of those things that happen in life, and it happened for a reason. . . . I'm a fatalist. I wish I had won it, but when I look back on it, I ended up a better person because I lost it. To me that might be the shining light that comes out of it."

15

GHOSTS OF AUGUSTA

"Destiny, the alchemy of fate and luck."

Jane Mendelsohn, *I Was Amelia Earhart*

Above the lush Florida forests, the out-of-season hotels, and the empty beach tapering into the distance, the sky was a gunmetal gray, shot through with sheet lightning. Terrifying white forks split the ocean. At Great White Shark Enterprises, Frank Williams was in his office with the blinds drawn. He was recovering from the migraine that had caused him to spend most of the morning lying prone in the darkness. A big man, with wavy gray hair, fair skin, and a booming voice as cosmopolitan as Norman's, he is as tenacious in business and as much in thrall to wealth and the good things in life as the Shark is. But, like Norman, he is softened by kindness.

Williams has known Norman for nearly twenty years, but when he took on Norman's management early in 1994, few people thought it would last longer than six months. "He's not a great one for giving you continual pats on the back," Williams admits. "I mean, in four years he's told me perhaps three times what a great job I did for him. He's always ribbing me—'God, I think you could have done better'—spurring me on, type thing. At times it's been a very stormy passage." In the summer of 1997 they went for three months without talking until finally Williams couldn't stand it anymore and marched into Norman's office. "Is it over now?" he demanded. Norman looked up from his papers. "Is what over?" he asked innocently, knowing full well what Williams meant. Then they cleared the air and were friends again.

"When I first joined Greg as his manager, Steve Williams said to me, 'From now on there will always be conflict, every day,' " Frank Williams remarks. " 'If there's a hard way and an easy way, Greg will find the hard way.' Now, that's not 100 percent true, but there's a lot of truth in it. But that's what makes champions champions. They are different, they do go against the tide."

If a man's character could be judged by the contents of his office, it would be nearly impossible not to like Norman. Laura's decor is almost poetically beautiful. From the Persian rugs to the dappled elevator casing, the fragrant bathrooms to the shark sculpture on the boardroom table, there is nothing in the building that doesn't look as if it cost a million dollars, and yet, with the exception of the giant blue mural of Norman beside the autograph signing room, the overall picture is one of elegance. Even the pervading smell, of clean, expensive wood, is unforgettable.

Norman's office is large but not disproportionately so. Behind his chair stands a vibrant painting of the rich red earth of the Australian Outback, and an organizer testifies to his frantic schedule. The walls are hung with framed photographs of the Shark with Nicklaus—"To a great pro and friend, best regards, Jack," with Clint Eastwood, Nigel Mansell, Ben Hogan, and Nelson Mandela, and there are letters from Bill Clinton—"I really appreciate you making time to play with me. . . . I've been one of your biggest fans for a long time"—and Al Gore, among others. His shower is an appropriately macho blend of black marble and fluffy cream towels, and his bookshelves are dotted with little models of his various planes and boats, photos of his family and dog Foster, and books on game-fishing records, wine, and fish.

Williams reaches up to his own bookshelf and takes down the most gratuitously cruel item of media coverage published since Norman's collapse at Augusta in 1996. A German magazine has used photo-manipulation to show Faldo putting a Green Jacket on Norman's shoulders. Williams has never forgotten the morning after the Masters nightmare. When he arrived at the office, he and Nina, Norman's secretary, took one look at each other and burst into tears. "Greg came in and was a pillar of strength. You'd never have thought anything had happened. I don't know to this day how badly it affected him, I really don't. He does not dwell on the past. Ever."

It was a changed Greg Norman who went to Hilton Head Island after the Masters. This being the most damning of all his defeats, he steeled himself for the worst, for the most vicious criticism and savage personal attacks. He wasn't prepared for compassion or kindness or for the ten thousand faxes and letters that poured into Great White Shark Enterprises and onto his boat *Aussi Rules*—moored near the MCI Classic—at a rate of one every three minutes. He wasn't expecting a national outpouring of emotion and empathy. "I'm sick of getting tears in my eyes reading them," Williams said. "So many of them are about kids. So many of them are about how Greg was such a perfect role model for how to handle adversity."

"My son said I'm still his hero, so that's all I ask," Norman said.

When phone calls, telegrams, and notes on his locker were added to the volume of support, Norman was visibly humbled and overwhelmed. "Laura said to me, 'You know, maybe this is better than winning the Green Jacket. Maybe now you understand the importance of it all.' It's extraordinary how I reached out and touched people by losing. . . . It's almost as though, like Laura said, that you've won some aspect of it all, but you didn't get the Green Jacket. It's like nothing that's happened and there are a lot of things I'll be able to cherish. . . . The thing that makes me gladdest about all of this is that I've seen life in a different light. That's what I'm happy about."

Everywhere Norman turned people were cheering for him, and his fellow professionals—the ones he thought were incapable of feeling anything but jealousy and scorn for him—shook his hand warmly and told him he was the best player in the world and that his graciousness in defeat was a credit to the game. Nicklaus, Floyd, and Couples all telephoned. "You know, I don't think Greg really realized how much people like him," Love said. "I think one of the things that's come out of this is that he knows now how much the Tour players did not want to see it happen to him and that they wanted him to know that they didn't want to see it happen to him."

Playing with Norman in a practice round, Price told him, "You've earned more respect and more friends by handling yourself the way you did in the adversity that you faced than if you'd won three Masters in a row."

Whether by accident or design, Norman was paired in the opening two rounds with Azinger, who, in the three years since he beat the Shark in the PGA Championship play-off, had endured a horrific battle with cancer. "I think I might have the perfect pairing for Greg, as far as putting things into perspective," Azinger said. "We grind it out, but the reality is, he lost a tournament, I could have lost my life. In that regard, I might have been the guy he needed to look at for two days."

Human nature being what it is, there was always going to be someone who took pleasure in Norman's misery, and at Hilton Head it was an inebriated man the local police identified as Thomas J. Yarrington. "Do you have a problem?" demanded Norman when Yarrington heckled him on the eighteenth tee on Saturday.

"Why'd you choke last week? You cost me a lot of money!" the drunkard yelled belligerently. Navarro pounced on him and wrestled him to the ground. "That's assault and battery, and I'm going to sue Greg Norman!" yelled Yarrington before being removed from the course and charged with disorderly conduct.

"WHY'D YOU CHOKE LAST WEEK? YOU COST ME A LOT OF MONEY!" THE DRUNKARD YELLED BELLIGERENTLY. NAVARRO POUNCED ON HIM. . . . "THAT'S ASSAULT AND BATTERY, AND I'M GOING TO SUE GREG NORMAN!"

But every minute more letters came from good people, genuine people, people who cared, so many of them that Norman, who tries to reply to all his mail personally, paid forty-five thousand dollars for full-page thank-you ads in *Golf World*, *Golfweek*, and the *Sydney Telegraph*. Notes came from George Bush, Byron Nelson, former Australian prime minister Bob Hawke, Christopher Dodd from the U.S. Senate, Augusta chairman Jackson T. Stephens, Harmon, Watson, Danny Sullivan, and Hoch, but often it was the ordinary people who said the most. "I have been playing golf since I was four years old," wrote ten-year-old David Tiffenberg from Florida. "I hate, hate, hate to lose, but if I won every tournament I would quit golf tomorrow. We can't always have our heart's desire, but failing can make us stronger. You are the best golfer in the whole world. Be happy and know that there are a million kids like me who love and respect you."

In response to Dave Anderson's lacerating critique of Norman in the *New York Times*, Robert M. Schmon wrote, "What makes Norman extraordinary and so utterly compelling to watch is not his indifference, but his obsession to win. This, mixed with his propensity for shot decisions that push the envelope, that are bold and often foolhardy, pull him apart from the ordinary, the safe and the bland, and into the wonderful world of our golfing fantasy and imagination."

By the time he finished thirteen strokes behind Loren Roberts and one ahead of Faldo on Sunday, Norman knew that there had been an intrinsic change in his personality. "The best thing is that I'm less cynical now, which is going to make my approach to the game much easier as years go by. It's easier to deal with situations when you know that people really care about you. It picks you up when you're feeling down. It's been an amazing few weeks. Missing two cuts, practicing at home, playing great, playing at the Masters, and then coming here. It's been a lifetime of experiences."

In retrospect it was strange how quickly Norman reverted from the state of grace he found in the immediate aftermath of the Masters to his former cynicism. It was not immediately obvious. He returned from a three-week holiday full of vim and vigor and in no time at all was on his Gulfstream jet, rushing from a whirlwind site inspection of the TPC at Sugarloaf to the Memorial Tournament, and telling the *New York Times*, "I want to be the hunted again. I want to have that six-shot lead again going into a Sunday of the U.S. Open or the Masters. . . . There'll be a situation where I'll be the hunter, sure, where I'll be a Faldo sitting four or five back. But I want that lead again, to be hunted, more for myself than for anything else."

He conceded that there had been strategic errors at Augusta. "I like my strategy 98 percent of the time," he said. "But when I think back at things I should have done at the Masters under those extreme firm conditions, maybe there are times, maybe half a dozen to ten shots out of seventy-two that you play differently. Think of the guys who have won the most majors—Jack Nicklaus and Ben Hogan—two of the most conservative guys who have ever played the game of golf. There's a reason why."

Racing through America at forty-five thousand feet, Norman was full of fun and laughter, the picture of health after a week of diving and catching sail-fish off the coast of Mexico with Laura and Nick and Sue Price, and two weeks alone on the waves in the Bahamas. He had even found time to play recreational golf at Cat Cay with his brother-in-law and two crew members. "In eighteen holes, I had eighteen beers," Norman said with a grin. "When we ran out of beer, we went home."

But when he reached Lytham for the British Open in July, all memory of these happy moments had vanished without trace from his mind. "I was a little bit down," Norman said. "I was not in the place I wanted to be. I did not have a good three-week break after Hilton Head. I didn't do anything that I planned on doing."

RACING THROUGH AMERICA AT FORTY-FIVE THOUSAND FEET, NORMAN WAS FULL OF FUN AND LAUGHTER, THE PICTURE OF HEALTH AFTER A WEEK OF DIVING AND CATCHING SAILFISH OFF THE COAST OF MEXICO . . .

To make up for it he had just taken another two-week trip to the south of France and the Mediterranean. He appeared to be enjoying life, but there were signs that he was suffering a delayed reaction to the Masters. There had, for instance, been the Greater Hartford Open debacle. The defending champion, Norman had been forced to disqualify himself on Friday night after finding he'd played a nonconforming ball during the tournament. He was in fourth place at the time. A series of frantic phone calls to Maxfli and PGA officials confirmed that the balls Maxfli had given him to experiment with, an XS-7, XS-8, and XS-9, but had forgotten to tell him not to use in competition, were not on the USGA's list of conforming balls.

"It's been a Jekyll and Hyde season for me," Norman said at Lytham. "I had a good start, but the last six or eight weeks have not been very stellar at all. I think it is a patch that I'm going through and hopefully I will dig myself out of that patch this week with a victory. Like any job, you get into a rut, that's all. You have to figure it out, do something different, take a vacation to stimulate what you're going back to."

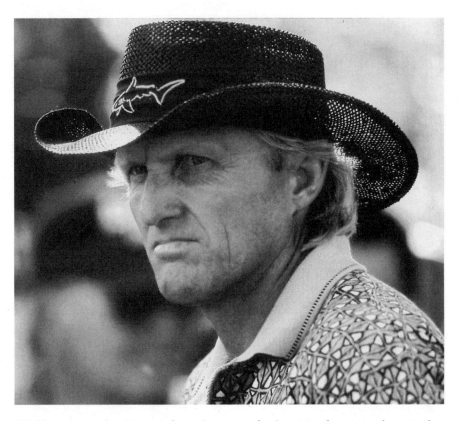

World weariness etches Norman's face as he turns to face his critics after missing the cut at the 1996 U.S. Open. (© Phil Sheldon)

At the British Open, Norman was stimulated enough to tie for seventeenth place, but back in the United States his life began to unravel. First he dispensed with the services of Harmon. "If you look at Greg's record in 1993, '94, '95, he was by far and away the best player in the world," Harmon says. "I don't know how anybody could play better than he played. But in 1996 he started to stray away from some of the things that I liked him to do, and he wanted to go back to some of the stuff he did back in '86—get his swing a little steeper, get his swing longer. He felt it took the pressure off his back. And for some reason we just started to grow apart, teaching-wise. . . . I worked with him up to the U.S. PGA, and then we decided to go our separate ways."

245

Norman and his erstwhile teacher Butch Harmon search for perfection. (© Phil Sheldon)

According to Harmon, their parting was personal, not swing-related. "Greg and I had a misunderstanding. He was upset about something I had talked to one of his companies about, and it just irritated him so much that he said, 'In the best interests of our friendship, I think it's better that we should go our separate ways.' Which actually, honestly, worked out good for me because I was not going to be able to teach both Greg and Tiger Woods."

It may have worked out for the best in the long run, but Norman's initial reaction to the "misunderstanding" was to go berserk. As long as he had worked with the Shark, Harmon had worn Greg Norman Collection clothing, emblazoned with Cobra logos, but when Cobra was sold and Woods was on the verge of signing with Nike, Harmon's agent suggested they get a Nike deal.

Harmon claims he told his agent to try to do a deal with the president of Norman's clothing company first, because he would be "very uncomfortable walking out on a tee with Greg Norman wearing Nike clothes." At the time, Woods was still an amateur, and Harmon says he felt loyal to Norman. Williams's version is a little different.

"Butch's agent rang and said, 'I'd like to get in touch with the guy at Reebok,' " Williams recalls, "so I put him in touch with Richie, who runs Greg Norman apparel, and he was apparently making demands of Richie for X amount of dollars and Richie got a little pissed off about it and told Greg, and Greg blew up. To Butch it was a very petty thing. To Greg it was a major thing because Greg is, 'You're either for me or you're against me. You're either 100 percent—not 99 percent, 100 percent—with me or you're not with me,' and that's the way he is. Butch tended to blame me. Butch said some pretty nasty things about me, too, and I never did anything but good for Butch. I made him a lot of money. And that was the whole reason Butch left."

"It really wasn't that they were going to pay me," Harmon insists. "I was going to do a number of clinics or exhibitions for him at my fee and that's how I would get repaid for wearing the clothes, which Richie had no problem with. But, unfortunately, when the story got back to Greg, he was told something totally different and he just flew off the handle. He got extremely upset with me and that's really what the whole deal was about. Since then he has apologized to me and said he was totally wrong, he was given the wrong information, and the thing that he said that made me feel so good was, 'I don't know why I was so mad because you have the right to get any deal you can get.' As I told him later, 'Greg, I was trying to do the right thing by you.' "

While the Harmon situation simmered away in the fall of '96, Norman busied himself with another feud, this one with David Graham. At Lytham, Norman had attended a meeting on the Presidents Cup, a Ryder Cup-type duel between the United States and the Rest of the World, during which Graham was unceremoniously ousted as captain.

"The Presidents Cup was about the worst insult I ever had in golf," Graham, the former U.S. Open champion, told author Lorne Rubenstein. However, he was less concerned about the circumstances that led to his being forced to resign than about the role Norman played in the situation. This was not entirely unreasonable. Norman had been very vocal about Graham's organizational abilities, or lack thereof. "We're all very concerned," he said in late June. "It's like walking into a room full of fog—you don't know what the heck's going on. You've got to get the team camaraderie going early. It's like we're not even playing a golf tournament."

Two years earlier Norman had been forced to withdraw from the event when he had hemorrhoid surgery. When he showed up on the last day to support his team, CBS asked him if he would wear a microphone for the telecast. Graham put his foot down. "The Presidents Cup is not Greg Norman's tournament," Graham said nastily. "It's a twelve-man team, it's not Greg's team." Norman was spitting mad.

During the second Presidents Cup, Graham received two phone calls from the Shark, one of which was an attempt to convince him that Norman had not instigated his departure. "The second was to tell me what he thought of me in no uncertain terms, that our friendship was over and that he never wanted to talk to me again," Graham recalled. "I said, 'Hey, your choice.' I don't know why he said those things."

Probed by Rubenstein, Norman admitted it was true. "David was way out of line for telling you that," he said. "It was a private conversation. But I did tell him those things. Did he also tell you that at the end of our conversation he apologized for accusing me of wrongdoing?"

In actuality, Graham did not own up to saying sorry at all. "I've even told Greg on the phone that if he could prove to me that he was not responsible, then I certainly owe him an apology," he explained. "But on the other hand, I can't stop thinking that I've known Greg Norman for over twenty years, and he was the number-one-ranked player in the world, and part of the responsibility of being the number-one player in the world is to ask, 'Now, what's right and what's wrong in this situation?' . . . The thing that hurts me the most is that he didn't try to stop it."

At the end of the day it didn't matter who was the ringleader at the meeting, only that victory was so important to the members of the International team that all twelve of them sanctioned the casting aside of Graham. Player described the way those dozen players handled the situation as "a total disgrace, a humiliating embarrassment" for Graham, which had damaged the image of the game. The PGA Tour bowed to pressure from the foreign players and Thomson was installed as captain.

"A lot of guys were gunning for him," Clayton says of Graham, who has been left scarred by the experience. "He'd pissed Ernie Els off because he had criticized Ernie the time before for not playing when Ernie had committed to play in the Dunhill Cup, and it's pretty hard to piss Ernie off. A lot of guys, when they came back from the first Presidents Cup, said he hadn't done that great a job."

Williams says that Norman, whose team lost by a point to the United States, was taken totally by surprise when he was made the scapegoat for Graham's departure. "At the British Open meeting, apparently one started complaining, 'Well, David never tells us anything and he's so arrogant and he made my wife leave in the middle of the banquet,' and then another guy chipped in and then they all chipped in and they all had their own little grievances about Graham."

Elkington and Price backed him up. "It had nothing to do with Greg," Elkington said.

A year later Graham remains bitter about Norman's perceived role in the mutiny. "It'll take more than that son of a bitch to put me out of business," he said.

All in all it amounted to a blood-pressure-raising September for Norman. Alan Fine, the sports psychologist, once said that Norman was a man who thrived on obstacles. In 1996, Norman also found time to have a blazing row with Finchem, cornering him in the lobby at the Westfields Conference Center in Virginia during the Presidents Cup. Shortly before the start of the singles matches on Sunday, the U.S. Tour commissioner had announced the formation of a "federation" that would sanction three World Tour-type events in 1999. "I've had it up to here with Tim Finchem," Norman raged the next day. "It's the end of the rope for me. He hung me out to dry."

HE WAS PARTICULARLY ANGRY THAT FINCHEM APPEARED NOT ONLY TO HAVE STOLEN HIS WORLD TOUR IDEA BUT HAD ALSO TAKEN ADVANTAGE OF FOX'S INTEREST IN GOLF.

He was particularly angry that Finchem appeared not only to have stolen his World Tour idea but had also taken advantage of Fox's interest in golf.

"Hopefully, Greg and I can work through this," Finchem said feebly.

Norman's response to this series of controversies was to endeavor to prove that when he had "forty million bucks" to keep him happy, he really meant it. "With my performance thus far in 1996, which includes a win at Doral, my career earnings are now over $10 million," he wrote on his Internet site. Two weeks after the Hartford incident, he had signed an $18 million

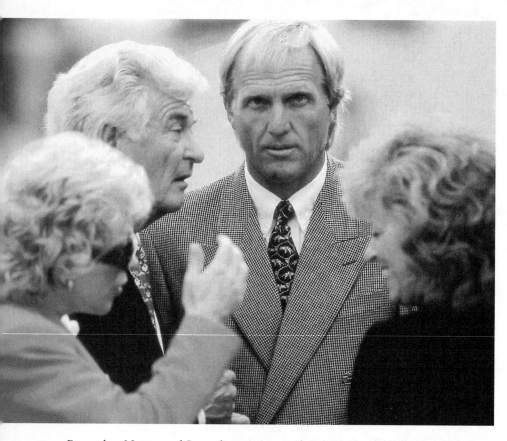

Power play: Norman and Laura discuss strategy with Bob Hawke, the former Australian premier, and his wife during the 1996 Presidents Cup. (© Phil Sheldon)

deal with Maxfli, and he skipped the World Match Play to close a deal in Chicago. He arrived late in the week for the prestigious season-ending Tour Championship, failing to appear at the pro-am, first citing mechanical problems with his jet and then saying, "I just had to reshuffle some things," and he then left before the final round.

He was still seething over the World Tour business. "It's like somebody cutting off your arm," Norman said, adding that the incident had sapped his enthusiasm. "You can try to mend it but you never really get it back."

On Norman's parking plaque at the Tour Championship, somebody had written, "Gone Fishin'."

250

Greg Norman, shiny under the glare of the television lights, sat on a sofa beside Laura wearing an expression that could have been bemused rapture but might just as easily have meant "Too fucking little, too fucking late." It was September and an Australian presenter was waving a big red book. "Greg Norman, this is your life," he cried as he wheeled out Arnold Palmer, Bob Hope, and the usual procession of childhood acquaintances Norman had probably hoped he would never see again.

Then they brought out Toini and Merv. Norman embraced his mother warmly and gave a quick, cool hug to his father, taking care to not allow his immaculate Nehru suit to actually touch Merv's body. "So," enthused the presenter, "did you think Greg would end up as [the world's best] golfer?"

"He could have spread out into a few other things, but this one will do," Merv said.

For much of his adult life, Norman had tried to penetrate Merv's reserve, to cut down the emotional wall that would have allowed Merv to put his arms around him and say, "I love you, I'm proud of you." But to no avail. A product of his generation, Merv found it difficult to display physical affection and even harder to accept Norman's lavish lifestyle. "Sometimes I used to think, 'Wouldn't it be great to give my dad a big hug? God, wouldn't that be great? I haven't seen him in so long,' " Norman told *SI* shortly before the Masters. Instead, he went for months without calling him. "What's the point?" he said. "I can't get anything out of him anyway."

There is little doubt that Norman's personality—his obsessive drive and his constant need to reinvent himself in different superhero modes (savior, top gun, petter of sharks)—is inextricably bound to his relationship with his father. "My father made me the individual I am because of his strength of character, and my mother gave me the emotions," Norman says, and Laura is not alone in thinking that the events of Augusta and Norman's lifelong conflict with Merv might be linked.

"We tried to discuss what happened at the Masters," Laura says. "You know, I do not believe Greg choked. He works his butt off to win, he loves that feeling. Greg has been there too many times to choke. Some people say,

'Well, the whole thing with his dad came up, he wanted to please his dad too much.' Who could ever know what happened? It could be very complex, it could be very simple. Maybe he did want it too much and he put too much effort into it. The fact is, it didn't happen."

"In America, the cliché—maybe because there are so many fatherless kids in the ghettos—is that when you home in on a lineman at the Super Bowl, he always goes, 'Hi, Mom!' " says Callahan. "I think that if they homed in on golfers, they'd all go, 'Hi, Dad!' because I think it's a father's game. Deacon Palmer is the clue to Arnold. . . . Harry Player was that goldminer. . . . Payne Stewart, his father died and if you mention it today, he'll start weeping. . . . All the guys who have the most vinegar in them, the way to sweeten them up is to say, 'Tell me about your dad.' "

"THE KIND OF ROSETTA STONE TO ALL THESE GUYS, TO ME, IS THEIR DADS. THEY'RE ALL DAD GUYS WITH TWO EXCEPTIONS— FALDO AND GREG NORMAN. THEY'RE MOM GUYS."

Callahan's theory has Woods and Nicklaus as the ultimate dad guys. "When Charlie Nicklaus died, Jack lost weight, took charge of his life, got off the phone with Charlie, and became a man. Barbara will tell you that. The year his father died, Tom Weiskopf, whom everyone regarded as a wasted talent, became the best player in the world. The kind of Rosetta Stone to all these guys, to me, is their dads. They're all dad guys with two exceptions—Faldo and Greg Norman. They're mom guys. Faldo's mother probably couldn't break an egg, but she'd be in the kitchen and he'd be on the porch, he's practicing his swing, and she's saying, 'Give me one more knuckle.' And Norman's mother was a player. But mom guys in golf are pretty rare."

Williams compares Merv to the father of Venturi, who scoffed at his son's dreams and then, when he became successful, told him to prove it wasn't a fluke. Only on the day that Venturi came to him and said, "Dad, I don't know if I'm going to be able to play golf again, I think I'm going to lose three fingers," did he reveal the depth of his feelings. "Don't worry," he told his son. "I've seen the best, and it was you."

"The doctors could have cut my arm off, it wouldn't have mattered," Venturi said.

"I think it's that kind of relationship," Williams says of Merv and Norman. "I think his father wants him to achieve again and again, and I think he's doing what Venturi's father did to him. We all like to get recognition from our parents—it's the ultimate recognition. I don't know if Greg has ever got the feedback that he would like. . . . I'd say his father's not used to hugging people. But I've always found Merv okay. I think he's a strict, down-the-line, black-and-white guy."

"His father was a rather severe, tough individual, whereas his mother was a very gentle, very supportive individual," Marshall recalls. "I would say Greg had a lot of conflicts with his father. His mother was a wonderful woman. . . . I think his father probably found it hard to turn to Greg and say, 'Well done, that was bloody good.' Whereas, his mother was very supportive."

Tom Ramsey has been one of the few to have seen a different side to Merv. "I think his father's a tremendous fellow, really a good and genuine man. I really like his father. I relate to his father very well. I find his father very much a warm people person, and I think Greg is not a people person, even though that's his image."

"There were a lot of things said about his dad not being supportive," Laura says. "His father is very proud of him. He doesn't know sometimes exactly how to show it, but he has his own way of doing it. It's just that he's from the old school. He doesn't understand Greg's lifestyle, the way Greg is. Greg is very flamboyant in a lot of ways; his dad is extremely conservative. So there's conflict there, but it isn't that his dad didn't support him. He did, but his mother was the golfer. She was the one who, while his father was working, would drive him to the golf course and pick him up."

At the same time she admits that Norman's desperation to please his father is a likely key to both his character and his success. "It could be that because he was looking for approval and wanted to show his father how good he was, that's what spurred him on. One psychologist could say, 'That's the reason'; another could say, 'How come those guys who have really supportive fathers that were golf coaches are so good?' I think it's unfair to make an assumption of that. It's very possible that Greg could have become so successful for that reason, but I just think Greg is a very driven person. He wants to be good at everything. So whether that originated from trying to please his dad or not, I don't know. I think that Greg could also get to the point where he could start thinking, 'Is it my dad?' I don't think he really knows. And I don't think that anybody will ever know."

Partly because of his background and partly because of the animosity his wealth and attitude arouse on the PGA Tour, Norman has, he feels, always struggled to form close bonds with other men. "I feel sorry for Greg," Laura told Reilly. "What's happened is really sad. I know Greg would love to have a close male friend, someone to get drunk with and just tell anything. But there's nobody."

What made this statement slightly disturbing is that, for years, Norman had talked about his friendships with everyone from Nicklaus to Price, and yet when it came down to it, he seemed to feel he had left his real friends behind in Australia. "My best friends, outside my wife, are the people I pay a salary to," Norman says.

Edwards didn't find this surprising in the least. "Curtis Strange used to be his best friend . . . won't talk to him anymore. Curtis Strange used to joke with me and refer to Greg as 'our buddy.' 'Hear what our buddy did the other day?' But that's what he does. He likes to surround himself with the top people, and then when they're no longer the top people or they put him off, they're out. There was a football player who was a great running back with the New York Giants, Tucker Fredrickson. He was one of Greg's big mates in Palm Beach. I asked someone the other day, 'Have you seen Tucker Fredrickson?' He said, 'Oh, he and Greg aren't talking.' And I thought, that doesn't surprise me at all. It just follows the course with Greg. And it's too bad. That's why he's lonely. That's why he doesn't have any friends."

Even Norman's friendship with Nicklaus had cooled. "I don't see Jack that much," Norman explains. "His life and career have gone in a different direction. I hardly ever see the man. Yeah, we're still friends, but not like Nicky Price or Ray Floyd."

"Greg's an extremely loyal person," Elkington told Hodenfield. "If you're on the right side of him, fine. If you're on the wrong side, he won't give you the time of day. That's the way a lot of people are in Australia. We don't buddy up with everybody. And in his position, everybody wants to be his friend."

"I get hurt when I read in the paper that he hasn't got any friends," Williams says. "I mean, he has twenty or thirty friends that work for him. I don't think Greg realizes how good some of his friends are." He sighs heavily. "There's a part of Greg that's very private. I consider myself a friend of his, but there will always be a part of Greg that I will never get to know. I think he just holds that last bit back. But I know that if I were ever in trouble or I needed him, he'd be there. Good friend to have. Terrible enemy. I get very emotional about Greg, I really do. I don't like to be emotional—he's the only male that I am emotional about, apart from my kids—but he brings it out in me for some reason. I feel passionately about him, and a lot of the people around him do."

But either Norman doesn't see that or he chooses to overlook it. When Laura first came out on Tour, she recalls the wife of a top player telling her not to expect to have many friends if Norman became the best golfer in the world. Now she feels it's true. "Part of it is Greg's personality. Greg makes a wonderful friend because he's a very giving, caring, considerate person, but I think people are intimidated by him. They're just not sure how to approach him and over the years he's become a little defensive, so maybe he's more unapproachable now. And I think as you get older you don't need as many friends. You don't have as much time for them. In our life, anyway."

"GREG MAKES A WONDERFUL FRIEND . . . BUT I THINK PEOPLE ARE INTIMIDATED BY HIM. THEY'RE JUST NOT SURE HOW TO APPROACH HIM AND OVER THE YEARS HE'S BECOME A LITTLE DEFENSIVE."

The strange thing is that people who care deeply about Norman and feel they share a bond with him are everywhere. "He's a great guy," says Elkington, who enjoys fishing, hunting, and sharing a beer with Norman. "He's fun to be around," Price talks glowingly about their relationship. "People don't see the side of him that I see and a lot of his close friends see. He's a very generous and warm person. In our time as friends, we've had a really good time together and he enjoyed every minute of it. What people don't realize is that he's very generous to kids, to other Australian guys, and to other professionals."

Longmuir has remained a loyal friend to Norman, and Norman to him, throughout the years. "He's terribly misunderstood," the Scotsman says. At the 1995 British Open at St. Andrews, he bumped into the Australian in the locker room, not realizing that Norman was suffering excruciating back pain and had played poorly as a result. "There wasn't any talk of his bad finish, it was just, 'You'll make the cut,' " Longmuir remembers. "We got to chatting. I'd had a bit of a bad time with my personal life and he mentioned it, said he had heard. Just then a couple of R&A officials came down into the changing room. And this is what you have to understand about Greg to understand the man. We were having a personal conversation and these two officials walked up and said, 'Greg, could you give us your autograph?' I thought he was going to punch their lights out. He said, 'Just wait over there, please,' and then we continued talking with these guys listening. I felt so awkward. I don't get much time with him and it was a precious moment. And to have these guys break in on it."

Away from the Tour, with its broken dreams and fleeting bonds, Norman's home life is secure, happy, and relatively normal. He works extremely hard at being a good father, offsetting his long absences by spending quality time with his children when he is at home, helping them with their homework or taking them fishing. At tournaments and at home, Morgan and Gregory come across as well-mannered and well-balanced kids. "I don't think people realize what a wonderful father Greg is," Laura says.

"One of the most fascinating things in my life now is being a parent," Norman says.

Williams envies Norman's relationship with Laura and his ability to communicate with his children. "He's loving, affectionate, firm, converses with them at length. I think he's a much more involved father with his children than perhaps his own father was. I think that's an education process from Laura, because Americans . . . show their feelings. They're not afraid to embrace or kiss, whereas the English and the Australians and people of that extraction are. So I think in that respect, Laura has been exceptionally good for Greg. You know, he portrays this macho image. I'm not sure he's as macho as he makes out. I think he's much more caring and feeling than he lets on. I think he has an enormous amount of softness in him that he doesn't want to show."

"I think there's a sensitive guy in there," Elkington agrees. "Not supersensitive, but I think he cares about things."

"As you get more successful, you become more reclusive in a lot of ways, so you become very close to the people around you," Laura says. "Greg and I have become so family-oriented and toward each other that we really are best friends. The way we're different is that he's like the Energizer Bunny. Gregory and I are homebodies, and Morgan and Greg are more 'Let's see how much we can do in one day.' That's great because we keep each other in balance. If I were like him, we would go until he ran out of juice."

When he is at home, Norman rises at 5:00 A.M., answers his e-mail, takes his children to school, exercises, eats breakfast, and is off and running. His Hobe Sound house, built in 1902, sits on eight acres of land between the ocean and the Intracoastal Waterway. It has a gym, a beach house, two guest flats, a putting green, a basketball court, and Labradors—VB, Foster, and Miller—named after beers.

"His house is beautiful," says Edwards. "I mean, it's everything money can buy. He's got all the toys. . . . But I think he's very lonely, if you want the truth."

"His home life is very ordinary," Williams says firmly. "It's a big home, beautifully decorated, but it's a house which, although opulent, is very comfortable. When you sit down, you don't feel as if you're in a show house. . . . [Greg] cooks the barbecue, helps with the washing up, helps around the house."

"Our home is a home," Norman says. "It's not overstated."

Laura describes their life as simple. "People expect our house, for some reason, to be glitzy. Our house is really a home. We've got two kids who have friends over all the time. Our house is just big overstuffed furniture. It's really comfortable, nothing pretentious at all." But in the midst of all this ordinariness, there is the extraordinariness that famous people have a tendency to see as normal. The *People* magazine version of down-to-earth existence. "When we added on a new wing to the house," Laura continues, "from the main house to the children's wing, I put in this gallery, and that's where the trophies are now. I don't have golf pictures up in the house or the office. The trophies are with us, as they should be, but they're not all over the house. At the end of the day, Greg and I are just normal everyday people. Our lives are very high profile because of Greg's job, but we are no different than we were before Greg became successful. Even though we have a butler, I send him home and we do the cooking, and Greg helps with the dishes and we go out and walk the dog. We do all the things that other people do."

To her, Norman's best quality is "his sensitivity toward his family, the way he is with the children, the way he is toward me. His biggest strength is his mind. He's the one person I've seen who I believe could do anything he set his mind to. His weakness is probably his vulnerability. He does get upset about the things that are said about him. When he's out on the golf course, he hears things and he gets angry. Now, I wish he wouldn't let that stuff bother him, but he does, and he gets back to his old days of being an Australian kid who wants to come out fighting. That part of him is a weakness. He lets too much outside stuff affect him."

16

THE POLITICS OF ENVY

"Greg, as I say, thrives on the press. If the press stopped writing about Greg, or he didn't get the attention he gets, it would be like taking the sun away from a flower."

James Marshall, March 1997

For weeks clean-cut Secret Service men had been there, with their hammers and fiber-optic phone lines, poring over the beach cottage with a magnifying glass. They were preparing for President Bill Clinton's visit. Following the success of their friendly game of golf at New South Wales Golf Club in Sydney in November, Norman and Clinton now spoke on "a weekly basis" on the phone, and Norman had invited the thirteen-handicap, golf-mad president to spend a night at his home in Hobe Sound before they teamed up for a two-day, member-guest tournament at the Medalist in March 1997.

Because the events of the '96 Masters had entered international vernacular, Clinton had spent much of the previous year cautioning anyone who expressed optimism at his lead in the polls with the words "Remember Greg Norman." It didn't bother Norman. He himself was a staunch Republican, but he maintained they got along well. "There's really a nice chemistry between us," he said. "I think we share some personality traits. We have a similar attitude toward life. I think he's a real man's man."

He was looking forward to showing the president around the Medalist. "It's a great honor but it will be very low-key," Norman said. "The president wants to play golf, work out in my gym, putt on the green in my backyard,

259

have a few cold beers and a couple of quiet dinners. He values occasions when he can be a regular guy."

Clinton was continuing a long tradition of White House golfers, but Norman's depiction of a close friendship between them was met with a degree of skepticism. "There's an awful lot that, I'm afraid, is total utter bullshit," Marshall says sorrowfully. "Who said he talks twice a week to Clinton? I would personally doubt it. And if Greg said it, I certainly wouldn't believe it. See, he's given to gross exaggeration sometimes. Sometimes it's hard to draw the line between what's fantasy and what's real. . . . That [story] that it was the air force or golf. It's a load of bullshit. Greg no more would have qualified academically to get into the Australian Air Force than fly to the moon. Greg was no Einstein when he left school, and that story that has been perpetuated over the years that he was either going to be a fighter pilot or a golfer is sheer garbage."

IT WAS AFTER MIDNIGHT AND LAURA WAS IN BED, BUT SHE GOT UP TO WATCH FROM THE WINDOW AS THE MOTORCADE ROLLED UP THE DRIVE.

Ramsey is of a similar mind. "I think he's opinionated about too many things other than golf, when he doesn't have the background or the education to be."

"Greg was fortunate that he was blessed with a gift for playing golf," Marshall continues. "That has been his passport to success in life. Greg is not the sort of person, in my view, about whom you could say had he not been a golfer he would have been a rocket scientist or a doctor. . . . I think, if you take away all the facade and all the bullshit, Greg is just a very ordinary guy. He's not a Peter Thomson, who would have been highly successful in any field. He's not a Graham Marsh, who is a very bright guy. Greg likes to be larger than life."

That said, preparations continued apace for the president's visit on March 13. "The Secret Service looked at everything," Laura says. "There was this patch of grass and they said, 'If he's going to walk from here to here, we need to have you put in some paving stones if you wouldn't mind.' They were very nice about it. And we said, 'No problem.' "

When Clinton finally arrived, he was late. It was after midnight and Laura was in bed, but she got up to watch from the window as the motorcade rolled up the drive. Clinton stood on the front steps talking to Norman. Food had been prepared for him over at the beach cottage, but he wanted to come into the main house. Contrary to popular belief, he refused a beer and drank a Diet Coke. He was plainly exhausted and kept yawning. Laura drifted in and out of sleep, catching snatches of conversation.

"I've always been impressed about the man being a man," Norman said enigmatically, "but as I said to him, 'You're just a damn good person.' " They discussed "life," China, and the Constitution, on which Norman had a few thoughts.

A little before 2:00 A.M., Laura woke with a start as a dark figure loomed at the end of the bed.

"They've just taken the president away in an ambulance," Norman said plaintively.

Laura sat up in bed with a shriek. "I said, 'Come on, that's not funny,' " she recalls, "because he knew my biggest fear was that [Clinton] would get food poisoning or get shot while he was at the property. You know, something awful. He said, 'Word of honor, they've just taken him away in an ambulance.' And I can't even describe what that feels like; the president

"AND I CAN'T EVEN DESCRIBE WHAT THAT FEELS LIKE; THE PRESIDENT OF THE UNITED STATES HAS FALLEN DOWN YOUR STEPS! GREG CAUGHT HIM, THANK GOODNESS."

of the United States has fallen down your steps! Greg caught him, thank goodness, because he would have gone back and hit his head, but it was a traumatic time."

At 1:20 A.M., Norman had been escorting the president to his quarters when Clinton tripped on a step that had been colored to blend in with the concrete landing and tore the quadriceps tendon in his right knee. By 1:45 he was on his way to a hospital in Bethesda, Maryland, for an operation. He would spend up to eight weeks in a leg brace and his summit with Boris Yeltsin would have to be postponed.

Chaos reigned at the Norman household as the rest of America woke up to pictures of an ashen president emerging from the hospital in a wheelchair. Helicopters circled Norman's house, photographers camped out in the bushes, boats ferried tourists past the infamous steps where the president took a tumble, and Norman was inundated with interview requests from every talk show in the country—all of which he turned down—all wanting to know exactly how Clinton came to suffer a freak accident at the home of golf's most star-crossed player. "Every time I turned on the television, there was this picture of him, and I kept thinking, 'My God, this happened at our house,' " Laura says. "It was an awful feeling."

On the other side of the planet, far from Norman's glamorous, power-brokering existence, Charlie Earp sat on the peaceful, lager-scented balcony of Royal Queensland. He was contemplating his former pupil's future. "If he could win one of the majors, it would make a big difference to Gregory Norman," he said. "Dear God, let him win one."

He was a little put out that Norman had traded his more traditional methods for newfangled teachers like Harmon and, more recently, Lead-better. "I just teach natural stuff. I don't go in for any of this biomechanical business," he says. "The golf swing's been going for three or four hundred years, and the things they're trying to do! Robot stuff. I'm what Greg would probably refer to as an eye coach. I can see the problems. A lot of the old coaches can. I just don't go for the gurus. They're just trying to teach everybody to play the same way. Everybody's different to me."

In October 1996, Norman had gone to see Leadbetter at Lake Nona at the suggestion of Price. They had spoken on the phone once before when Norman wanted advice on improving his short irons, and Leadbetter had told him to point his thumb at his ear at the top of the backswing. "He doesn't like to get into detailed mechanics. He's such a great natural athlete, he just likes to stand up to the ball and hit it."

When Norman came to see him about a full-time coaching arrange-ment, Leadbetter was struck by how different he was from his image. "He's actually quite an introvert. You know, he's really a nice guy and he's got a lot of high values. He's a workaholic, too. He's certainly a fun-loving guy, but he's very private, too. He really has very few close friends. He's very family-oriented."

Inevitably, they discussed the Masters. "To be honest, the problems he had last year at Augusta were more physical than mental," Leadbetter says. "They became mental after a period, but initially they were physical. He didn't have any trust in his swing." Watching him hit shots, he thought Norman's swing was too flat, too tight, and too restricted, and that the clubface was shut. "Coming into the ball, he really had to manipulate his body out of the way to try to hit it. So he was losing a lot of distance and really didn't have a lot of control with his irons, which was very noticeable at Augusta last year. I suggested that we narrow his stance, get him turning behind the ball, and get him freed up to the point where his swing is somewhere between where Butch Harmon got it and where he used to be many years ago. The turning action is really what's helped his spine and his back in general. And he's very confident. "He says, 'Hey, my swing feels great, David. . . . I'm feeling good about it.' "

Likening himself to Nicklaus, Norman told *Golf World* that he had switched to a flatter swing for exactly the same reasons the Bear did after the 1986 Masters—because he was unhappy with his swing. "At first it worked," reported Norman, "but soon he was struggling. . . . In my case, I was fed up with golf after a slump in 1991. That was when Butch Harmon convinced me to take an extrawide stance and make a flat swing. Like Jack, I played great for a while. However, let me go on record for the first time and say that this swing always felt unnatural, led to overrotation of my forearms, hips, and shoulders, and was hard on my back. This flatter action failed me at last year's Masters, where I mis-hit shots under pressure."

In an intriguing twist, Edwards says that Harmon told Watson and him that, before he turned to Leadbetter, Norman had asked Nicklaus if he would consider coaching him. "Jack said, 'Greg, I'm not a coach, I'm a golfer. I'm not one of those Leadbetters.' "

In December, two weeks after he started working with Leadbetter, Norman won the Australian Open by eight shots. In the first weekend of

EDWARDS SAYS THAT HARMON TOLD WATSON AND HIM THAT, BEFORE HE TURNED TO LEADBETTER, NORMAN HAD ASKED NICKLAUS IF HE WOULD CONSIDER COACHING HIM.

January, he collected a million dollars for beating Hoch in the Andersen Consulting World Championship of Golf—one of those surreal multimillion-dollar events nobody cares about, with a format that demands a Mensa membership. At that point he had been the No. 1 in the world for 291 of the 560 weeks the rankings had been in existence. Curiously, he had won the world money list just once in its thirty-year history, in 1986. Nicklaus had topped it seven times.

Two months later he lost a three-man play-off for the Dubai Desert Classic, handing the title to an Australian rookie by the name of Richard Green. It was his first full tournament since October, and he was relaxed and charming after a three-month break to rest his ailing back. During that time he had taken a two-week, golf-design trip through Asia; dropped into Morocco for twelve hours for a dinner engagement; changed from a wound to a two-piece ball; put a little work into the World Pitch and Putt Company; prepared to open a chain of restaurants called Greg Norman's Down Under Grille in Myrtle Beach, South Carolina; Orlando; Palm Beach; etc., and endorsed a golf aid called the Secret.

"Greg doesn't need Lead, he's got the Secret," Faldo said facetiously.

In the back of Norman's mind, Augusta loomed large, the crucible of humiliation to which he had to return. He was already receiving huge quantities of supportive mail. After the 1996 Masters, he had taken more time off than ever before, had dropped to 149th in greens in regulation, seen his scoring average rise by three-quarters of a shot per round, and missed four cuts for the first time in his career. Asked at Doral how he was going to deal with this year's Masters, he said simply, "I never run away from anything, guys. I've always stood facing the music." He grimaced. He had a baseball cap on and his blond hair dripped with sweat. "I accept the fact that I made a mistake. It was all my fault. If you people want to keep talking about it, writing about it, so be it. It's not going to affect me. I look forward to going back to the Masters with just as much passion as I had before things happened last year."

He had decided that his Tuesday press conference at Augusta was positively the last time he was going to speak about it. Until then he resigned himself to discussing it at The Players Championship. He was less happy to talk about Clinton. "I think from my wife's point of view and mine, we were looking forward to having a friend over for a couple of days," Norman said, making the president's visit sound like a pajama party, "and as it turned out, that friend hurt himself. But looking behind every dark cloud, there is a silver lining. Maybe slowing him down a little bit might have been good for him."

At one stage Finchem arrived to help Norman dispel the notion that a cross word had ever passed between the two of them. They sat like a couple of born politicians making the kind of candyfloss talk that politicians specialize in. "There never has been a feud between the two of us and there probably never will," Norman assured his audience.

"Probably," beamed Commissioner Finchem.

"Probably," said Norman with less certainty.

The World Tour furor had driven Norman closer than he had ever been to retiring. "I could see him saying, 'To hell with this. I don't need this,' " Williams says.

"Retirement," Norman said immediately when he was asked at the TPC what the long-term prognosis was for his back. "I think that would be the best bet. I can tell you that when I didn't play golf for three months, I never had a hip problem, never had a back problem. Believe me, I enjoyed waking up every morning without having an ache and a pain and having to stretch out to get myself going for that day. So that's the answer."

And then the Masters was upon him.

Of all the golfers on earth, there are only two men capable of controlling, and even manipulating, the emotions of the press, through a subtle blend of charisma, charm, and brazen self-confidence—Ballesteros and Norman. At Augusta, Norman was at his best, thanking reporters profusely for their support since the previous Masters, and then later dropping it in that he hadn't read a golf article in a year.

"Whenever a guy says, 'I don't read it,' you get a picture of him poring over it with a jeweler's loop," Callahan remarked.

Jenkins made fun of Norman's post-Augusta '96 comments that he made only two mistakes all day and that he had so much confidence in his own abilities that "if I wanted to be a brain surgeon and take the time to study that, I could," suggesting that he would lose the '97 Masters when he (a) blows a ten-shot lead . . . while hitting only three bad shots, and (b) dies after thirty-six holes while performing brain surgery on himself."

It turned out that Norman had spent the previous day with Tony Robbins, a motivational speaker, who had worked with Olympic swimmers, Andre Agassi, and the military. Robbins told him that most athletes have one or two keys they use to motivate themselves. Norman, it transpired, had forty-eight. Describing one, he explained, "If you keep thinking about the worst round you've ever had in your life, you're going to keep playing that same shitty round. I don't want to keep thinking about it. Flush it on out."

He looked so thin and hollow-eyed that several people asked if he had lost weight. "I don't think so," Norman said. He had just spent two hours in a traffic jam and astounded Laura by managing to refrain from attacking the dashboard or screaming curses out the window. He returned to his day with Robbins. "One thing he did say . . . was that I had two worlds going on. I had the outer world and the inner world. And I've been worrying about the outer world. I've got to get back into worrying about my inner world."

Three days later Norman missed the cut at the 1997 Masters. When his ball rolled off the apron of the fifteenth green into the water on the second day, he abandoned hope. "He didn't want to play after that, it appeared," said Nicklaus, his playing partner. "It took all the wind out of his sails."

When the blood began to gush from the bull's neck, Norman leaned forward, a broad smile on his rugged face. The dying animal bellowed in agony but in Madrid the cheering crowd drowned it out. They cheered again when the matador bowed and presented the Shark with his hat, a great honor. A Spanish newspaper showed Norman craning forward in a state of high excitement, face alight.

In the year since the Masters disaster, there had been a revolution on the PGA Tour—namely, the arrival of Tiger Woods. In April, Woods had electrified the golf world by winning the Masters by a staggering twelve strokes. In the space of eight months he had acquired some sixty million dollars in endorsements and become a global phenomenon, and he was as far ahead of most players, in terms of power, charisma, and technique, as Nicklaus had been in his heyday and Norman was at his best. At 330 yards he was almost fifty yards longer than the Australian off the tee, and Norman said that every course was a 68 for him. "I remember the days when courses were par-68 for me, too," he said wistfully.

Despite Norman's insistence that he cherished the arrival of the new No. 1 golfer in the world, it was no coincidence that he altered his schedule to take in events he hadn't entered for years, like the St. Jude Classic in Memphis and the Spanish Open in Madrid.

"Greg's playing in the Spanish Open as a favor to Seve, and then Seve's going to play in Greg's tournament in Australia," Williams said. "They've been friends for years."

Ballesteros appeared to have slept through the entire relationship. He claimed that his manager, Roddy Carr, had asked him if it was okay if Norman played in the tournament. "I said, 'Fine,' " Ballesteros said. "Greg has been the number-one player for many years and it is good for the tournament. Apparently, they made a deal that I go and play in Australia. I never said that. Maybe Roddy Carr will play in Australia."

In November, Ballesteros, after making strings of prima donna demands for air tickets, hotels, $100,000 appearance fees, and assorted luxuries for his wife, children, and nanny, would renege on the deal to play three events in Australia. "Greg is furious," Williams said, knowing that the Spaniard would get away with murder, while Norman's softness would render him unable to sue.

Back home in the United States, a row was beginning to sizzle over Norman's comments following Jumbo Ozaki's victory in the Chunichi Crowns tournament in Japan at the end of April. At the second hole in the final round, Norman accused Ozaki—who is more powerful than the prime minister in Japan—of improving his lie in the rough. It was a brave but ultimately foolhardy call. "All I did was issue a warning to Jumbo as a friend," Norman said. "I told him, 'You can't put your driver behind the ball and then pull out an iron.' I didn't accuse him of doing anything."

All of these things added to Norman's grim countenance and defensive attitude. Throughout the season, as he emerged victorious from two events and signed more multimillion-dollar deals, he hardly cracked a smile. "There's an evolution through time, an evolution through two decades of pressure," Norman told *Golf*. "In [the] Australian Open, people compared me to Tiger Woods, who was smiling all the time. Hell, when I was twenty-one years old and didn't have a care in the world, I smiled a lot, too."

The change in him was the subject of frequent debate. He was noticeably more abrupt and on edge. "People think that you just go out there and play golf and have a good time," Norman says, "but there's so much more to it, so many sacrifices. So obviously I'm very cynical because of that, which I hate. It's a shame because my nature has changed and my attitude has changed, which saddens me most out of my life . . . I know I'm not the same guy now that I was seven years ago. I'm not the same guy now that I was twenty years ago. I'm not the same guy I was a year ago."

THE CHANGE IN HIM WAS THE SUBJECT OF FREQUENT DEBATE. HE WAS NOTICEABLY MORE ABRUPT AND ON EDGE.

"There are two Greg Normans," Harmon explains. "Away from the golf course, he's great. He's fun to be around, he's tremendously adventurous—shark fishing and landing on carriers. He loves to push everything to the limit. I thoroughly enjoy being around Greg away from the course. At the golf course, he seems to be irritated all the time. He doesn't seem to be having a good time. He always seems to be upset, whether it's with himself or with somebody else, and I don't like that side of him. I wish he'd go back to the way he used to be. There's nothing wrong with being intense. If you look at Tiger Woods, he's intense when he's playing, but you see him smiling and laughing. You never see Greg like that in a tournament and I think that's hurt his golf game. I think his intensity has caught up a little bit with his nervous system over the years."

"I've seen him get very angry," Williams admits. "There's a lot of anger in him, a lot of anger. I don't know why he does get so angry sometimes."

Stewart Ginn, Norman's friend from the early days in Australia, felt he knew the exact cause of the Shark's unhappiness. "Of course he's changed," he says. "I think the pressures have got to him. I feel sorry for him. I've seen him in situations where he's got a mobile in one hand, he's got a beer in the other, three people are waiting in the hotel lobby, two people are in the room with him, he's leading the tournament by five or six shots, and we're trying to go out to dinner. He's got no peace. None. He's turned harder in a lot of ways because he's had to. I think a lot of people are jealous of what he has. I feel sorry for him. But the thing I like is that we can still have a laugh together."

It was hard to tell whether what happened at the Kemper Open was the result of these pressures or one of the indirect causes of them. Standing on the tee with Tom Lehman on the morning of the third round, Norman listened idly as the starter introduced him and said he was one of the game's great players. "But if he ever invites you to his house to view his trophy collection, I would advise you to respectfully decline," Bill McGuire continued, in a tongue-in-cheek reference to the Clinton incident.

Martinez, Lehman's caddie, was amused. "I thought it was kind of funny. I thought it was overblown, but you're in Washington, D.C. The place is full of clowns and criminals. I laughed, but then I looked at Greg. Greg was not laughing. He kind of turned and looked at the guy, and he glared at him for about two or three seconds. Then he turned and hit his tee ball, and the guy introduced Tom and Tom hit his ball. I looked at Greg and he's making a beeline for the tent where they keep the drinks [to confront McGuire] and there was some serious talking that went on. He was not happy. Then he got off to a bad start because it seemed like he was so agitated."

Norman was not merely agitated, he was furious. Back home in Florida, Clinton's little accident had spawned a thriving—not to mention embarrassing—industry in T-shirts and coffee mugs, and it had worn on his last nerve. He chewed McGuire up one side and down the other and then went after Lehman and started horribly.

"What really got to Greg was that he was in contention . . . and he was very psyched up," Laura explains. "He hears this and it just sent him off the edge. And I don't blame him. A lot of people said, 'Well, he overreacted.' They don't understand that when these guys are trying to win a tournament, their mind is very much into what they're doing. . . . Greg was just standing there perfectly innocent, and this man said something very stupid at a time when Greg was focused on his golf. Then they say there was nothing wrong with what the guy said. That was so totally wrong and it was unfair to Greg, it really was."

Not altogether surprisingly, the *Washington Post* gave Norman a roasting. "This kind of humiliation was totally unnecessary," Tony Kornheiser wrote. "McGuire tried to make a joke, and Norman ran over him with a tank. . . . It's not like he intimated that Norman pushed Clinton down the steps. . . .

Golfers and tennis players amaze me with their sense of entitlement. . . .
What should the guy have said, 'Ladies and gentlemen, here's God'?"

The next day, when a spectator heckled Norman with some nonsensi-
cal remark that sounded like, "Chum it in the water, Greg," he flipped the
guy the bird.

From Kemper, where he shot 67 to finish third, Norman went to Congressional for the U.S. Open. On the eve of the tournament, when the mud-
slinging was at its height, the Normans took Gregory and Morgan to the

"McGuire tried to make a joke, and Norman ran over him with a tank. . . . What should the guy have said, 'Ladies and gentlemen, here's God'?"

White House to meet the president. It was a
beautiful day, and afterward Norman suggested
they show their children, who have been
brought up as Catholics, the church where they
were married. "It was lovely," Laura says. "The
priest blessed our rings. It was very special because it's been sixteen years. The priest said it
was so nice to see someone come back because
they almost never do."

"I've never seen a couple work harder at a
marriage," Williams says.

That night Norman held a press conference to announce, to general amazement, that
he was trading in his Gulfstream IV jet for a $40
million Boeing 747. He had also signed a seven-
year agreement to be an ambassador for Boeing.
According to Norman, who covered 442,600 kilometers in 1996, the bigger
plane would allow him to take more staff and make fewer refueling stops, as
well as provide space for a boardroom, a private suite with toilet and shower,
a gym, and an advanced satellite communications facility.

"Has it occurred to anybody that this deal might be a better deal than
the one he's got at the moment?" Williams demanded as the *Australian* re-
flected the general reaction with a montage of Norman's house, his custom-
built boat, his jet, his Harley, and the Boeing 747, illuminated like a prop in a
David Copperfield show. "He can have all the comforts of home," Williams
said of the Boeing, for which Norman paid cash.

Williams was on his way back to Australia to take up the reins of
Norman's company there as executive vice president, while Bart Collins,
the smooth, IMG-molded American who had headed Norman's company

in Australia, was returning to the United States as president of Great White Shark Enterprises. Despite reports to the contrary, it was an entirely amicable arrangement. "Everybody," Norman beamed, "is extremely happy at my company."

On Thursday, Norman's father was admitted to a hospital with heart trouble. On Friday, Norman missed the cut. On Sunday, the *Post* ran a column in which readers were invited to offer their opinion on the Kemper controversy. "There's no excuse for Greg Norman's boorish behavior," railed Mark Nelson from Vienna. "Palmer and Nicklaus are always class acts. Norman's me-against-the-world bit is wearing thin."

"Gee, I wonder if Jay Leno and David Letterman know that 'it is just wrong . . . to make jokes' about the president's activities," said Steve Durante from Potomac.

Most of the letters were critical, variously describing Norman as juvenile, petty, sour, mercurial, arrogant, egotistical, and self-absorbed. Curtis Werner, aged seven, was one of only four supporters. "If it makes you feel any better, I would love to come over and see your trophies," he told Norman. "However, my dad wants me home by nine."

In Australia the media seized on Norman's latest blunder with glee, quoting the *Post* in full and making spiteful insinuations about choking. "Where once he held a special place in people's hearts for his thrilling, take-no-prisoners approach to tournament play, and the stoic way in which he accepted the slings and arrows of outrageous fortune when he came unstuck," Charles Happell wrote, "he is now threatening to try their patience."

The *Herald-Sun* began a column with "Message to Greg Norman: 'Go away. Take your private jet back to Florida. Come back when you have rid yourself of your hubris.' "

Over the winter the Normans had held a family vote to decide whether they should move back to Australia permanently. It had to be unanimous and since Gregory, now eleven, didn't want to go, the idea was put on hold. But Norman had given up trying to appease the Australian press or anyone else. "They kill me," he says. "Two years ago, I was so close to never going back down there."

Ten days after being condemned for missing the U.S. Open cut, Norman made three closing birdies to win the St. Jude Classic in Memphis.

The more one analyzes it, the more Norman's life resembles a hall of mirrors, a shifting corridor of reflections and split images. There is the granite-jawed, Lone Ranger figure the public sees, surrounded by jets, Ferraris, butlers, and heads of state, forever poised on the knife-edge between agony and ecstasy. There is the unstintingly kind, private, and down-to-earth man his friends know—the friends he doesn't always believe he has. There is the Norman his family knows, and then there is the Norman only Norman knows.

Norman cherishes this secret corner of himself. So certain is he that he is the only one acquainted with his true nature, he doesn't even believe that Laura is privy to it, far less the media. "The media don't have a clue about Greg Norman," the Shark says categorically. "I pick up newspaper articles and read about Greg Norman and what he's like and what he's done, and they're 100 percent not true. . . . And that's what, believe me, out of everything, irritates you to death. If I retired now, my only regret in life would be the media and the slant they put on things. Because I know the majority of it isn't right."

"I think it's really sad that his ability to sit down with the press and open himself up has really backfired on him," Laura says. "They think they know him but they don't know him at all."

To Norman, there are three major misconceptions about him:

(a) He is egotistical. "I don't have an ego," Norman said at Doral when he was asked if he was bothered by the prevailing Tiger mania. This gave rise to the joke, "Greg Norman doesn't have an ego. He has two."

(b) He is arrogant. "I know I'm not an arrogant guy," Norman says. "I'm actually the other way. I'm not one who enjoys the hype. I never have. I've never enjoyed the limelight. I hate the limelight. All that stuff I don't enjoy. I don't like cameras in my face. But people think I do." Laura supports this: "There is a bit of an arrogance about Greg, but anybody who's very good in their profession has a bit of arrogance. His confidence in himself might come across as being egotistical, but that's a misconception. . . . When we go to functions at school with the children that he's not used to, Greg sort of stays in the background. He's very shy in a lot of ways, still."

(c) He is materialistic. "I'm not a materialistic individual," Norman says. "I mean, I can buy and sell things in a heartbeat. I don't get attached to materialistic things."

Herein lies the essence of Norman's problem: He sets himself up to be targeted. There is every reason to believe that he is, as Williams says, the same big-hearted kid that he was at seventeen, but over and over he provides fodder for those who would prefer to be amused by his perception of himself as a country boy at heart.

"I've never been afraid to ask a question," Norman says. "I've never been afraid to go up to a president or a Jack Nicklaus, because most of the time people love to give advice when they're of the stature of the president of the United States or a Jack Nicklaus or the prime minister of Australia. They enjoy being recognized as someone special."

He sees no contradiction between this and his desire to be accepted as the boy next door. When Jana Wendt of Australia's Channel Seven suggested that one of the "bugbears" Australians had with him was "that you have such a well-developed sense of your own worth," Norman interpreted that as a compliment. "A wave of joy and gratitude swept over his face," reported *Inside Sport*. "Thank you," he said. "I'm glad someone has finally realized that. Because yes, I do. Like I said, I'm very in tune with myself and my business, and what I can do and produce for people."

"I KNOW I'M NOT AN ARROGANT GUY," NORMAN SAYS. "I'M ACTUALLY THE OTHER WAY. I'M NOT ONE WHO ENJOYS THE HYPE."

Remarks like these convey all the characteristics Norman claims to despise and reveal none of the traits the people closest to him love: his generosity, compassion, and consideration. "He's a very kind man," Earp says. "He'd do anything for you. If he thinks he owes someone a favor, he does it. He can't stand nonsense, can't tolerate it. But he can make an excuse for someone, forgive them. I've got a video of his fortieth birthday. Very private, very caring, tears. His mother read a poem and he loved it. He has to be the other way because he's a salesman for golf."

"I've been a good friend of his for ten or twelve years," Cott says, "and from what I've seen, he deserves everything he's got. You can talk about all the toys, but he's out there working all the time. It annoys me: I hear 'Greg Norman this' and 'Greg Norman that,' but if they worked as hard as he does, they'd probably be up there, too. He's just such a down-to-earth, great guy. He's so generous, he's so funny. Laura and the kids are his whole life. It's an honor to be around them because they're unique people."

Collins once said that the only common thread in Norman's life is Laura. Through every storm, she has always been there for him, supporting him unconditionally. "I don't know anyone who doesn't love Laura," Williams says.

"The only person who really knows me is my wife, and I bet you she doesn't know me completely," Norman says. "She hasn't seen sides of me I know I have, that I don't think she needs to see. I don't mean that in a bad way. Like I tell her, 'You've never seen me mad yet.' Nobody's ever seen me mad yet, except a couple of people."

"His family comes first," Cott says. "Second is his golf."

More than anything Laura would love Norman to slow down, to consider being a businessman, working nine to five. "She'd like to have me home forty-nine weeks of the year, instead of twelve weeks of the year," Norman grins. "Sure she would. More for the kids' sake, because it's hard on the kids. But she does a great job in running that side of things. We're a perfect couple. She understands what I have to do, I understand what she has to do. We work very closely together. Sometimes it's not the quantity of time, it's the quality of time. Again, it's a delicate balance. There might be some people out there who couldn't do it, and if it wasn't for Laura, I probably wouldn't be where I am. Then again, if it wasn't for me, she wouldn't be where she is."

Greg Norman was higher than nature ever meant man to be, and he was still climbing. Muscles straining, breath uneven, he heaved himself up until finally he stood on top of the Sydney Harbour Bridge, where Paul Hogan once worked as a rigger. Far below him the Opera House jutted like a toy fan into the twinkling waters of the harbor, and yachts flecked the bay like stars. "Action!" cried the director. Above Norman's head, a cameraman leaned from the hovering Channel Seven helicopter and prepared to shoot.

Norman had arrived in Australia at 6:30 the previous morning, flying into Sydney in his Gulfstream IV jet. "Why don't I live here?" he asked a couple of hours later, relaxed and laughing as he enjoyed a meal in Rose Bay. "He's very emotional about Australia when he first comes back," says Williams. "Until the media start on him."

Later, when Williams jokingly suggested that Norman spend the afternoon watching the Australian PGA, he jumped at the chance. "Do you know," said the Shark, sprawled out in the sunshine in a T-shirt, shorts, and sneakers, "I've never done that?" Williams was flabbergasted. At the New South Wales Golf Club, Norman wandered happily through the crowds, signing autographs and watching other players compete.

Driving back through Circular Quay a few hours later, they stopped at a traffic light. Beside

ALL OF A SUDDEN, THE GROOM'S EXPRESSION CHANGED. HE SHOT OUT AN ARM. "THAT'S GREG NORMAN!" HE CRIED. "THAT'S GREG BLOODY NORMAN!"

them, a wedding party had gathered on the steps of a cathedral, the bride in white, the groom immaculate in a suit. All of a sudden, the groom's expression changed. He shot out an arm. "That's Greg Norman!" he cried. "That's Greg bloody Norman!"

Norman grinned out the window. "He seems pretty excited," he said.

The lights went green. Cott, who was driving, moved off. "Hold on a minute," Norman said. He jumped out of the car and walked over to the wedding party, with its flowers and suits and radiant faces. There, on the steps of the cathedral, he kissed the bride, put his arm around the groom and posed for a few photographs. "That's when Greg's at his best," Williams said. "That's when he's happiest."

On Sydney Harbour Bridge, an icy wind blasted Norman's strong brown face and pushed back his blond hair. In six days' time, the man who had been No. 1 in the world for the best part of a decade—and its most charismatic, exciting, loved, and inexplicably flawed exponent—would tie the Australian Open with scores of 68, 67, 66, 73, then lose to Lee Westwood

275

on the fourth play-off hole. Now he faced the cameras with a smile. "I look forward to seeing you all at the Greg Norman Holden International on February 5 through 8, 1998," he said. "In one of my favorite cities in the world—Sydney, the Olympic city."

It was November 1997 and Norman was reaching the end of another triumphant season, during which he had overtaken Woods as No. 1 in the world. When he won the World Series in August, sweeping four shots clear of Mickelson with a stylish and aggressive performance, Price called him the greatest player of the last twenty years.

"Greg Norman is one of only two people who transcend the game," Clayton says. "Tiger Woods is the other. Even Nicklaus didn't do that."

Norman used to feel that he would play his best golf in his forties. In 1993, when he devised his secret seven-year plan, his focus was the year 2000, by which time he would be forty-five, his children would be almost ready to leave the nest, and retirement, from golf at least, might be a possibility. But lately, he had begun to wonder if he shouldn't bring it forward—if the misconceptions, the needling, and the constant reminders of his failures and belittling of his achievements were really worth the fleeting moments of ecstasy.

"There's never been anybody who tried harder than Greg, and he gets precious little credit for that," Thomson says. "He's got great courtesy and manners. People win things, and there's a temptation to rest on your laurels and take up the soft life. That's an easy way to go, and to his great credit Greg has never done that for an instant."

Perhaps this is the key to Norman's continued survival in the face of blows that have felled greater men like oaks—hard work, plain and simple. Or, perhaps, as Cott says, he has been saved by his priorities: family first, golf second, and business and fishing somewhere in between. But never once has he shied from the harsh benchmark of history, the one that says that despite winning almost eighty titles around the world in snow and wind, on links and park land, despite meeting triumph and tragedy with dignity and equanimity, he must be lumped in with those who were almost great.

"I look at our careers," Price says, "and I've won three majors and he's won two. And that's weird. To me, he's an eight-major person. I look at Faldo [with his six majors] and I think, 'Greg should have won more than he has.' Faldo's got a very clinical game, but he's a plodder. He doesn't have the ability to hit the ball three hundred yards if he wants to, or stop a five-iron on a dime. He doesn't have the flair that Greg has."

"When you look at his career, when you look at everything about the man, he's one of the greatest players we've ever seen," Harmon says. "And yet everyone is judged by the majors. I don't agree with that. I think his statistics speak for themselves—his scoring averages, his Vardon Trophies. . . . Those are the things that count."

"It wouldn't surprise me if he won a major at forty-five or fifty," Clayton says. "He's so much fitter than I imagine Nicklaus ever was. Phenomenally fit, still got a great game. But if he stopped now, how would history measure his career? I think there is a parallel with Weiskopf. Their careers will probably be judged the same way. So in the end do you lump them in with Larry Nelson, or do you just say, they were great players who could have won more majors? Then again, put Nicklaus where Norman was and he'd have won eight majors. So can he be called a great champion? I don't know. He's definitely a great golfer. He can hit shots not many guys can hit or ever will. Best driver of the golf ball there ever was. Great bunker player. Terrific iron player. Good putter. Gutsy. The crowds love him. Charisma. Everything the game cries out for."

"Lord knows, he's a good player," Middlecoff sums it up. "But he does a lot of funny things."

To Norman, majors mean a lot, but they are not everything, not life and certainly not death. "My sweetest victory was my first one, the West Lakes Classic," he says, "because I would never have won the British Open if I had won that one first. Then comes Royal St. George's and then maybe Turnberry."

Through it all Norman has soldiered on, golden, proud, adventurous, thrilling, damaged, and compulsively watchable. "There've been times when I haven't wanted to go on," Norman admits. "But when you really think about it, why deprive yourself because of other people's opinions? I love doing what I do. I don't care what anybody else thinks about me. I do what I think is right for me, my wife, my family, and my friends. And if I keep that priority, everything else will fall into place."

After four rounds of the Australian Open, Norman's name was in its customary place—at the top of the leaderboard. Soon it would be Christmas, and he would take a much-needed break with his family, enjoying a little tranquillity before it all began again in the new year. "Quite honestly, if I retired tomorrow, they're going to forget about me in a very short period of time," Norman says. "But all I've done and all I've structured for myself and my family, I've got for the rest of my life, and that's the most important thing. That's when you go and really savor what you've done because you've got time to sit back and reflect. And I'll enjoy that, I really will. There'll be no better feeling."

INDEX

A

Agassi, Andre, 266

AGU *see* Australian Golf Union (AGU)

Ali, Muhammad, dinner with, 36, 132

Alliss, Peter, 119

American Brands, bought Cobra, 204

Anderson, Dave, 134, 243

Andrassy, Jay Jr. (Laura's brother), 99

Andrassy, Laura *see* Norman, Laura

Andrassy, Richard (Laura's brother), 99

Appearance money, 74, 83, 88, 89, 100, 146, 171, 172, 267

Aspley High, school attended by Greg, 6, 8, 9, 12

Augusta: Home of the Masters Tournament (Eubanks), 226

Aussi Rules, fishing yacht owned by Greg, 161, 218, 241

Australia

    birthplace of Norman, 1–2

    relationship between Greg and, 170, 173, 271

    richest man, Kerry Packer, 171, 217

Australian Golf Union (AGU), 18, 171

Australian Golf Writers Association, 32

Australian Rules, game based on Gaelic football, 2, 5, 8, 9, 10

Azinger, Paul, 142, 144, 186, 195, 196, 198, 242

B

Baker-Finch, Ian, 147, 170

Ballesteros, Seve, 22, 25, 31, 33, 46, 49, 58, 61, 72, 78, 84, 88, 102, 103, 107, 126, 134, 136, 137, 147–148, 149, 161, 173, 179, 189, 265, 267

    appearance fees, 267

    comparison to, 77

Barden, Jimmy, 40

Barker, Sue (British tennis player), 44–46

Barner, Ed, manager of Miller and Ballesteros, 30–31

Barnes, Brian, 84

Baws, Howie, 115, 122

Beard, Frank, 110

Beck, Chip, 112

Beman, Deane, PGA Tour commissioner, 147–148

Bender, Pete

    caddie for Greg, 104, 105, 110, 112, 117, 118, 120, 121, 136, 142, 143, 161

Blackmar, Phil, 124

Boers, Tom, 227

Brand, Gordon J., 116, 118, 119

British Tour, 83–84

Brown, Ken, 37–38, 58, 83, 85

Bush, George, 242

C

Caddies

    Greg's treatment of, 178

    relationship between golfers and, 87, 143

Calcavecchia, Mark, 153, 155, 156, 157, 163, 169, 188, 195

Callahan, Tom, golf writer, 134, 236, 238, 252, 265

Carr, Roddy, 267

Cepelak, Brenna, 228

Clark, Howard, 34, 84

Clayton, Mike, 39, 65, 128, 139, 170, 218, 238, 276, 278

Clifford, John, 23, 24

Clinton, Bill, 240, 264, 269

    fall and knee injury, 261

    visit to Norman home, 259–262

Cobra Golf, Inc., xiii–xiv, 113, 185, 204, 205, 206, 216, 246

Cochran, Russ, 176

Cogill, Glen, caddie for Greg, 11, 20, 23, 25

Coleman, Pete, caddie for Ballesteros, 72, 77, 78, 79, 161
Collins, Bart, 270, 274
Cott, John, chauffeur, 215, 273, 276
Country clubs and golf courses
    Atlanta Country Club, 90
    Augusta National, 52, 53, 82, 101, 102, 150, 154, 175, 187, 222-238, 264
    Beverley Park, 18
    Blue Monster, 162-163
    Carnoustie, 105
    Castle Pines, 158
    Fanling Golf Club, 46
    Grand Golf Course, 171
    Grange (Adelaide), 23, 24
    Inverness, 124, 126, 138, 195
    Lochinvar, 180
    McCleod Country Club, built for women by women, 21
    Medalist, 259
    Mount Isa Golf Club, 4
    Muirfield, 137, 138, 183, 189, 212
    New South Wales Golf Club, 259
    Olympic Club, 198
    Pebble Beach, 94, 107
    Pinehurst, 37
    Riverside Oaks, 158
    Royal Birkdale, 81, 85, 90
    Royal Canberra, 145
    Royal Lytham, 33, 49, 119, 244
    Royal Melbourne, 143, 175
    Royal Queensland, 11, 14, 17, 20, 21, 124, 136
    Royal St. George, 33, 60, 83, 187, 255, 278
    St. Andrews, 33, 90, 98, 100, 120, 131, 166, 169
    St. Michael's, 171
    Shinnecock Hills, 110, 111, 212
    Stadium Course, 206
    Sugarloaf, 218, 243
    Sunningdale, 90, 128
    Turnberry, 37, 115, 117, 119, 207, 278
    Victoria Golf Club, 28
    Virginia Golf Club (Brisbane), 8, 26
    Walton Heath, 147
    Wentworth, 90
    Winged Foot, 92, 93, 94, 97, 98, 103, 167, 206
    Woodlands, 179
Couples, Fred, 194, 227, 241
Cousteau, Jacques, 159
Crampton, Bruce, 18, 23, 24, 25, 26
Crenshaw, Ben, 112, 212, 230, 233
Crow, Tom, vice chairman of Cobra, 113, 185, 186, 218

D
Dabell, Norman, 155
Daly, John, 207, 208
Daniel, Beth, 74
Dassu, Balovino, 35
Davis, Rodger, 25, 111, 126, 230, 231
Devlin, Bruce, 18, 24, 25, 26, 117, 120
Diaz, Jaime, 198
Dibnah, Corrine, 14
Dobereiner, Peter, news correspondent, 82, 98, 223
Dodd, Christopher, 242
The Dogged Victims of Inexorable Fate (Jenkins), 119
Draovitch, Pete, physiotherapist, 184, 185, 215
Dunn, Willie, 111
Durante, Steve, 271
Dwyer, Roger, 17, 18
Dye, Pete, 217

E
Earp, Charlie, 14, 16, 19, 20, 21, 22, 32, 34, 90, 91, 96, 113, 133, 136, 138, 169, 174, 175, 186, 262
    Greg's mentor, 5
Eastwood, Clint, 240
Edwards, Bruce, caddie for Greg, 152, 153, 155, 156, 157, 163, 164, 176, 177, 178, 179, 257, 263
Elkington, Steve, 179, 180, 225, 249, 254, 255, 256
Els, Ernie, 191, 209, 248
Erskine, James, 171, 202, 203, 207

Espinosa, Al, 94
Eubanks, Steve, 226
Evans, Clive, 9
Evans, Gary, 187, 188, 194

F
Faldo, Nick, 30, 58, 68, 78, 84, 116, 117, 118, 150,
 158, 164, 165, 166, 167, 173, 175, 183, 186,
 189, 191, 192, 194, 195, 196, 203, 218, 222,
 228, 229, 230, 231, 232, 233, 237, 240,
 243, 252, 264
Feinstein, John, 182, 184
Fergus, Keith, 53
Ferguson, Mike, 20, 170
Fernandez, Vicente, 61
Finchem, Tim, 208–210, 213, 249, 265
Fine, Alan, 249
Flanagan, Kevin, 13
Flash, first mate on fishing yacht, 161, 215
Floyd, Maria (Raymond's wife), 112, 241
Floyd, Raymond, 61, 72, 111, 112, 113, 117, 199,
 232, 254
 comparison to, 51
Flynn, Bill, 111
Forsbrand, Anders, 117
Fredrickson, Tucker, 254
Frost, David, South African golfer, 165, 169,
 195, 228

G
Gale, Terry, 17, 18
Gallacher, Bernard, 70
Gallagher, Jim Jr., 198, 199
Gamez, Robert, 164, 169, 195
Gilmour, Scotty, 51, 69, 110
 erstwhile caddie to Greg, 87, 88
Ginn, Stewart, 35, 39, 60, 62, 170, 268
Golden Bear International, Nicklaus
 company, 41
Golf
 course design venture by Greg, 171
 courses, specific. see Country clubs and golf
  courses
 tournaments see Tournaments

Golf My Way (Nicklaus), 9
Gordon, Ian, authority on sharks, 159
Gore, Al, 240
Grady, Wayne, 14, 20, 152, 153, 154, 155, 156, 157,
 170, 218, 230
Graham, David, 23, 25, 26, 46, 89, 100, 247,
 248, 249
Great White Shark, label put on Greg by
 press, 54, 57
Great White Shark Enterprises, 93, 207, 215,
 239, 241, 271
The Greatest (motion picture), 36
Green, Hubert, 117, 120
Green, Richard, 264
Greg Norman Collection, clothing company,
 216, 246, 247
Greg Norman Foundation, 172
Greg Norman Junior Golf Foundation, 172
Greg Norman's Down Under Grille, chain of
 restaurants, 264

H
Hammond, Donnie, 102
Happell, Charles, 271
Harmon, Claude, Master's champion, 180
Harmon, Claude "Butch" (Claude's son), golf
 coach, 180, 181, 183, 184, 187, 189, 199, 223,
 226, 228, 232, 234, 242, 245, 246, 247,
 262, 263, 268
Hauser, Melanie, golf writer, 147
Hawke, Bob (prime minister of Australia), 171,
 175, 242
Hay, David, 5
Hay, Dr. Bob, 5
Hay, Peter, 5
Hayes, Mark, 117
Heard, Jerry, 110
Hinkle, Lon, 53
Hobday, Simon, 34
Hoch, Scott, 150, 227, 242, 263
Hodenfield, Chris, 11, 40, 109, 254
Hogan, Ben, 126, 194, 236, 240, 244
Hogan, Paul, "Crocodile Dundee," 171, 274
Hope, Bob, 251

Horne, Gail, teacher of Greg, 9
Hovi, Seth (Greg's grandfather), 1
Hovi, Tyyne (Greg's grandmother), 1
How We Won the Open (Bender), 121, 155
Hutton, Jamie, sick teenager helped by Greg, 144, 145, 146

I
IMG *see* International Management Group (IMG)
International Management Group (IMG)
  Greg's decision to walk away from, 203
    xiv, 68, 89, 101, 122, 132, 133, 150, 170, 171, 172, 174, 175, 185, 186, 200, 201, 202, 203, 204, 205, 207, 215, 216, 218, 270
Internet site, 218, 229
Irwin, Hale, 93

J
Jacklin, Tony, 51, 137
Jenkins, Dan, 119, 131, 138, 212, 265
Jimenez, Mark, caddie for Azinger and Tway, 196
Job, Nick, 61
Johnston, Alastair, 204
Johnstone, Tony, 59
Jones, Bobby, 94, 218, 233
Jones, Brian, 170

K
King, Cyril, 22, 64
King, Gary (Cyril's son), 64
King, Greg (Cyril's son), 64
King, Michael (Queenie), 40, 62
  remained loyal to Greg, 85
King, Steve (Cyril's son), 64
Kite, Tom, 102, 103
Koch, Gary, 117, 119
Kornheiser, Tony, 269
Kostis, Peter, 237

L
Langer, Bernhard, 58, 72, 74, 102, 121, 124, 189, 191, 192, 194

Lawrence, Don, ghostwriter for *My Story*, 83
Leadbetter, David, coached Faldo to victory, 166, 175, 232, 238, 262, 263
Lee, Jackie, 51
Lee, Robert, 117
Lehman, Tom, 143, 269
Leonard, Sugar Ray, 132
Levy, Lawrence, 144
  photographer, 74, 115, 122, 124
Lietzke, Bruce, 183, 188
Longmuir, Bill, 24, 35, 37, 40, 41, 44, 62, 66, 69, 75, 76, 79, 84, 86, 91, 109, 255
  remained loyal friend, 85
Love, Davis III, 160, 180, 185, 208, 241
Lu, Little, 47
Lu, Mr., 47
Luters, Lt. Maris "Weasel," 224
Lyle, Sandy, 52, 80, 84, 129, 143
Lyons, Greg, 10

M
Mackay, Roger, 147
Mackay, Sommie, amateur golfer, 16, 17, 26
Mahaffey, John, 120
Mandela, Nelson, 240
Mansell, Nigel, race car driver, 146, 163, 174, 240
Mansell, Roseanne (Nigel's wife), 163
Marsh, Graham, 23, 25, 74, 98, 100
Marshall, James, 28, 30, 31, 33, 34, 37, 41, 44, 45, 46, 47, 48, 49, 60, 78, 86, 87, 101, 132, 173, 203, 253, 260
  became interested in golf management, 29
  best man at Greg and Laura's wedding, 59
  dispute with sponsors, 51
  end of five-year relationship with Greg, 66–67, 68, 72
  idea of "the Shark," 69
  prediction of Greg's millionaire status by, 35
  protective of Greg, 38
  reaction to pregnancy news, 66
  signed contract with Greg, 32
Marshall, John, twin brother of James, 36
Marshall, Lois, wife of James, 33, 49, 68

Martinez, Andy, 143, 269

Mayfair, Billy, 213

McCarron, Scott, 228

McClelland, Doug, 24

McCormack, Mark, 68, 69, 122, 142, 203, 204
  analysis of rivalry between Faldo and
    Norman, 167

McCumber, Mark, 213, 236

McGuire, Bernie, 215, 217

McGuire, Bill, 269

McWilliam, Billy, 18, 19

Mickelson, Phil, 222, 227, 228, 276

Middlecoff, Cary, 140, 237, 278

Miller, David, 190

Miller, Johnny, 31, 53, 149, 194, 237

Miller, Lou, 37

Mitchell, Andrew, 141

Mize, Larry, 108, 134, 136, 137, 138, 139, 142, 169,
  174, 181, 195, 238

Montgomery, John, 208

Montgomery, Scott, 208

Mount Isa Mines, 2, 3, 5

Murdoch, Rupert, Australian media tycoon,
  208

Murphy, Kevin, 13

Murray, Doug, 19

Murray, Jim, sports columnist, 91, 108, 126,
  235

My Story (Norman), 83, 86

N

Nagle, Kel, 21, 62

Nakajima, Tommy, 102, 118, 119, 120, 121

Navarro, Tony, caddie for Greg, 186, 206, 213,
  215, 242

Nelson, Byron, 128, 131, 242

Nelson, Larry, 278

Nelson, Mark, 271

New South Wales PGA, 18

Newton, Jack, 23, 30, 36, 50, 62, 83, 98, 101,
  154, 169, 170, 172, 173, 237

Nicklaus, Barbara (Jack's wife), 139, 165, 241,
  252

Nicklaus, Charlie (Jack's father), 252

Nicklaus, Jack, 9, 14, 21, 53, 54, 61, 98, 101, 102,
  103, 104, 110, 111, 117, 119, 120, 132, 137, 139,
  140, 144, 151, 155, 156, 157, 158, 160, 161,
  162, 194, 229, 238, 240, 244, 252, 254,
  263, 267, 271, 273, 278
  comparison to, 24, 26, 34, 37
  won sixth Green Jacket from Masters, 104,
    107

Nicklaus, Steve (Jack's son), 103

Nicolette, Mike, 82

Nobilo, Frank, 223

Norman, Greg
  achieved lowest aggregate score in British
    Open history, 192
  America and, 90–91, 110
  analysis of weaknesses and problems in
    golf, 101, 199, 236–237
  announced World Golf Tour, 208–211
  Australia and, 170
  best season in '86, 131
  birth of daughter, 74
  birth of, 1
  blossomed under Marshall's guidance, 38
  boating and, 160, 161, 162
  bought sod farm, 217
  breakdown of relationship with Norton,
    204
  burnout admitted, 175, 181
  called Great White Shark by press, 54, 57
  car accident of, 20
  Cathay-Pacific deal, 47
  charitable acts, 144–146
  chemical poisoning of, 213
  childhood of, 2–12
  comments on British Tour players,
    83–84
  competitive nature of, 75
  conquering fears as child, 10
  danger, relish for, 100, 146
  defeat against Tway, 126, 138
  defeat used as springboard to victory, 158
  devotion to family, 83, 262, 274
  earnings, 23, 80, 90, 124, 133, 146, 174, 204,
    214, 249, 267

Norman, Greg (*cont.*)
    effects of losing on, 113
    end of five-year relationship with Marshall,
        66–67, 68
    endorsements, xiii, 34–35, 66, 133, 150, 185,
        186, 218
    environmentalists against, 159
    fatherhood and, 109, 256
    favorites, 110
        book, 184
        Roosevelt quotation, 166
    first Australian to win British Open since
        1965, 122
    fishing disaster of, 64
    friendship with Nicklaus cooled, 254
    generosity of, 77, 172
    goals to become millionaire, 13
    golf course design venture, 171
    houses owned by, 108, 139, 140
    IMG split and, 203–204
    indulgences and purchases by, 35, 36, 65,
        132, 133, 139–140, 146, 216–219
    influenced most by mother, 4
    Internet site, 218
    invitation to Masters, 52
    invited to join PGA of Australia circuit, 23
    kidney stone, 79–80
    Laura's effect on, 76
    lifesaving efforts of, 11
    long dry spell in career, 179
    loss of teeth in, 5
    lost Masters, 56, 107, 234, 241
    lost play-off in all four majors, 198
    love for lists, 229
    lucrative business ventures, 216–217
    made decision to take up golf, 8–9, 16
    managed by IMG, 68–69
    marriage to Laura, 59
    Masters scores, 101
    media and, 34, 37, 54, 61, 69, 70, 91, 100, 108,
        122, 131, 134, 137–138, 142, 149, 159, 170,
        190, 209, 235–236, 240, 243, 269, 271,
        272
    met Laura Andrassy, 47–49

missed cut for Masters, 266
most devastating loss, 138
move to Sydney, 19
nicknames of, 11, 39, 98
office decor, 240
optimism toward future, 278, 279
paid cash for Boeing 747, 270
payments to caddies, 78
PGA Player of the Year, xiii, 229
Player of the Year, 214
play-off against Zoeller, 95–98
practical joke played on, 200
preference for individual sports, 8
proposed to Laura, 56
quest for Green Jacket, 131–148, 150, 165,
    222–238
quiet revolution in life, 184
recruitment strategy for employees, 161
relationship with Sue Barker, 44–46
restaurants, 264
robbed, 73
Rolls Royce cars and, 59, 66, 83, 109, 194,
    219
Royal Queensland and, 17–21
shark hunting by, 57, 158–159, 268
signed contract with James Marshall, 32
sponsors, 73
surfing adventures of, 12
surgery on knee, 81
temper of, 61–62
thoughts about Tiger Woods, 189, 267–268,
    272
toyed with thoughts of retirement, 265
treatment of caddie by, 87–88
victories, 26, 34, 51, 58, 81–82, 90, 98, 108,
    115, 121, 128, 129–130, 131, 143, 158, 183,
    192, 206, 263–264, 271
water-skiing accident, 99
whirlwind tour, 200
won first pro-am title, 23
won first trophy in golf, 10
Norman, Gregory Michael (Greg's son), 99,
    181, 196, 256, 270, 271
Norman, Janis (Greg's sister), 2, 4

Norman, Laura (Greg's wife)
  after British Open win, 122, 194
  asked about women following Greg, 70
  became ill after Mize defeat, 141
  birth of daughter, 74
  christening of son, 99
  comments
    on Greg's hurt by friends, 209
    on Greg's winning streak, 131
    on jealousy by others, 220
  compared Marshall to jilted lover, 68
  effect on Greg, 76
  home life, 256-257
  IMG split and, 203
  impressed her in-laws, 63
  involved in business decisions, 215
  marriage of, 59
  met Greg, 47-49
  money raised for charity by, 172
  Norton's conflict with Greg seen as lover's
    quarrel by, 205
  office decor, 240
  President's visit to home of, 259-262
  proposal by Greg to, 56
  reflections on Greg's qualities, 257-258
  support for Greg, 274
  wanted Greg to spend time with family, 171
Norman, Laura (Greg's wife) xiii, 16, 66, 67,
    71, 72, 73, 79, 80, 82, 90, 95, 107, 108, 109,
    113, 115, 116, 137, 138, 140, 146, 157, 161,
    162, 163, 165, 173, 175, 181, 184, 187, 191,
    204, 213, 220, 223, 227, 231, 232, 235,
    236, 241, 244, 251, 255, 256, 266, 269,
    270, 272
Norman, Mervyn (Greg's father), 1, 2, 4, 5, 10,
    15, 16, 31, 32, 60, 61, 128, 217, 251
  admitted to hospital, 271
  compared to father of Venturi, 252, 253
  muted response to son's achievements, 41,
    175-176
  overjoyed at son's British Open win, 124
  son did not follow footsteps of, 6
Norman, Morgan-Leigh (Greg's daughter),
    82, 109, 120, 137, 231, 232, 256, 270

  birth of, 74
Norman, Toini (Greg's mother), 1, 2, 4-5, 9,
    10, 12, 15, 16, 19, 26, 31, 32, 50, 59, 128,
    217, 251
  caddied for son, 61
  interest in golfing by, 8
  parents of, 1
  reaction to Greg's marriage, 60
  win at ladies' club championship, 124
Norman's Yacht's, Inc., 218
Norton, Hughes, agent
  end of relationship with Greg, 202-206
  xiii, 89, 95, 101, 122, 132, 165
Norwood, Bev, 203
  IMG vice president, 122

O
Oak Pointe, waterfront home to the
    Normans, 108
O'Brien, Larry, 41
Oddy, Drake, caddie for Calcavecchia, 155
Olazabal, Jose Maria, 209
O'Leary, John, 40, 84, 85
O'Meara, Mark, 150
Order of Merit, 86, 147
  Australian, 27
  European, 52, 80
Ozaki, Jumbo, 158, 188, 267

P
Packer, Kerry, Australia's richest man, 171, 217
Palmer, Arnold, 21, 51, 52, 53, 68, 89, 91, 105,
    108, 132, 140, 194, 209, 236, 237, 251, 271
Palmer, Deacon (Arnold's father), 252
Pate, Jerry, 83
Pavin, Corey, 189, 191, 212
Pelham Golf Yearbook (Stanley), 57
Penske, Roger, 139
Perrin, Steve, life saved by Greg, 11
PGA of Australia, 147
PGA Tour, in America, 27
Pillage, Derek, manager of Lyle and Trevino,
    37
Player, Gary, 21, 22, 25, 51, 194, 248

Player, Harry (Gary's father), 252
Precision Golf Forgings, 16, 17
Price, Nick, 89, 91, 102, 104, 140, 161, 165, 189, 203, 209, 210, 211, 213, 214, 223, 227, 232, 237, 241, 244, 254, 255, 262, 276
Price, Sue, 244
Prodger, Andy, caddie to Faldo, 88

Q
Queensland PGA, 23

R
Rafferty, Ronan, 188
Ramsey, Tom, 29, 38, 77, 78, 100, 200, 253, 260
Rankings, 264
 see also Order of Merit
Rawkins, Peter, 3
Reilly, Rick, 120, 138, 166, 229, 233
Robbins, Tony, motivational speaker, 266
Roberts, Loren, 243
Roberts, Sam, (Sandy's son), 172
Roberts, Sandy, television broadcaster, 172-173
Rodriguez, Chi Chi, 236
Rogers, Bill, 194
Rotella, Dr. Bob, 1, 237
Rough Guide to Australia (guidebook), 2
Royal Australian Air Force, career turned down in, 15
Rubenstein, Lorne, 247, 248
Rugby, enjoyed by Norman, 2-3
Runyan, Paul, 56

S
Sanders, Doug, 116
Sarazen, Gene, winner of 1932 British Open, 194
Schmon, Robert M., 243
Schofield, Ken, 34, 85, 211, 212
Seitz, Nick, 149
Selvey, Mike, 190
Senior, Peter, 147, 188, 190, 191

Shark Attack (Norman), instruction book, 50, 105, 180, 218
Shark Shootout, 200, 208
Shearer, Bob, 24, 27, 46, 77
Simpson, John, 68
Simpson, Tim, 160
Singh, Vijay, 195
Sluman, Jeff, 180
Snead, Sam, 14, 236
Sony World Rankings, 147
Spearman, Mitchell, 175
Sponsors, 73
Stadler, Craig, 124
Stanley, Ian, 45
Stanley, Louis T., 57, 59
Starling, Steve, 158, 159
Stephens, Jackson T., Augusta chairman, 242
Stephenson, Jan, 74
Stevens, Paul, "singing caddie," 51
Stewart, Payne, 112, 124, 150, 152, 170, 252
Strange, Curtis, 53, 144, 147, 158, 254
Stuve, Gary, boat captain, 160, 161, 162, 215, 225
Sullivan, Danny, 242
Sutton, Hal, 112

T
Tarde, Jerry, 209
Tewell, Doug, 148
This is Your Life (television program), 4
Thomson, Peter, 25, 26, 28, 29, 30, 32, 43, 62, 98, 114, 122, 172, 173, 209, 236, 238, 260
Thorpe, Jim, 89
Thorpe, Mike, 124
Thursday's Child, charity, 144
Tickner, Chris, 25
Tiffenberg, David, ten-year-old who wrote kind letter to Greg, 242
Tod, April, 140
Todd, Ian, 68, 204
Torrance, Sam, 40, 80, 84, 85
Tournaments
 Alfred Dunhill Challenge, 211

Andersen Consulting World Championship of Golf, 263–264
Australasian Tour, 24
Australian Masters, 65, 81, 90, 133, 169, 174, 207, 216
Australian Open, 17, 40, 41, 50, 57, 63, 74, 79, 88, 89, 143, 171, 199, 200, 214, 263, 267, 275, 278
Australian PGA, 98, 131, 150, 275
Australian Skins, 200
Australian TPC, 145
B&H International, 85
Bay Hill Classic, 82
BellSouth Classic, 218
British Open, 37, 49, 60, 68, 72, 83, 86, 102, 115, 116, 119, 120, 128, 132, 133, 137, 141, 147, 152, 166, 174, 176, 183, 187, 188, 190, 192, 194, 196, 231, 244, 245, 249, 255, 278
British PGA Championship, 33, 62, 82
Canadian Open, 72, 98, 108, 183
Cannes Open, 88
Chunichi Crowns, 267
Doral Ryder Open, 162, 163, 186, 208, 225, 264
Dubai Desert Classic, 211, 264
Dunhill Cup, 100, 131, 169, 213, 248
Dunlop Masters, 58, 71
Dunlop Phoenix, 74, 89
ESP Open, 145
European Masters, 211
European Open, 74, 128, 131, 147
European Tour, 37, 78, 211
French Open, 51, 72
Grand Slam of Golf, 200
Greater Hartford Open, 244
Greater Milwaukee Open, 158
Greg Norman Holden International (formerly Classic), 202, 218, 276
Hennessy Cognac Cup, 73
Heritage Classic, 144, 145, 212, 214
Hong Kong Open, 47, 51, 65, 81–82
Houston Open, 179
Irish Open, 41, 51, 72, 211

Italian Open, 51, 59, 146, 147
Japanese Tour, 39
John Player Classic, 119
Johnnie Walker Classic, 211
Johnnie Walker World Championship, 186
Kemper Open, 90, 108, 269
Kuzuba International, 32
Las Vegas Invitational, 108
Martini International, 33, 34, 41, 46, 57, 69
Masters, 52, 53, 54, 56, 82, 128, 141, 165, 222–238, 241, 259, 263, 264, 265, 266
MCI Classic, 241
Memorial Tournament, 41, 90, 174, 212, 243
Nestle Invitational, 164, 206
New South Wales Open, 23, 89, 131
Palm Meadows Cup, 170
PGA Championship, 92, 102, 124, 147, 177, 195, 198, 229, 242, 248, 254, 266
Players Championship, 82, 133, 206, 226, 264
Presidents Cup, 247, 248, 249
Queensland Junior Championship, 11
Queensland Open, 23, 100, 131
Ryder Cup, 46
St. Jude Classic, 27, 267
Scandinavian Enterprise Open, 41
Scandinavian Open, 51
Shark Shootout, 200, 208
South Australian Open, 131
Spanish Open, 51, 267
State Express Classic, 72, 83
Swiss Open, 45
Sydney Open, 45
Taiheiyo Masters, 200
Tournament Players Championship (TPC), 158, 179, 243, 265
Uniroyal International, 37
U.S. Open, 60, 72, 89, 91, 93, 94, 98, 102, 103, 107, 110, 113, 119, 141, 147, 179, 187, 207, 212, 236, 247, 270, 271
Victorian Open, 65
West Lakes Classic, 23, 26, 27, 39, 40, 41, 90, 170, 185, 278

Tournaments (*cont.*)
Westchester Classic, 112, 147, 152
Western Australian Open, 131
Western Open, 98, 176, 186
World Cup, 27, 45, 77, 84, 147
World Match Play, 46, 51, 75, 77, 88, 128, 129, 131, 250
World Series, 211, 213, 276
Trevino, Lee, 47, 61, 111, 112, 137, 150, 165, 230
Tway, Bob, 111, 112, 125, 126, 138, 139, 165, 169, 174, 195, 227

U
United States Golf Association (USGA), 72, 93
U.S. Federal Trade Commission, investigation of World Golf Tour, 209
USF&G Classic, 164
USGA *see* United States Golf Association (USGA)

V
Van Sickle, Gary, 186
Vardon Trophy, 214, 278
Venturi, Ken, 145
Verdi, Bob, 134, 151
von Nida, Norman, 21

W
Wadkins, Lanny, 110, 112
Waldorf, Duffy, 228
Watson, Dennis, 111
Watson, Tom, 54, 61, 87, 94, 102, 105, 107, 111, 117, 137, 152, 161, 164, 190, 195, 242
Webb, Mel, 236
Webster, Dr. Rudi, 71
Weiskopf, Tom, 51, 137, 150, 151, 176, 206, 252
Wendt, Jana, 273

Werner, Curtis, 271
Westwood, Lee, 275
Whiting, Hugh, 217
Whitten, Ron, 218
Williams, Frank
agent, 27, 132, 140, 200, 202, 203, 205, 207, 208, 215, 216, 217, 223, 231, 239, 249, 252, 256, 257, 265, 267, 268, 270, 273, 275
arrested as payback for practical joke, 201
Williams, Steve, 147, 240
caddie for Greg, 128
Wilson, sporting goods company, 34
Wind, Herbert Warren, 54
Winning Ways (Webster), 71
Wolstenholme, Guy, 28, 29, 32
Wood, Craig, lost play-off in all four majors, 198
Woods, Tiger, 24, 25, 26, 101, 180, 189, 194, 205, 246, 252, 268, 272, 276
endorsements, 266
managed by IMG, 68
paid record appearance fees, 171
Woosnam, Ian, 116, 117, 119
World Golf Tour, 208–210, 249, 250, 265
World Pitch and Putt Company, 264
World of Professional Golf (McCormack), 167

Y
Yarrington, Thomas J., drunken heckler, 242
Year of the Shark, 212
Yeltsin, Boris, 261
practical joke incident involving name of, 201

Z
Zen of the Martial Arts, favorite book, 184
Zoeller, Fuzzy, 92, 93, 94, 95, 120, 188, 206
play-off, 95–98